CW01214550

THE ART OF YOUR START

The Complete Leadership Playbook for
Onboarding, Assimilation, and Integration

Daniel J. Mueller

PRAISE FOR ART OF YOUR START

The following endorsements are organized by last name, in alphabetical order.

"*The Art of Your Start* is a great read and one I highly recommend for leaders at all levels. It's a great reference manual for various stages in one career: starting a new job after promotion, starting with a new company, and onboarding a new executive. Daniel's decades of experience shine through in this exceptionally well-crafted work."

Rob Andrews
Chairman and CEO, Allen Austin Executive Search

"*The Art of Your Start* provides an excellent and relatable template for leaders at all levels to excel. The real-life stories and challenges of strong-performing executives and how they worked to navigate the curveballs of the corporate world are powerful and effective. This book encourages self-reflection and provides solutions to challenges we will all face as we continue the pursuit of career growth and life-changing opportunities."

Danny Austin
Senior Vice President, Imperial Dade

"'Success is where preparation and opportunity meet.' Bobby Unser. Written by one of the earliest and most active pioneers of the executive leadership coaching industry, *The Art of Your Start* offers invaluable insights, practical tips, and proven strategies to help leaders seamlessly transition into new roles. From day one, you'll discover how to navigate the complexities of your new environment, reflect on your responsibilities, and align yourself.

"This book goes beyond basic onboarding checklists. It delves deep into the psychological aspects of assimilation, empowering you to overcome challenges, build confidence, and establish yourself as a valuable contributor. It will help you gain insider knowledge on how to quickly adapt to the team dynamics, contribute fresh ideas, and make a lasting impact in your new role."

Adrian Borcoci
Senior Management Consultant

"As a leader who works in the context of a church, it is crucial for me to grow and be shaped and developed so I can effectively minister to the large and diverse congregation that I serve. Daniel Mueller's book *The Art of Your Start* gives leaders a playbook to manage themselves well, develop strategy, focus on what is most important, plan for growth, and adapt to change. I am grateful for the wisdom contained in its pages."

Dave Brandolini
Executive Pastor, Austin Ridge Bible Church

"*The Art of Your Start* is an indispensable guide for organizational leaders, offering invaluable insights and practical tools for success in their roles. With a clear and comprehensive structure, the book covers every aspect of starting and thriving in a new leadership position. It emphasizes the significance of intentionality, hard work, and the integration process, providing stories of both triumphs and failures to illustrate best practices. This book is a must-read for leaders at all levels, from those just starting out to seasoned executives, and it will undoubtedly equip them with the knowledge and skills needed to excel in their positions."

Darin Brannan
CEO and Venture Capitalist

"As a leader, starting a new role in any company can be a daunting task. Onboarding is crucial for both the leader and the organization to ensure a smooth transition and a successful start. *The Art of Your Start* is a comprehensive guide that provides leaders, managers, and team members with the tools and strategies to effectively onboard new additions to the organization. Through insightful advice and practical tips, Daniel breaks down the onboarding process into simple, manageable steps, utilizing his BUILDS™ framework. What sets this book apart are the recommendations targeted at not only the leader, but their manager and their team members. *The Art of Your Start* is a must-read for anyone who wants high confidence in making a positive impact in their new role, and to create a strong foundation for sustained success."

Craig Epstein
VP of Operations, Michael & Susan Dell Foundation

"Daniel's combination of storytelling and truth-telling makes this book easy to read, and the wisdom he shares through his stories is memorable. I have often thought about concepts Mr. Mueller imparts weeks or months later, when I've found myself in a situation he had described. I'm certain that in his decades of experience, he's seen just about everything, so I trust his guidance and strategies. This book is one to keep and reference as the stages of your career advance over time."

Jill Graham
Co-founder, Roots Analytics

"I highly recommend *The Art of Your Start* to any new leader or anyone involved in the onboarding, assimilation, and integration process. This book is packed with practical advice on how to navigate the first year in a new leadership role, and it is written in a clear and engaging style.

"The author, Daniel Mueller, draws on his own lengthy experience as a corporate executive coach and his research on leadership failures provides readers with the tools they need to succeed. He covers a wide range of topics, including setting expectations, building relationships, and managing change. I found the book to be particularly helpful in the areas of cultural assimilation and integration. Mueller provides valuable insights into how to understand the company's culture and how to build relationships with key stakeholders.

"Overall, *The Art of Your Start* is an essential resource for any new leader. It is a well-written and informative book that will help you succeed in your new role, and benefit from the wisdom Mueller has assembled, which I have also personally benefited from."

Loran Gutt
Chief Strategy Officer, Auctane

"This book is a treasure trove of actionable wisdom drawn from Daniel's decades of leadership coaching at the highest levels. His clear, systematic approach is both a roadmap and a valuable reference for any executive making a transition or leveling up."

Mike Murphy
Murphy PLLC

"We have benefited greatly from Daniel Mueller's guidance in onboarding new members of our executive leadership team. This book captures a lot of the real-world experience and wisdom that Daniel has accumulated over multiple decades of coaching CEOs and executives.

The BUILDS™ playbook in Section 2 serves as a practical guide to the first twelve months in a new executive role, both for the executive and the manager supporting the new leader. Highly recommended!"

Antti Nivala
Founder and CEO, M-Files

"*The Art of Your Start* delivers practical and actionable advice on how to best position yourself for success at a new job. The author masterfully sprinkles anecdotes throughout the book, which give life to the insightful strategies for building relationships and delivering results. What I particularly appreciate about this book is its emphasis on self-reflection, understanding your strengths and weaknesses and being mindful of them as you onboard. The author's expertise shines through in his ability to provide a comprehensive roadmap to onboarding, from identifying common pitfalls to building on strengths necessary for success in any field. I highly recommend this book for anyone starting a new leadership role or who just wants to launch their career to the next level. Invaluable!"

Damien Perera
VP, Mergers and Acquisitions, Auctane

"As Daniel notes, starting a new role requires an approach that is both science and art. Daniel's proven expertise captured in *The Art of Your Start* provides real and tangible steps for the critical first twelve months. He provides practical guidance to ensure you move at the right pace, with the right plans, and with the necessary support throughout the organization to provide the best opportunity for success. And that success is earned with the right techniques to build an effective culture that enables teams to perform far beyond one individual's contributions.

"The planned and thoughtful techniques are critical not only to succeed in the early stages of a new role; they should be followed throughout the evolution of the business and your own leadership role.

"I'm excited and honored to recommend *The Art of Your Start* as a must-read for any aspiring leader."

Bob Pritchard
Chief Revenue Officer, M-Files

"One of the highlights I have had in Texas was competing in cycling on the road. One event and leadership lesson that comes to mind is the Hotter'N Hell Hundred race, which occurs in August in Wichita Falls, TX with gusting winds and one hundred–degree temps. After battling the elements and your personal challenge not to quit for ninety-nine miles, the 'last mile' winds up to the finish. This particular finish line had the road split into two lanes with a concrete island in the middle. At forty miles per hour and shoulder to shoulder, you can imagine the finish was not pretty, with cyclists crashing and some not knowing to go left or right. The lesson I learned that day was to know how to finish. I think when you start leading, you should also have an idea of knowing how to finish!

"Daniel has helped hundreds of leaders understand the importance of not just competing well but more importantly finishing well!"

Andrew Rauch
VP of Growth, Improving

"Daniel has coached hundreds of executives through what is the most difficult part of any job, the start. That experience is priceless and should be treasured by every executive looking to accelerate their career."

Joel Trammel
Co-founder, The American CEO

"*The Art of Your Start* is the 'roll up your sleeves' handbook to your success in a new role. It helps both the new employee and manager avoid the all-too-common pitfalls which lead to expensive and painful failures. I've personally benefited from Daniel's wisdom, and I highly recommend his book filled with stories, humor, templates and tools that can be mined for years."

Scott Whyte
Partner, HEP Private Equity Firm

"*The Art of Your Start* is a must-read for any leader, at any level, at any time in their career. Daniel's proven track record, methodology, and ability to create a heightened focus with success-minded clarity are unmatched. It is a pleasure to see Daniel continue to share his deep experience and tremendous guidance."

Andrew Wilmott
President, Fusion

Copyright © 2024 by Daniel J. Mueller

THE ART OF YOUR START

All rights reserved. No part of this publication may be reproduced, distributed, or transmitted in any form or by any means, including photocopying, recording, or other electronic or mechanical methods, without the prior written permission of the publisher, except in the case of brief quotations embodied in critical reviews and certain other noncommercial uses permitted by copyright law. For permission requests, write to the publisher, addressed "Attention: Permissions Coordinator," at info@beyondpublishing.net

Quantity sales and special discounts are available on quantity purchases by corporations, associations, and others. For details, contact the publisher at the address above.

U.S. trade bookstores and wholesalers, email info@BeyondPublishing.net to place an order.

The Beyond Publishing Speakers Bureau can bring authors to your live event.

For more information or to book an event, contact the Beyond Publishing Speakers Bureau at speak@BeyondPublishing.net

The author can be reached directly at BeyondPublishing.net

Printed in the United States of America. Distributed globally by BeyondPublishing.net

BEYOND

New York | Los Angeles | London | Sydney

ISBN Softcover: 978-1-63792-417-4
ISBN Hardcover: 978-1-63792-416-7

DEDICATION

To the exceptional leaders whom I've had the honor of coaching over the past thirty-plus years: this book is dedicated to you.

Your drive and commitment to excellence have been a source of inspiration and motivation for me. I am grateful for the opportunity to have witnessed your journey as you stepped into new leadership roles and for the privilege of having coached you through the challenges you faced. If you recognize your story within these pages, please know I changed the names to protect your confidentiality.

To those who persevered through difficult transitions and went on to excel in your roles, I am in awe of your determination and grit. And to those who encountered setbacks along the way, your resilience and ability to learn from those experiences have been invaluable. It is through working with all of you that I have gained the knowledge and insights I share in this book. I am honored to pass on these strategies and tactics to the next generation of leaders. Thank you for shaping my understanding of the art (and science) of effective leadership assimilation and integration. Journey well.

To my beloved wife, Patty: I want to express my heartfelt gratitude for your unwavering support and patience during this year-long writing journey. Your love and encouragement are invaluable. Without you by my side, none of this would hold much meaning. Your support is a testament to your selflessness and loving devotion. I could not have asked for a better life partner, and I thank God for you daily.

TABLE OF CONTENTS

Endorsements	2
Dedication	11
Foreword	15
Preface	17
Introduction	19
Section 1: The Problem	26
1. The Science and Art of Starting	27
2. Out of the Starting Blocks	36
3. Preparing to Run	49
4. Expectations	60
5. Common Mistakes	68
6. Section 1 Conclusion	82
Section 2: The Solution	84
7. The BUILDS™ Playbook	86
8. Build Trust!	94
9. Understand Needs!	107
10. Involve Stakeholders!	114
11. Listen to Concerns!	125
12. Deliver Results!	137
13. Serve with Excellence!	155
14. Section 2 Conclusion	166

Section 3: Valuable Resources	170
Phase 1: Resources for Build Trust, Understand Needs, and Involve Stakeholders	171
15. Recommended Reading	172
16. Relationship-Building Tactics	175
17. Stakeholder Meeting Tactics	186
18. Structure for a Hundred-Day Plan	191
19. The DISC Behavioral Assessment	199
20. Gaining Mentorship	215
Phase 2: Resources for Listen to Concerns and Deliver Results	229
21. Assess Yourself	231
22. Remove Blind Spots	233
23. Unleashing Leadership Excellence Assessment	249
24. Leadership Development Plans	267
Phase 3: Resources for Serve with Excellence	274
25. Serving Up	276
26. Section 3 Conclusion	292
Epilogue	294
Bibliography	296
Index	297
About the Author	303

FOREWORD

The Art of Your Start is a must-read for organizational leaders for three compelling reasons.

First, as a leader, you will likely start a new role at some point in your career. Second, as a leader of leaders, you will hire others who could benefit from learning the art of starting a new role. Third, it will better equip both you and others for successful integration and assimilation into your organization.

I personally had the author as my coach in my last role. He tried to help me with the onboarding process, but I did not follow his recommendations, and the results were suboptimal, to say the least. I told myself, "I've got this," but I was behind from day one. I lost both credibility and self-confidence with each passing day.

This time around, I have implemented this playbook to the letter. The results have been nothing short of amazing. As I write this, I am in my tenth month, and continue to see the benefits of following this one-year success plan.

The Art of Your Start is a hard-hitting and no-nonsense guide that is not for the faint of heart. Coach Daniel's direct style requires thick skin. He does not shy away from the realities of the leadership assimilation and integration journey. I can personally attest that the perils are very real, and generally unforeseen until it is too late. It is much better to invest the time upfront to learn what he calls the art, and science, of onboarding, assimilation, and integration.

What I also found especially helpful is this book is designed for both the hiring manager and the newly appointed leader, with specific sections dedicated to each audience throughout the chapters. It is actually two books in one: for you, the leader in your first year in a new role, and for you, the manager of this leader, or of any leader for that matter. It emphasizes the importance of intentionality and hard work in our leadership journey and serves as a valuable reminder of what it takes to be a successful leader at any level in an organization, from frontline managers to the CEO.

Organized into three sections, this book presents the problems, solutions, and valuable resources for starting and thriving during the first year in a new leadership role.

In Section 1, you will learn about the importance of being intentional in the onboarding, transition, and assimilation process and discover best practices through stories of successes and failures.

Section 2 offers a clear and easy-to-follow framework, called "the BUILDS™ playbook," which provides critical actions to take during the first twelve months of your new role.

In Section 3, you will find powerful tools and resources that will help you build upon previous learning and master this process.

I see *The Art of Your Start* as an essential resource for all organizational leaders. Coach Daniel provides practical guidance and tools to help us succeed in our roles. He'll steer you in the right direction. If you are starting a new leadership role, or responsible for helping someone do so, this book is for you.

Loran Gutt
Vice President of Corporate Development
Auctane, a Thoma Bravo Portfolio Company

PREFACE

In the shadows of towering achievements and brilliant minds, I've witnessed the silent tragedies of exceptional leadership careers sabotaged by flawed onboarding, assimilation, and integration. This book is my beacon to those lost in that morass and those driven to reach their full potential.

My first experience of great leaders failing during this process was in 1987, when I began specializing in executive coaching. John E. Paget, CEO of Intelogic Trace, hired me to be his CEO coach, and for nearly three decades I would help him pick up the pieces of limited executive success. By most standards, being a direct report to tech industry titans such as Jack Welch (GE), John Sculley (Apple), Rick Hamada (Avnet), and Bob Huang (Synnex) would be impressive enough. But John had the potential to be a peer to Welch, for example, yet never made it because of a missing skill set that you are about to acquire through *Art of Your Start*.

Personally, John was one of the most successful people I've ever known. As evidence, I point to his 50+ years of happy marriage, awesome, tight-knit family, and many true friends. John passionately and humbly served others, engaged in significant community service, and was involved in many philanthropic endeavors. At his funeral in 2018, people from all walks of life sang his praises. Professionally, to a person, people loved working for John. During the course of his career, I interviewed practically every direct report he ever had, and to a person they respected and admired his leadership. However, he consistently found himself passed over for top roles and holding shorter-than-desired tenures.

Why? John, like most leaders, never studied the art and science of starting a new leadership role until, in 2012, he gave up chasing corporate roles and came to work for me as one of my CEO coaches. At that time, I had seventy-five executive coaches in my stable, and John immediately shot up to number one, far surpassing me and everyone else. He was a very quick study, and I am convinced if he could've read this book along the way, he would have been a household name along with Welch, and *Art of Your Start* would've been authored by Paget instead of Mueller.

The first version of this book, now out of print, was called *The Critical 180* and designed to inform on best practices during the first six months in a new role. Ten years ago, that was cutting-edge thinking for onboarding books, which were, and still are for the most part, focused on the first three months in a new role. As a result of this eBook and other expert systems, I saw my clients' failure rate decrease, but not to the degree I expected. Despite my book, expert systems, and best coaching, a disproportionate number of clients *still* met the same fate: involuntary and premature exits, albeit in their second six months in the role. "How is this possible?" I asked myself. I resolved to find a cure for this problem—and you will find that cure within these pages.

The Art of Your Start is a playbook that will give you, the newly appointed leader, the greatest chances of significant success throughout the entire first year, and beyond. Part of each chapter is for you, and part for your manager and other stakeholders responsible for retaining top talent. For bosses, mentors, and coaches, this book will help you better assimilate and integrate leaders into organizations, and ensure your mutual long-term success.

Whether you are a seasoned CEO with many roles under your belt, or a first-time organizational leader, my vision is that this book becomes your indispensable ally in reaching your fullest leadership potential.

INTRODUCTION

Counterintuitive.

This is perhaps the best word to describe your first year in a new leadership role. Often, most of what you think you know won't serve you during this critical period.

Leaders, despite their vast experience, may face unique challenges in a new environment, requiring adaptability and open-mindedness for a successful first year.

To exemplify the unexpected challenges in new leadership roles, consider my trip to Turks and Caicos with my wife, Patty. My client, Tom, a Chief Investment Officer with a home there, had recommended its beautiful golf course. Upon arrival, we found the car's steering wheel on the opposite side, beginning a series of unexpected difficulties.

Navigating foreign roads may seem easy, but it can be challenging. We encountered honking and near accidents when we drove on the "wrong" side in Turks and Caicos, forcing me to rethink every move. This highlighted that old habits can be unhelpful in new situations, making many decisions counterintuitive and reliance on past experience potentially disastrous.

Assimilating and integrating into a new organization during your first year is much like navigating in foreign territory. Numerous obstacles can stand in your way, some as obvious as a right-side-of-the-car steering wheel, while others are easy to miss. In a new environment, your instincts may be thrown off, and decisions may often be counterintuitive. That's why there's a plethora of leadership terminations and resignations in the first year.

This book aims to guide leaders in adapting to new roles and help their managers support them. It will be beneficial in your current situation and future career advancements.

As an executive coach, I've seen capable leaders struggle while transitioning into new roles. Regardless of your position, your failure to adapt significantly impacts you, your team, and the company.

Leader failure injures the organization. It affects peers and subordinates and may cause "casualties" beyond the leader. It also harms those involved in leader selection. Hiring failures often return to haunt the hiring manager.

As an employee and potential hiring manager, ensuring effective onboarding, integration, and assimilation for your hires reduces your liability. I suggest distributing this book to first- and second-line managers and senior leaders in your organization. Reading it can help prevent "accidents," serving as a type of insurance against failure.

As a former corporate executive coach for Heidrick & Struggles, I learned that, according to a study commissioned by their former CEO, Kevin Kelly, 40 percent of new leaders they placed were fired or quit within eighteen months.[1] My research indicates a 20 to 25 percent failure rate in the first year. Eileen Kamerick, a former client, resigned as Heidrick's CFO due to leadership failures. This supports the saying, "People join companies and leave bosses." More on Eileen later.

Being "placed" in a leadership role by a recruiter doesn't ensure success. While the retention rates for such placements may be higher, it doesn't guarantee smooth cultural assimilation. Hence, some progressive search firms now provide onboarding coaching to those they place.

Even if recommended by a senior executive or board member, you're not immune to failure. Strong relationships can quickly deteriorate.

---

[1] Brooke Masters, "Rise of a headhunter," Financial Times, March 30, 2009, https://www.ft.com/content/19975256-1af2-11de-8aa3-0000779fd2ac.

Sometimes, the champion of a new leader leaves soon after their hire, disrupting the support dynamic.

Relating to the Turks and Caicos example, adapting to a new leadership environment can be risky. Changes, such as the departure of a friend-leader or the arrival of a new one, are like navigating new roads with unfamiliar rules and signs. Misinterpreting these circumstances can lead to minor or major collisions. Hence, your first year in a new role is not "business as usual."

Without caution, you can miss signals and signs, leading to avoidable accidents ranging from minor to fatal. As a leader in a new environment, it's crucial to slow down, understand the surroundings, and learn the rules.

This one-year process is like initiating a new sailor for an America's Cup team. Despite the past experience, each boat is different and requires an adjustment period. Learning the ropes before heading into the open sea minimizes risk. If you are a competitive racer, it's best to test your crew on calm seas before a race with high stakes. The onboarding, assimilation, and integration process is both an art and a science. Study it like you would any skill. No matter how much you already know, the stakes are very high, and there is plenty to learn as you take control of a new high-performance vessel.

Careful planning for successful entry and mastery is crucial. Newly appointed leaders face many potential threats during their first year. Avoidable mistakes can make you vulnerable, so it's essential to prepare thoroughly. From start to finish, effective onboarding, assimilation, and integration is a full twelve-month endeavor. The question to ask yourself is this: "How can I go beyond just surviving my first year and truly thrive and establish myself as a key leader and influencer in the organization?"

Starting a leadership role is like preparing for a 10K race. You prepare physically, mentally, and spiritually, aware of the stress, pressure, and expectations. Thorough preparation, a clear playbook, the proper mindset, and the right resources are vital.

Like a runner, the start of your role sets the pace for the finish. Your first year is unique, requiring a strategic approach, much like pacing oneself for a race. This is a marathon, not a sprint.

The Art of Your Start addresses two groups: new leaders and those bringing them in. The goal for both groups is the same: make zero onboarding, assimilation, and integration mistakes during the first twelve months. Those who approach this year with caution and planning often succeed, while those who rush in without preparation tend to fail.

The stakes, higher for senior leaders, can affect career trajectory and net worth. Your "career equity," based on your successful job history, dictates your career progress, market demand, job opportunities, and wealth creation potential. The reward for successfully navigating multiple leadership roles is substantial.

Because the stakes are so high, it is normal and natural to expect the newly hired leader to produce immediate results. This is akin to having your first mile of the race be your fastest mile. Danger. Everyone wants immediate results, yourself included, but what is wanted and what's realistic are two different things.

New hires may feel pressured to deliver immediate results to prove their worth, while hiring managers may have similar expectations. However, these ideas can lead to counterproductive actions. Everyone gets one chance at a great start, which, as in a race, requires avoiding poor choices that can lead to metaphorical muscle cramps or torn ligaments.

Higher-level leadership positions often pose the greatest difficulty for seamless assimilation and integration. Both the organization and the new leader tend to be set in their ways. Will there be a clash of values, culture, expectations, style, or vision? Will the organization embrace the change this leader will try to bring? Will there be a disagreement over strategic direction? Will there be an acceptable change to roles and responsibilities? A lot can go wrong.

Immediate results need to be subordinate to successful assimilation and integration into the role, culture, key relationships, and so much more. This doesn't happen quickly. That is why this book goes way beyond traditional onboarding. It is a much longer process than many think.

Starting a race moderately, despite being able to sprint, is tough. A healthy fear of failure helps top athletes pace themselves. Similarly, corporate leaders face their own races. The initial pace can quickly become uncontrollable, leading to failure.

I would like permission to coach and advise you through this process that few have mastered. It's not every day that a leader changes jobs. Even if it has been successfully done a dozen times before, usually, it has been at lower levels. The higher up the organizational ladder you climb, the more a careful and thorough warmup will matter. New leaders can't rapidly change an organization but must quickly adapt to its culture and their superior's expectations. In this first year, you and the hiring manager are assessing each other, creating a delicate dynamic that requires great skill to navigate successfully.

Just like in a race, mental preparation is essential before starting. The first few miles are crucial, just as the initial twelve months are critical for assimilation and integration. A strong start significantly impacts your performance throughout the journey.

Entering a new leadership role involves a significant investment of time, energy, and reputation. Successfully transitioning is vital. The first year sets the stage for future success, making it a pivotal opportunity. The hiring manager's impression of you during this time can make or break your relationship. Unfortunately, there's a one-in-five chance of failure within the first year. Let's ensure you defy those odds.

In the early stages, take slow and steady strides, being patient. Expectations are generally lower during this time. Both leader and hiring manager should have reasonable expectations for the first few months. It may feel odd to pace yourself when others seem to be moving quickly, but it's crucial to grasp the culture, build relationships, and understand expectations before picking up speed. As you observe your peers running hard and fast, it's important to remember that each person must run their own race. Your focus should be on consciously pacing yourself and not letting others dictate your speed. Your peers who have been in their roles for a while can afford to run at a faster pace, as they have already gained what they need. Run your own race and stay true to your own timeline.

Let's go back to my marathon analogy for a moment with a quick story.

The sound of the starter's pistol jolted the crowd of several thousand behind me. With a burst of energy, I crossed the starting line and found myself leading the pack. However, the experienced runners swiftly overtook me, leaving me behind. It was a rookie mistake to position myself at the front, thinking it would give me a great start. This strategy backfired as I exhausted myself trying to keep up. Similarly, it's important to recognize your more seasoned peers have a different pace that may be challenging to match right away.

Introduction to "The Manager's Corner"

At the end of every chapter, there is a special section dedicated to the manager.

Failed assimilation and integration come with a significant cost to both the organization and the leader. The average tenure of leaders in new roles is decreasing, leading to increased costs of failure. Financial losses can include decreased company value, diminished competitiveness, and a tarnished reputation.

Internally, failed assimilation and integration can result in lower morale, loss of top talent, and challenges in filling roles. Overcoming these issues requires proactive measures. Organizations must provide greater support to new leaders to ensure successful transitions.

After a candidate accepts an offer, there is a common tendency to relax. However, this is a critical time to increase investment in your new leadership talent and go the extra mile for successful assimilation. Reading this book is a good starting point, even if you can only read the last paragraph of each chapter. It is specifically written to you.

Most importantly, don't delegate this responsibility solely to the people and culture department. As the manager, you are ultimately accountable for the success of your new leader.

Mastering the art and science of onboarding, assimilating, and integrating leaders is crucial for both organizations and the leaders themselves. Unfortunately, many do not give it the attention it deserves, leading to rough starts and unwanted turnover. Embracing this process can significantly improve talent retention and drive organizational performance. Realizing it is a year-long journey that you own is a great first step.

SECTION ONE
THE PROBLEM

This section looks at the most common problems all leaders face in their first year in a new role.

There are certain leaders who are gifted at artfully starting new roles. The problem I see is that most think they fall into this category, yet few are truly "artful starters."

Therefore, to master the art of their start, most need to first take a scientific approach, breaking down this process into easy-to-follow phases and employing a specific proven methodology. The good news: it is an easily learned science and can be approached as such. So, why title this book *The Art of Your Start*? Because it is both an art and a science. Simply following a prescriptive playbook will not ensure success. Thus, here you will find a very prescriptive methodology AND some great latitude for creativity as you onboard, assimilate, and integrate. From CEO to frontline leader, the problems, solutions, and resources are the same, but applied "artfully" in different ways. It just takes time and intentionality, which is what you are demonstrating by reading and applying this material.

For those who are already acutely aware of all the problems inherent during your first year in a new role or job, feel free to skip this section and go right to "Section 2: The Solution."

For those who are managers of new leaders, heads of people and culture, board members, and CEOs, you can speed through this book by reading the last paragraph of each chapter, entitled "The Manager's Corner."

CHAPTER 1

THE SCIENCE *and* ART OF STARTING

Steve just started a new role as a vice president of a major division. This book says that he has ninety days to deliver major "quick" wins. However, the culture is extremely slow moving, he is not being brought in to make major changes, and nothing is obviously broken. Blindly following my generic guidance would lead him to fail. He is rightfully tailoring and adjusting his approach to best meet the culture. He finds himself constantly pulling back from making changes he sees as "nice but not necessary" and is getting great performance feedback from his manager. As his onboarding coach, I am watching him artfully adopt my playbook to best meet the demands of this unique environment. You should too.

Executive onboarding coaches like myself have studied the dramas that play out when newly appointed leaders crash and burn because of poor onboarding, assimilation, and integration practices. No matter how many times you've started a new leadership role, there are always unique factors that can derail you if you're not careful. Understanding the science behind this art will equip you with a powerful set of tools to use for yourself as you transition, or to ensure the effective assimilation of a leader you are hiring.

Even the Best Can Get Fired

Everyone knows examples of top talent not working out, whether involving internal moves within the same organization or new jobs in new companies. Each leadership move should be considered as a new role, such as when one organization has merged with another. The same onboarding principles apply. Changed roles mean new responsibilities, expectations, and people with which to interface. In many cases, that garners amplified constructive criticism from peers and superiors. Which stakeholders to pay the most attention to can be a dilemma, and as you know, hidden agendas abound.

As an example of such dangers, Stephen, a CHRO, hired me to onboard a new CFO for his one-billion-dollar PE-owned entity. An enlightened people and culture leader, he was aware of the 20 to 25 percent failure rate for newly appointed leaders. I did my job, and the CFO assimilated well, despite a night-and-day difference in style from the last CFO. My six-month engagement ended, and I lost touch with Stephen.

Six years later, I reconnected with Stephen after a merger between his company and one of its competitors. Stephen was no longer employed there. I asked why. In his words:

"I thought everything was fine. I kept my job, title, staff, and responsibilities. However, I failed to pick up the subtle clues that things were different. It's hard when you have the same desk and chair. I was moved out without even realizing it was happening."

Assimilation takes on a new meaning when you consider this story. Even with Stephen's experience at onboarding (he understood the science), his performance didn't align with new company expectations. He was quietly shuffled out. Similar stories are everywhere. Your organization may undergo a change in leadership in the next few years. Will you be ready to do all that is needed to assimilate?

Learning from Others' Mistakes

As you're undoubtedly aware, it's often better to learn from other people's mistakes instead of making your own. Here is one such lesson.

A few decades ago, Craig was a highly successful CEO in Toronto, Canada. He is now retired, just sitting on boards and investing in companies. Pre-Zoom, I made monthly trips from Austin, TX, to Toronto for sessions with him over the course of five years.

Craig grew exponentially. He was a rock star. Then one day, he received an offer he didn't want to refuse and sold his multi-billion-dollar company. When I asked him what his plans were, I was surprised by his answer.

"Daniel, I want to find a bigger role."

"But you don't need to work anymore," I replied. "You can do anything you want."

"Yeah, I know. But it's not about the money. It's about the challenge. I want to run a bigger company, maybe in the USA."

"Okay. Well, I will be happy to help you find one. I also do this thing called executive career coaching, and I help top leaders like you make an effective career transition and find an ideal new role."

Craig was not interested. He had this paradigm of me as an executive leadership coach, helping him to be a more effective in place leader. I couldn't change his mindset, so he went off on his own to be his own career coach.

Being your own career advisor is as dangerous as being your own onboarding coach. There are many pitfalls. Bob Snelling, the former CEO of Snelling Personnel, co-authored with me *Recruiters: The Inside Story*. He is a legend in the executive search industry who, many decades ago, was THE guy who coined the word "recruiter." Bob is known for often saying, "The worst thing you can do is get only one job offer." Why? Lack of choice. It is a go/no-go decision you must make, which is suboptimal. Ideally, you have one or two other offers to compare, contrast, and negotiate. Well, Craig got ONE job offer. It met his criteria of being a bigger, more impressive role so, of course, he took it.

When Craig accepted this CEO role from a major US-based company, I fully expected him to keep me as his coach. After all, that was my niche. When he told me that he wanted to get settled in his new role first, I was disappointed.

A month into his new role, Craig took a call from me and gave a euphoric update on all the changes he was making. I thought to myself, "Slow down." All I managed to say was, "Wow, you've been busy!"

I reached out again two weeks later for a follow-up call. After another set of positive updates, I asked, "What are you struggling with the most right now?"

Craig hesitated, then told me, "Well, I just had an argument with Nathan. He's a board member giving me a hard time about a reduction in force that I want to do."

I stopped him right there. "Wait a minute, Craig. You can't be getting into an argument with a board member this early. Bring me in and let me coach you. I know this onboarding stuff really well. Let me help you make a smooth transition into this role."

He pushed back. "Let me work through this first."

Again disappointed, I agreed to call him back in two weeks.

The next time we spoke, it was a super short conversation. "Okay, come to New York," he said. I knew he was in trouble.

The next week, as I landed at JFK, I mulled over what I would say. Something like, "I think you're heading into trouble. I researched the company. They aren't known for integrity. They have an aggressive, dog-eat-dog culture, radically different from the relational one you built in Toronto. Be careful!" But I never got the chance.

Traffic was bad, and I pulled up to his building on Long Island with only fifteen minutes to spare. To my utter amazement, Craig was walking out the front door carrying a box. I thought, "Unbelievable. You can't make this stuff up." He put the box in his trunk and drove away. Stunned, but totally curious, I parked my rental and mustered the courage to go inside. In the back of my head, I had a feeling Craig was not coming back, but who knew?

Mentioning Craig's name caused the receptionist to stop like a deer in headlights. She made a call. Moments later, Arthur, the chairman of the board, came out and introduced himself. Arthur was also the founder of the company. He was the reason the culture was so toxic, and I immediately became nervous. I braced myself as we entered an imposing boardroom with a thirty-foot conference table. Feeling sure I was about to get a grilling, I braced myself for questions like, "What makes you a coach? What are your credentials? What is leadership coaching anyway, and why should we pay you?" As he directed me to my seat and took his place at the head, I quickly prepared my answers. I knew I only had a short time to allay any concerns he had—and boy, did he look skeptical! If body language could yell, he was screaming at me.

"Are you Craig's coach?" Arthur asked.

"Yes, sir," I stammered.

"Craig won't be meeting with you today. But let me ask you a question. Who the (expletive) has time to blog? Do you teach your clients to blog?"

"No," I answered honestly. Blogging was relatively new back then, and Craig was ahead of his time. I realized this wasn't about me and relaxed. Then I flashed back to Craig putting the box into his trunk, and I knew what had happened.

"Craig's no longer here," Arthur continued, "and we can't (expletive) figure out what the (expletive) happened. He came so highly recommended, but he was doing (expletive) frontline employee training in time management and blogging about that and many other trivial things. What the (expletive) has that got to do with running a (expletive) multibillion-dollar company?"

Craig never used expletives. This is not a judgment, simply an observation of a cultural mismatch that was obvious in the first thirty seconds with Arthur. How could Craig have missed such an obvious red flag? Ego is a dangerous thing when selecting a new role, and Craig's ego and "bigger-is-better" attitude had gotten the best of him.

After thirty minutes of Arthur ranting, I was free to go. Wow! Clearly, there was a huge cultural disconnect. Arthur's vulgar language alone was enough to prove this. Craig was a sophisticated Midwesterner known for his ability to connect with frontline employees. Arthur was a brash, rough-around-the-edges New Yorker who had grown his company from zero to billions with an abrasive, demanding style. Craig's insistence on making the reduction in force without full board support was enough to push Arthur over the edge in less than two months. Ouch.

Hindsight Is 20/20

Reflecting on Craig's time at Arthur's organization, my debrief with him provided valuable insights. Craig employed his usual rapport-building techniques with employees, yet they were misinterpreted within Arthur's culture, especially by Arthur. Additionally, Craig prioritized safeguarding the cash and wanted to cut the organization's alarming rate of expenditure. Arthur disagreed. While Craig believed he had performed excellently (a sentiment shared by me), his actions were not in alignment with Arthur's expectations.

Recognizing when the gameboard has been reset can be challenging. Changes and new developments call for a comprehensive approach to onboarding, assimilation, and integration to ensure all factors are considered. Craig's example highlights the importance of avoiding conflicts during the initial months in a new position—especially with your manager.

An onboarding, assimilation, and integration coach is an invaluable resource when utilized effectively. However, it is crucial not to wait until you encounter problems to seek assistance. A common pattern I observe is clients using their biweekly, half-hour integration sessions to share an overwhelming stream of "good news." Here's a word of advice: It is more beneficial to use that time to identify "red flags" and address areas that require improvement. While we want to support your achievements, our ultimate goal is to see you successfully complete your first year and be there for long-term celebrations.

Gaining a New Manager

As you face a change in leadership, you should treat the situation much as you would if starting a new job in a new company. The good news is that you already have a proven track record at your company. However, this existing track record may work against you, as the new manager will surely seek opinions about you from key stakeholders, and some of what they hear may not be favorable, depending on whom they ask. Furthermore, newly appointed managers typically prefer to bring in their own team members, which is a natural inclination.

You might think to yourself, "I will surely be acknowledged as a loyal employee who has served diligently and performed exceptionally well." Undoubtedly, loyalty and performance are important. However, the primary cause of departures among established team members is often the failure to establish a connection with the new manager. The advice may seem straightforward, but it can be challenging to implement. Focus on building a strong relationship with your new manager. Positive rapport often outweighs other factors. Whether justified or not, this is reality.

Lastly, allow me to share an exercise I conduct with my onboarding, assimilation, and integration clients, which I learned from those top leaders starting a new role. Within the first thirty to sixty days, I ask them to rank their direct reports from #1 (most valuable "keeper") to the least favorable ("likely need to replace"). Then, I ask about their plan for the lowest-scoring direct report.

If your manager left today, and you received someone new, how would they rank you? The great rapport you currently have with your existing manager may not put you in good stead with your new boss. This makes the case for treating this as if you just started a new job.

The Manager's Corner: *The Science and Art of Starting*

First, let me say that we should stop calling it "onboarding," which is generally thought of as the very earliest part of what is, in fact, a one-year onboarding, assimilation, and integration process.

Creating a positive and effective process is your responsibility. In my experience with over two thousand clients in the past thirty-five years, the majority did not receive significant intentional support beyond the initial list of introductions, job descriptions, and projects from their managers. This is particularly prevalent at the VP level and above, where it is assumed that senior leaders inherently know what to do. While junior leaders may receive better attention during onboarding, assimilation, and integration, I strongly believe that investing more effort here is crucial. Considering the significant resources dedicated to attracting and hiring top talent, it only makes sense to prioritize a world-class onboarding, assimilation, and integration process.

The "honeymoon" period often appears to be one-sided. Believing that things are going well, you may give the new leader space to acclimate, feeling relieved that they are on board. However, it is important to pause and consider if there is early disenfranchisement occurring. Don't accept the "all-is-good" response at face value. Are you actively investigating potential obstacles they may be facing? Are you working to remove barriers for them? Have you created a safe environment for your new leader to share their initial experiences and impressions with you?

Internal promotions pose challenges too. It takes time for new leaders to grasp shifts in expectations. Providing a gentle nudge or a few words can help them realize that despite the familiar environment, certain things have changed, requiring adjustment.

Internal promotions can be perceived as easier since the leader is already familiar with the organizational culture. However, they can also pose challenges, as they come with perceived biases, existing alliances, detractors, and other factors that may hinder the widespread acceptance of the leader's new role. This often happens, particularly among former peers.

If you are a board director reading this, note that you play a vital role in supporting the success of a newly appointed CEO. Research indicates that first-time CEOs face challenging odds, with only a fifty-fifty chance of surviving beyond their first year. As a CEO, it's important to recognize that there is a 20 to 25 percent likelihood of your new direct report either being fired or resigning within their first year. These statistics emphasize the need for proactive measures to ensure successful leadership transitions and retention of key talent.

To ensure the success of new leadership talent, stakeholders must make concerted efforts. Reading relevant books and hiring onboarding coaches can help. However, active involvement from managers (including the board) is critical. Instead of assuming smooth progress, you should actively identify and address assimilation and integration challenges.

CHAPTER 2

OUT OF THE STARTING BLOCKS

To run a successful race, serious athletes use heart rate monitors and watches to track their performance. At the start, you may notice a faster pulse due to excitement and pent-up energy. Your goals and the desire to achieve a personal record increase your heart rate. Yet it's crucial to begin at a slow pace to avoid pushing your heart into the anaerobic red zone, as it becomes difficult to regain control. A good coach's advice: "Run your own race; don't let others' pace dictate yours." The same is my advice for you: "Start slow, get into a sustainable cadence, and maintain your own optimal pace."

It may seem like everyone is passing you, and you know you could go faster and keep up if you tried, but you also know that you'll flame out before the finish line if you do. Instead, you lower your expectation of keeping up with the faster runners. You set a pace you can maintain for the many kilometers ahead. You may finish with a new personal record; you may not—but you'll finish. That's the most important thing to keep in mind.

Just like in running, it may feel disheartening as others pass you at work, though you know you could keep up if you pushed yourself. However, you must understand that pushing too hard will lead to exhaustion before reaching the finish line. Adjust your expectation of keeping up with faster "runners" and set a sustainable pace for the long distance ahead. While achieving a new personal record is possible, it is not the sole focus. The crucial thing is to finish the race. Always remind yourself, "This is a marathon, not a sprint."

When embarking on a new leadership role, adopting the mindset of a long-distance runner is valuable. Your objective is to reach the finish line, running your own race. You hold sole responsibility for setting your pace. It is useful to reflect on the expectations others have of you. A saying worth remembering is, "Never will the expectations be lower for you than in your first one hundred days."

Experts believe that the challenges of surviving in a new role are more significant now than ever before. In 2002, I conducted significant research on this subject. To quote one such resource: "Leaders everywhere confront a set of irrevocable imperatives, changing realities driven by profound social, political, economic, and technical changes. Our world, not to mention the business world, is in the midst of transformational change, calling for new leadership".[1] Two decades and a pandemic later, this is more true than ever!

Another reason for your survival being in greater jeopardy now is that boards of directors, shareholders, and key stakeholders have less patience compared to previous eras. Presently, there are substantial political and business pressures, and venture capitalists, private equity firms, and public shareholders are less inclined to adopt a "wait and see" or "benefit of the doubt" approach when it comes to organizational performance. Consequently, this directly impacts you in profound ways and greatly increases pressure on you to produce results.

In the current landscape, elevated expectations, intense competition, and rapid promotion of new leaders are driving high turnover in leadership roles. Companies, in the past, focused extensively on internal talent development. However, as the rate of change in

---

[1] Daniel Goleman, Richard Boyatzis, and Annie McKee, *Primal Leadership: Realizing the Power of Emotional Intelligence* (Boston: Harvard Business School Press, 2002), 246.

business accelerated and as tenure decreased, there was a shift towards hiring from the outside to fill gaps quickly. This shift, however, has its drawbacks, including potential cultural misfits and higher costs.[2]

In my experience, overconfidence emerges as a significant risk factor in all cases. Let me instill a sense of healthy caution to prevent you from being overly confident in this area that few have studied, let alone mastered.

Overconfidence Will Trip You Up

Onboarding, assimilation, and integration failures predominantly occur among individuals joining a new company. The primary reason for this is that established leaders possess significantly more knowledge about their organization compared to newcomers. Familiarity grants advantages such as understanding organizational politics, culture, formal and informal communications, and the true measures of performance. In contrast, leaders hired externally lack these advantages. Reflecting on this reality, it becomes evident that there is a compelling case for intensifying efforts to develop the next generation of leaders within the company itself. Most junior leaders express strong eagerness for development, and the more we invest in their growth, the better it is for everyone involved.

In my role as a corporate leadership coach, I often collaborate with the board, CEO, and head of HR to develop the executive team. When a new executive is hired, I am frequently tasked with their onboarding, assimilation, and integration. A recurring pattern I observe is overconfidence. These leaders often join with a sense of business as usual. They are frequently recruited from other companies and given better compensation and a higher title, boosting their ego. Based on my

---

[2] Peter Cappelli, "Talent Management for the Twenty-first Century," *Harvard Business Review* 86, no. 3 (March 2008), https://hbr.org/2008/03/talent-management-for-the-twenty-first-century.

experience, it takes longer for these types of leaders to admit difficulties. Equally, hiring managers don't want to admit that despite a significant investment made in a search firm, an ill-suited candidate was selected.

My advice: Approach this process with humility. Adopt a "listen and learn" mindset and set aside your ego. Walk humbly among your superiors, peers, and subordinates. For the new leader, there's no need to prove yourself. Remember, you were selected and chosen for this position. Avoid boasting about your accomplishments or past experiences. A saying worth remembering is, "No one cares how much you know until they know how much you care." Show genuine care and concern for understanding the needs of those you are there to serve. Embrace a servant leadership mindset (more on that later) and prioritize meeting their needs rather than your own.

Allow me to share a case study.

Enrique assumed his role after a year of searching for the perfect leadership position. Brimming with excitement to lead an organization, his passion for being a change agent overwhelmed him, and he immediately sought to address numerous issues within the company. Within a month, he initiated three major projects, followed by sweeping organizational changes within the next three months. Unfortunately, after six months, the CEO decided to let him go, citing a poor cultural fit. When I met Enrique, he was bewildered and couldn't comprehend how he ended up unemployed. From my perspective, it was evident that his intense drive, unleashed without much restraint, proved to be too overpowering for the organization to handle.

To avoid excessive confidence, retrieve your past performance reviews, 360-degree assessment reports, and leadership test results from previous employment. Review the identified weaknesses on your list. This exercise can help ground you and provide a reality check. Additionally, reading this book can serve as a "cause to pause," prompting you to reflect on the potential challenges, unexpected turns, and lack of guidance you may encounter while navigating unfamiliar territory.

This is not business as usual.

Alignment Is Essential

Frequent frustrations voiced by my clients involve the challenge of securing time on their new manager's calendar. The lack of regular communication with higher-level superiors is a clear route to misalignment. When roles, responsibilities, and expectations are not in sync, relationships can swiftly veer off course.

One might assume that getting the attention of your manager in the initial three to six months of a new role would be straightforward. However, this is often not the case, and there are common reasons. The primary factor is that your manager experiences a sense of relief, knowing that someone is now responsible for your function. Consequently, they believe they can shift their focus to other neglected areas that have accumulated during the time it took to find and hire you.

Another common observation is that many adopt a "lone ranger" approach in an attempt to prove themselves. Even experienced individuals can become overconfident when entering a new role. They may think, "I've got this." Believing they fully understand the organization's needs, they proceed to execute their plans brilliantly. However, the issue lies in the fact that it is *your* plan rather than a *shared* plan.

Time after time, with terminated leaders, I ask, "Did you stay aligned with your manager?"

Invariably, the response is, "Yes, initially. However, I mistakenly assumed that the early direction provided to me was meant to be continued. Consequently, I stayed the course, unaware that expectations had shifted without my knowledge until it was too late."

Indeed, change is inevitable, including in expectations. Weekly check-ins with your manager are invaluable for establishing and preserving alignment with their goals and expectations. If your manager is too occupied to meet with you at least once per week (or twice per month, at the very least), it should raise a red flag. Addressing this issue before it becomes an accepted pattern is crucial. Otherwise, it can lead to disastrous consequences for your relationship.

You may argue, "But my manager only schedules one-on-ones twice per month." While that frequency may work for others, as a newcomer, maintaining alignment is paramount. Two weeks is too long between check-ins, especially during your first three months in the role. It may be inconvenient, and you may feel like a burden, but it is essential. Your manager may also not be enthusiastic about it, as they have other pressing matters to attend to. However, you will appreciate the benefits later on. I am challenging you to strive for perfect alignment. If there is another effective way to achieve it, I've not seen it. Unfortunately, many promising relationships deteriorate due to this issue. When my onboarding clients report canceled one-on-ones, we see it as a significant red flag and take proactive measures to emphasize to the manager the importance of maintaining a regular cadence.

One of the challenges you may face is your ego getting in the way. You may be hesitant to appear weak or needy, as you were brought in to alleviate the burden on an already overwhelmed manager with numerous direct reports and objectives that may be off track. You want to be the hero and save the day, rescuing your manager from the challenges they have faced in your absence. However, it is crucial to remember that many have taken this approach, received praise initially, but then found themselves unexpectedly exiting the organization due to a lack of alignment with the very manager they tried to support.

It's important to recognize that regular one-on-one meetings are not the sole solution for achieving successful alignment. Verbal dialogues can often lead to misunderstandings. Another effective approach to maintaining alignment early on is through a written hundred-day onboarding plan, which I will fully discuss later. This plan outlines actionable steps and is regularly reviewed together with your manager. It holds great value and helps ensure that alignment is maintained as priorities and expectations may evolve. Comprehensive documentation of your job description, key priorities, and expected deliverables, including milestones and metrics, is essential. Dedicate extra effort to establishing and sustaining complete alignment on your objectives right from the start.

Issues with Managers

At times, a lack of alignment can be attributed to the manager. They may struggle with effective communication or have poor time-management skills, resulting in limited availability. In certain situations, you may find yourself dealing with seemingly hopeless circumstances that are beyond your control, such as being hired by someone already facing performance challenges of their own. In these instances, it is crucial to diligently identify and address such issues early on. You may need to proactively reach out cross-functionally to drive alignment across areas outside of your manager's control, securing buy-in for these efforts. Additionally, if you are not the CEO, remember that you have a manager overseeing your manager. Maintaining communication with that person is valuable. While the specifics of fostering this relationship with your manager's manager fall into the realm of "art" rather than a prescriptive playbook, building trust with your manager enables you to have those meetings. This can further allow you to assess any gaps in alignment between them. Although delicate and sensitive, those who successfully cultivate and maintain this high-trust relationship with their manager tend to outperform the norm.

Dysfunctional Relationships

You may encounter a trust issue from the start. Your manager may not have been in favor of hiring you, but external factors or persuasive individuals influenced the decision. Regardless of the context, the problem remains evident: lack of contact leads to a lack of alignment, ultimately resulting in failure in the role. The solution is equally straightforward: maintaining regular contact provides the opportunity to realign shifting priorities and expectations. Consistent realignment offers the best chance of success for everyone.

Your manager may struggle with delegation, being excessively hands-on, and not allowing you the freedom to perform your job effectively. In this case, having an uncomfortable conversation to establish clear expectations becomes necessary. Accepting this dysfunctional behavior could result in your peers perceiving you as ineffective, leading to negative feedback that reaches your manager and beyond. Ultimately, this can lead to being labeled as a low performer and confined to a limited role.

Numerous potential scenarios could lead to failure, but it is your responsibility to ensure that you don't succumb to them. You are not a victim of circumstances. Remember, you're either part of the solution, or you're part of the problem. Perfect managers do not exist; each has their own strengths and weaknesses. Your task is to identify these strengths and weaknesses and skillfully navigate the areas of weakness to achieve complete alignment on expectations.

In summary, it is crucial to take proactive measures in identifying and addressing potential issues early on in your relationship with your manager.

Common Failure Points

At this point, you may be experiencing a sense of unease as you contemplate the potential challenges that lie ahead. However, my role is not to provide comfort. As the well-known phrase goes, "Only the paranoid survive." By highlighting the various issues that can arise, you become better equipped to identify emerging problems, take appropriate actions, and proactively address them before they evolve into significant obstacles on your path to success.

At a high level, there are several common circumstances that frequently lead to onboarding, assimilation, and integration failure, such as:

1. Inadequate skill set for the job: Similar to spraining your ankle at the starting line, you may discover that the job is different or the requirements have changed, leaving you struggling to keep up.
2. Lack of high-trust relationships: Comparable to severe cramps during a race, failure to build trust with peers and your manager can hinder your progress. Address this issue early on to prevent further complications.
3. Organizational focus on retention: Like an unclear course, an organization that fails to prioritize retention during the first one hundred days may cause you to veer off track. Advocate for alignment if you sense you're off course.
4. Overexertion and burnout: Pushing yourself too hard too soon can lead to exhaustion and prematurely giving up. Pace yourself for the long run and prioritize sustainable progress.
5. Neglecting self-care: Failure to monitor your well-being, both physically and mentally, can result in breakdowns and falling short of your intended goals. Prioritize self-care and recharge regularly.

6. New manager appointment: If a new manager is appointed over you, treat it as starting a new job. Begin the onboarding, assimilation, and integration cycle again to ensure a successful transition. Mental preparedness is crucial to navigating unexpected challenges.
7. Treating the position as the same as your previous job: A new role requires a different approach. Approach it with the necessary strategy and planning, just as the successful completion of a race requires careful consideration.

Awareness of these common mistakes allows you to proactively mitigate risks and enhance your chances of a successful first year.

Passing the Trust Test

Building trust is a crucial aspect of any new relationship. As mentioned before, the saying "People join companies and leave bosses" emphasizes the significance of trust in determining one's success. Once trust is lost, it can be challenging to regain.

Let's consider Sheila as an example. Here is what she said:

"Knowing what I know now, I realize that success in a new role often depends more on luck than skill. My previous experience didn't go well. I was hired by a manager I had worked with before, but when they moved to a different role, I got a new manager who was difficult to connect with emotionally and logistically. Despite my efforts to get to know her, I couldn't seem to secure time on her schedule, and our meetings were uncomfortable. The lack of trust between us became apparent. I eventually gave up, failing to be intentional about building a strong relationship or showcasing my capabilities to her. As a result, I was pushed out of the company within a year. It was a disappointing outcome considering the job was a perfect fit for me, and I had the required skills. The main failure was the lack of a solid connection with my new manager. I should have been more proactive in building trust, and she could have made a more concerted effort as well. We both missed the mark."

Failure to establish a high level of trust with a new manager often results in terminations or resignations. It is crucial to invest effort in achieving and sustaining alignment and trust with your superior.

During the COVID era, many of my clients faced the challenge of not being able to meet their managers in person. However, they were able to overcome this obstacle by putting extra effort into building high-trust relationships through virtual means. Personally, I transitioned to a predominantly virtual coaching practice prior to COVID, and during that time, many individuals struggled with video quality and presence, resulting in amusing backgrounds and visual mistakes. Today, there is no excuse for poor video. It is essential to invest in excellent equipment, create a suitable background, and present yourself professionally. Numerous online resources are available to help improve your video presence. Being proficient in video communication is crucial during your first year.

In summary, there are four crucial actions to take right from the start:

1. Embrace humility.
2. Establish complete alignment with your manager.
3. Maintain a keen awareness of common failure points.
4. Foster high levels of trust.

By prioritizing these actions, you will be off to a great start.

The Manager's Corner: *Out of the Starting Blocks*

A common mistake I often observe when bringing in a new leader is neglecting retention efforts during their first one hundred days. The recruitment process does not end with the offer letter; it is only halfway complete. While the new leader has their responsibilities in securing long-term success, there are also actions that you should take.

Review the list of seven common failure points mentioned earlier. Being aware of these potential pitfalls can greatly benefit you. Keep in mind that a newly recruited leader may still have other job opportunities available to them. It is crucial to go the extra mile in providing a warm and supportive welcome. Do not let up on your onboarding, assimilation, and integration efforts until you are confident that the leader has successfully transitioned into their new role, assimilated into the company culture, and become fully aligned with the priorities of both you and your organization. From my point of view, this is a year-long process.

I have witnessed numerous instances where leaders accepted suboptimal roles because they were unable to secure their preferred positions. They reluctantly started in their second-choice role, only to receive their desired position a month or two later. Some individuals even return to their previous job, while others leave after experiencing unfavorable surprises and feeling disillusioned with the organization. It is important to recognize that there is no guarantee that your company's structure or culture will align perfectly with the new leader's vision. Even candidates who initially seem like a perfect fit may decide your organization's opportunity falls short of their expectations. It can be shocking and embarrassing for senior leaders when they have to inform the CEO or board about a resignation in such circumstances.

The success or failure of the new leader is a direct reflection of the person who selected them. Hiring managers should be cautious, as top leaders usually have backup options. It is wise to refrain from assuming that you have convinced the new leader to stay until they have been with your organization for a minimum of three to six months. If they decide to leave within a few months, they may not even list your organization on their resume. This is a common occurrence.

I encourage you to read this entire chapter as it addresses frequent challenges faced by managers like yourself in onboarding and assimilating top talent. It can provide valuable insights and help you reflect on your skills in this area. If you were to choose just one chapter to read from this book, I recommend this one for its significance and relevance.

CHAPTER 3

PREPARING TO RUN

If you've already started your new role, feel free to skip this chapter, as it primarily covers pre-start best practices.

Take Your Time

Before hastily jumping into your new role after signing the offer letter, it's essential to pause and consider a few crucial factors. While there may be eagerness and pent-up demand from your new manager, it's important to approach the transition thoughtfully and strategically.

Taking time off between roles is highly recommended for leaders. It allows you to clear your mind and properly prepare for the transition. A week may be insufficient; aiming for a minimum of two weeks is advisable. Even if you have been actively searching for a new role for months, it's crucial not to overlook the need for a mental reset. It is also essential to familiarize yourself with the onboarding, assimilation, and integration process before diving into something new.

Let's consider what happened to another top leader.

Recently, Larry left a role as head of corporate development. He resigned from one position and started the next with no breaks in between, which included packing up a house and family and moving cross-country. Within five weeks of starting his new job, he completed a fifty-million-dollar acquisition that had already been in the works.

Totally consumed, with no time to build relational bridges, he plunged headfirst into a big project. The relationships at the private equity firm that owned the company suffered, and two things happened. First, the acquisition was a huge success; second, Larry was exited after six months in the role.

Larry's experience serves as a cautionary tale. The intense pressure of the acquisition revealed Larry's operational weaknesses to the PE firm. Larry is now head of corporate development in a different role, and he has hired a strong number two who will handle all the operational details of transactions, offsetting his weakest areas. This was his plan in his previous role, but he regrets not executing it sooner. He had not taken any time to read onboarding books or get any significant coaching before he found himself drowning, all the while believing he was successfully treading water.

Taking time off between roles is essential for your well-being and preparation. It is highly recommended to allocate time for rest, reflection, and readiness. Prioritize your mental health, your personal life, and adequate preparation.

Start by reading this book and another recommended in Section 3 to study the art and science of onboarding, assimilation, and integration. Take time for introspection before your role begins.

I suggest you also answer these ten questions:

1. What past mistakes do I want to avoid in starting this new role?
2. What are my top ten strengths? (Write these out as a rank-ordered list.)
3. Which strengths should I focus on in my new role?
4. Which strengths should I be cautious of overusing?
5. What are my top ten weaknesses? (Write these out as a rank-ordered list.)

6. Which weaknesses should I avoid, especially in this new role?
7. How can I mitigate these weaknesses through hiring, delegation, or other means?
8. What is my playbook for the first thirty, sixty, and ninety days in the role?
9. Who are the key stakeholders I need to build relationships with immediately?
10. When can I schedule a one-week break (vacation) around the three-month mark to reflect, analyze my progress, and plan for the second quarter in the role?

Full Integration and Assimilation Takes Time

Even with the best onboarding, assimilation, and integration practices and the support of an experienced mentor, advisor, and/or coach, a significant number of leaders still fail. One reason is that most are not adept in starting new roles. It's a challenging process. Even leaders with decades of experience can make common mistakes in their first year. It can be difficult to readjust while relying solely on past experiences, as each company has its unique culture, people, and business dynamics, requiring a fresh approach.

Many Unique Factors

Each organization is unique, with its own culture, core values, and strategic direction. This can lead to clashes, disagreements, and challenges in aligning with the vision.

It is important to proceed with caution and be methodical. Your new peers may have their own agendas that could conflict with your objectives, so understanding and navigating those dynamics is crucial. Adapting to a new culture can be a significant challenge, especially if you lack experience in doing so.

As you step into your new role, you will encounter various challenges related to your direct reports. They are a diverse group with different strengths, weaknesses, and backgrounds. Additionally, there may be certain individuals or groups within the organization that are considered untouchable or critical to the mission. It's important to be aware of potential resistance or conflicts that may arise. Furthermore, you are likely to come across instances of poor performance that need to be addressed and improved.

Learning from Fast Failures

Fast failures are the opposite of quick wins.

Failure can be a valuable learning experience, but it's best to learn from the mistakes of others rather than experiencing them yourself. By studying some of the fastest failures I've encountered, you can gain valuable insights and avoid similar pitfalls. Here are a few notable examples.

Joe's Story

Joe, a highly qualified candidate, sought my assistance in finding a new leadership role.

After accepting what he believed to be the perfect job, Joe wasted no time starting his new position. When I reached out to him a few weeks later, he had already begun implementing significant changes. Eager to make an impact as the president of a major division within a well-known global publisher, Joe had suggested starting early to jump-start his ambitious ideas for organizational transformation.

Driven by his eagerness to take charge, Joe embarked on a flurry of activities within the first five weeks of his new role. He believed that immediate changes were necessary to improve revenue and overall performance. However, he soon realized that he was operating in a culture that strongly resisted change. The institution, led by PhDs, prioritized maintaining the status quo over driving performance. Joe's manager expected him to be a change agent while also avoiding any major disruptions. Balancing these conflicting expectations proved to be a significant challenge.

After just six weeks on the job, Joe found himself terminated. In our debrief, he shared his perspective: "They brought me in with the expectation of driving change, but it quickly became evident that the organization had a strong aversion to it. The intense political landscape and the entrenched good old boys' club were resistant to anyone challenging the status quo. Despite my best efforts, it seemed I never stood a chance to make the desired impact."

Joe failed to mention that he had a coach who tried to support him, but was too consumed with making changes to pause and listen. Despite having a few coaching sessions, he remained entrenched in execution mode, making it difficult to address the fundamentals of onboarding.

Joe's career never recovered from that failure. The experience damaged his self-confidence, and he never reached the same level again. His eagerness to make an immediate impact hindered his onboarding and preparation. He was mentally ahead of the race before it even began.

Starting fast can lead to failure. Moving too quickly increases the risk of mistakes. Leaders who rush overlook this important process. It's essential to allocate sufficient time and attention to these foundational aspects.

Patience is crucial. Allow yourself time without disrupting the organization too soon. Remember that organizations can be resistant to change, even if they claim otherwise. Following the playbook provided in Section 2 will dramatically increase your chances of avoiding failure.

Critical Success Factors

The reasons for success or failure in a new role vary for each leader. To protect your career, it is important to identify the necessary steps for your success and address any weaknesses that could hinder your assimilation. Each leader has their own unique "one thing" that is crucial for establishing themselves in the new role. While quick wins are important, certain factors determine overall success, which are specific to your situation. Selecting the right priorities is the art within the science.

Trevor's Story

Trevor's success story serves as a prime example of how to do it right from the start. In his words:

"When I got promoted, my coach advised me to reinvent myself. I shifted from being an expert closer to a manager, focusing on empowering my team rather than chasing deals. Although it was challenging to let go, I gained the respect of my team and rose higher in the organization. Coaching my team became a key factor in my success. While it's tough at times to watch them close deals, I resist the temptation and instead cheer them on. My focus now is on developing them into successful closers."

Trevor's journey from a closer to a team leader is commendable. With each promotion, he embraced the mindset of starting fresh in a new organization. He recognized the importance of tailoring his approach to the first one hundred days of each leadership role. A one-size-fits-all approach doesn't work. Adapting to a new environment requires energy and flexibility. That's why being well rested, prepared, and adaptable is crucial.

Standard onboarding, assimilation, and integration guidelines serve as a solid foundation for both internal promotions and external placements. However, it's essential to recognize the need for adaptation to suit the nuances of each specific environment.

Here are some quotes to inspire you to over-prepare:

- "There are no secrets to success. It is the result of preparation, hard work, and learning from failure." —Colin Powell
- "I don't believe in luck; I believe in preparation." —Bobby Knight
- "Success is where preparation and opportunity meet." —Bobby Unser

As a favorite saying of mine states, "I am sending you out like sheep among wolves. Therefore be as shrewd as snakes and as innocent as doves."[1] Navigate this process with wisdom and tact, avoiding overly assertive or demanding behavior. Maintain a balanced approach while gathering necessary information, ensuring a positive start to the relationship.

Three Key Asks Before You Start

At the very point of accepting an offer, I believe you should ask for:

1. An accelerated performance review: Request a performance review at the six-month mark to assess your progress and achievements.
2. Onboarding, assimilation, and integration coaching: Ask the company to provide or cover the cost of coaching to support your successful integration into the role.
3. Ability to run a thirty-day playbook: Allocate your first thirty days to specific objectives, including:
    a. Building relationships with key stakeholders.
    b. Assessing the needs of the organization.
    c. Developing a comprehensive hundred-day onboarding plan, to be finalized by the beginning of your thirty-first day.

---

[1] Matthew 10:16 (New International Version).

See Sections 2 and 3 for more specifics.

It is best to discuss these concessions BEFORE starting your new role and BEFORE signing the offer letter. This early negotiation allows for smoother agreement and avoids potential conflicts later on. Similar to a couple planning their marriage, it is ideal to establish expectations and agreements beforehand to minimize future obstacles.

By discussing and gaining agreement on your hundred-day plan, specifically the focus during the first thirty days, you can avoid being overwhelmed with immediate tactical execution and ensure you have the opportunity to follow your playbook outlined in Section 2. It is important to address this before starting your new role to manage expectations and prevent excessive project assignments. Have these discussions upfront. It is a wise decision and will set a solid foundation for entering your new role.

SUDs: Seemingly Unimportant Decisions

Once you have started, it becomes more challenging to negotiate the points I mentioned earlier. This can lead to making Seemingly Unimportant Decisions (SUDs) that can derail your career. Let me illustrate this with three examples of how SUDs negatively impacted the career of a leader who failed to heed this advice.

Juan's Story

Juan was recruited by the president of a large organization. During his first week, he was asked to identify issues beyond his area of responsibility, which took him out of scope and prevented him from executing his playbook. Unbeknownst to him, his boss had created much of the dysfunction in the organization. He was asked to report his findings to his boss's boss.

SUD #1: Misunderstood relational dynamics. When Juan shared his observations, which highlighted his boss's mistakes, it led to hidden ill will and created a challenging dynamic with his manager.

Next, Juan initiated a three-day off-site retreat for senior leaders without properly assessing the organization's receptiveness to change. The retreat, which included team building, open communication, and strategic planning, was perceived positively by participants who felt heard and empowered, as reflected in post-event surveys. This novel event was discussed enthusiastically for weeks. However, despite its success, my client faced severe criticism from his manager for not aligning with the established norms, indicating the change was too radical and premature. This resulted in a harsh setback for him. He was now firmly in the crosshairs of several key stakeholders.

SUD #2: Misjudging the organization's readiness for change. Juan had the right idea but the wrong timing and did not gain alignment for the counter-culture initiative from his key stakeholders.

Juan then pursued further changes within the organization, which largely helped address issues of low morale. For instance, he introduced an employee suggestion box without seeking prior approval. Although this measure was well received by the staff, he had to justify his action and once again faced criticism from his manager, who labeled him as a "loose cannon" for his unapproved initiatives. This highlighted Juan's underestimation of the organization's political dynamics.

SUD #3: Ignoring the politics inherent in every organization. Again, Juan had great ideas, and was innovative, creative, and a proactive problem solver, but he lacked full alignment from his stakeholders.

Leaders need to adopt a diplomatic approach and avoid moving too quickly or deeply without understanding the organization's dynamics. Juan was let go after only seven months due to his swift, transformative actions that were at odds with the organization's desire to maintain the status quo. Reflecting on his experience, Juan told me:

"They were more resistant to change than they thought. They wanted consistency but hired a change agent. In the future, I'll initially move slower, comprehend the political environment, and establish what I can and can't do. Ideally, I'll discern this even before accepting my next role."

The notion of Seemingly Unimportant Decisions is crucial, as they can appear frequently, especially during the first one hundred days in a new role.

The Manager's Corner: *Preparing to Run*

Twenty to twenty-five percent of leaders either quit or get fired in their first year, emphasizing the importance of ongoing vigilance and support. While the first one hundred days are critical, full assimilation can take six to twelve months, and full integration even longer. Never assume a leader has fully assimilated and integrated until they at least reach their one-year anniversary. Unfortunately, hiring managers often quickly forget about leaders they hired months ago, mistakenly presuming they are seamlessly assimilating and integrating into the organization.

Brian's Story

Brian hired me to assist him in securing a senior partner role in a venture capital firm on the west coast of the US. Despite our efforts, he ended up accepting a job offer from a VC firm in Boston, on the opposite coast. Brian had not yet relocated his family, so he kept exploring opportunities with VC firms in California. The partners at the Boston VC firm did not make significant efforts to make Brian feel valued or engaged. When he unexpectedly resigned after two months to accept a VC partner role in Silicon Valley, the Boston firm was shaken by the news. The lack of attention to retention and the assumption that they had already secured Brian's commitment contributed to the unexpected outcome.

To ensure the success of newly hired leaders, it is advisable to focus on retention for at least the first three months and continue monitoring their morale, job satisfaction, and overall well-being for the subsequent nine. Also, help them avoid Seemingly Unimportant Decisions (SUDs), which are explained earlier in this chapter.

Efforts should be made to retain the top talent you have invested in recruiting. As you know, your responsibilities extend well beyond their start date, and your continued support is critical to ensure long-term retention and success.

CHAPTER 4
EXPECTATIONS

Top leaders like you expect to make an immediate impact when entering a new role.

Expectations are Dangerous

Your expectations can derail your ultimate success. The first priority should be to lower your expectations. During the initial months in a new role, others' expectations of you are typically at their lowest. However, it is up to you to lower your own expectations. Expecting too much from yourself too soon may lead you to make decisions that seem right at the moment but ultimately harm your reputation and personal brand. Early on, you lack the luxury of trial and error. Exercise caution, particularly if there was an internal candidate vying for the same position. Some individuals will be eagerly waiting for you to stumble, ready to say, "I told you so. We should have hired X." In many of these cases, the speaker is referring to themselves as the superior candidate.

Your high expectations and ego can drive you to keep pace with or even outperform others. However, be aware that some individuals may encourage risky decisions. Their intentions are not necessarily malicious but rooted in the genuine hope of achieving the seemingly impossible. In your early stages, naivety can lead you to unknowingly tread a dangerous path. Consider the image of a hidden roadside bomb as a potent reminder. Proceed cautiously, prioritize safety, and navigate potential obstacles with care.

Organizations anticipate swift results from a leader who, on paper, is an ideal fit for their team. However, expectations are frequently unmet. Upon closer examination, the initial perception of a "perfect match" may prove to be a mistake. Frequently, leadership teams privately discuss concerns about newly hired leaders. Likewise, the new leader may start to question their decision. This can lead to friction between the new leader and the team.

Frequently, I've heard the lament, "They failed to disclose the true severity of the situation. It's far worse than I anticipated. I'm now discovering hidden challenges I wish I had known beforehand." Even more disheartening, I've encountered instances where individuals exclaimed, "They deceived me. They concealed crucial information. I was misled to believe X." In fact, I've heard multiple accounts of people stating, "I was outright lied to!"

Setting clear expectations on both sides is vital for a successful relationship. Beginning with an open and transparent yet highly diplomatic approach establishes a solid foundation for understanding and alignment.

Transparently navigating transitions can reduce the rate of leadership failures. Engaging in candid conversations during this period increases the likelihood of level-setting everyone's expectations.

Consciously lower expectations during this period.

Honeymoon Bliss

Honeymoons bring joy, but they don't accurately reflect ongoing reality. Similarly, in a new job, don't allow bliss to lower your guard and cloud your judgment. Resist thinking the honeymoon will last.

The first three months often form an exhilarating honeymoon period, where it appears that everything you touch turns to gold. Receptivity and accolades greet your every endeavor, and you are likely to feel a boost to your confidence as you achieve the many quick wins we'll talk about more in Section 2. However, it's crucial not to become too comfortable. Heightened self-confidence can lead to overestimation, setting expectations that become difficult to sustain. The only direction from such high expectations is downward. As a result, the second three months can be more perilous than the first. This is why I firmly believe the "three-month onboarding" paradigm is wrong. We need to reframe it as a year-long "onboarding, assimilation, and integration" process.

The honeymoon period is a natural, normal, and common occurrence. However, it turns into a negative syndrome if expectations surpass reality.

The Honeymoon Syndrome

The honeymoon syndrome, also known as the savior syndrome, refers to a dysfunctional situation where the initial success in a new role leads to exaggerated perceptions of one's abilities within an organization. This syndrome affects leaders at all levels, from frontline managers to the board. Surprisingly, even when a new board member is expected to be a valuable asset in resolving issues, they can turn into a nightmare for the organization.

During the recruitment process, some hiring managers fall into the trap of selection bias, believing that the candidate is "The One" who will miraculously solve all their problems. However, this leader rarely lives up to the initial hype, often leading to inevitable disappointment. Sometimes, a new hire begins with strong performance and exceptional talents, resulting in an increased load of responsibilities. They are viewed as capable of handling anything and the perfect solution for the organization's challenges. Unfortunately, many leaders crash and burn when overwhelmed with too much too soon. Others find themselves entangled in intricate corporate politics, as the following illustrates:

Lou's Story

Lou, the newly appointed head of operations, faced an incredibly challenging task within his first month: fixing a divided board. He was given a specific direction and instructed to develop a plan as quickly as possible. However, from the very beginning, Lou found himself dealing with the resistant CEO, who was apprehensive about confronting an issue.

By his second month, Lou diligently initiated a process with the board. The CEO was ecstatic with his work, hailing him as a hero. However, due to the project's all-consuming nature, Lou found himself with limited time to build critical relationships with stakeholders. These included the private equity firm that owned the company.

Lou struggled to navigate the complex dynamics between a seasoned private equity firm and the CEO. It didn't take long for Lou to realize his error: the lack of buy-in from the private equity firm. The CEO, unwilling to take responsibility, allowed Lou to shoulder the blame while ensuring he received a generous severance package. As Lou recovered from the experience, he reflected:

"I took on too much, too soon, neglecting my *Art of Your Start* playbook. Despite knowing what to do, the allure of high demand and importance clouded my judgment. I failed to assert myself and say 'no' or 'not yet,' resulting in being the fall guy in a power play and ultimately losing."

Lesson learned. Say "no" or "not yet" when necessary, proceed with caution, and avoid taking on too much.

Doug's Story

Doug, CEO of a PE-owned middle-market healthcare managed services company, hired me to be his coach. He proudly shared how he recruited an exceptional new board member. However, the honeymoon phase quickly faded as the board member began disrupting board meetings. He challenged Doug on minor matters, displayed aggressiveness, and dominated the previously smooth-functioning board. Doug soon wanted to end the working relationship with the board member, but it was easier said than done.

Sadly, Doug was ultimately fired less than two years after experiencing the initial high of being a seemingly flawless "savior." Remarkably, the board member played a significant role in advocating for Doug's dismissal.

A Perfect Storm

The honeymoon syndrome and its counterpart, the savior syndrome, create conditions for major errors by setting unrealistic expectations. Whether you are in your early "honeymoon" period or have been designated as the "savior" of an initiative, it is crucial to establish realistic expectations for yourself in the eyes of key stakeholders. As you are hiring others, take care not to ascribe to them superhuman qualities or be overly optimistic about what their contribution will produce in a certain timeframe.

All saviors eventually reveal their human nature, and all honeymoon periods come to an end, leading to a mixed bag of outcomes. Your responsibility is to manage and align expectations. In some cases, leaders who initially enjoyed widespread popularity may discover not everyone supported their selection. As decisions are scrutinized and doubts arise, it becomes important to address and clarify concerns. The Listen to Concerns part of your playbook in Section 2 goes into detail about this.

To manage the honeymoon period effectively, downplay expectations and the pace of accomplishments. Under-promising and over-delivering is the key. This approach helps prevent the perfect storm of exaggerated expectations for unrealistic achievements.

In short, avoid allowing yourself to be placed on the proverbial "pedestal," and don't put others on it either.

Stay Off the Pedestal

The savior and honeymoon syndromes share a common outcome: being placed on a pedestal like an amazing athlete who can conquer anything thrown at them. Reflecting on clients who have experienced this, the saying "the bigger they are, the harder they fall" comes to mind.

Here is some practical advice for when you're put on a pedestal:

1. Stay humble and keep your ego in check. As a top leader, positive feedback is common when starting a new role. However, be cautious not to blindly accept praise or let it inflate your ego. This vulnerable period requires vigilance. Challenge existing thinking, assess actions carefully, and avoid rushing impulsively. Downplay what you can do, both to yourself and to key stakeholders. Keep your ego under control.
2. Be cautious when taking on new commitments. It's better to say "not now" or "not yet" than to accept everything that comes your way. Focus on the highest priorities assigned by your manager. Pursue early, attainable wins. Follow the advice of Sam Morasca, a business mentor of mine: "Take small, quick steps." Take time to build relationships, understand critical organizational needs, and prioritize mission-critical tasks. Avoid setting unrealistic deadlines and only commit to what is essential.

3. Resist being seen as the solution to all problems. Every leader possesses strengths and weaknesses. It is crucial to maintain a realistic perspective. If you receive excessive praise, be willing to push back and level-set expectations.
4. Present yourself with reasonable transparency, acknowledging the combination of strengths and weaknesses that make up who you are.

Reasonable Transparency Is Needed

Throughout the selection process, it is crucial to acknowledge the presence of blind spots on both sides. Reasonable transparency regarding strengths and weaknesses should be shared by both you and the manager.

From the onset, recruiters and hiring managers should avoid presenting the organization as perfect, just as you should not pitch yourself as such. Ideally, both sides would be transparent, but that is often not the case. As part of interview teams, I make it a point to ensure that the strengths and weaknesses of both parties are known. Without this understanding, disappointment and "buyer's remorse" can arise, leading to early separations. It is crucial for everyone to have a clear understanding of what they are entering into before committing. Minimizing surprises increases the likelihood of a lasting relationship. Early on in my career, I learned that top leaders don't like surprises. I assume you are like this as well.

In conclusion, here is my best advice: Establish clear communication with key stakeholders regarding what you consider realistic right from the beginning. By doing so, you prevent expectations from exceeding reality, ensuring a positive start. It is better to under-promise and over-deliver rather than the other way around.

The Manager's Corner: *Expectations*

Those involved in selecting new leaders must be mindful of the inclination to view the final candidate as a "savior." We talk about this a lot in this chapter. The best organizations are not without issues; such companies do not exist. Great organizations are those that openly discuss and share any issues related to a role before a candidate accepts the position. Minimizing surprises for the new hire is crucial for a positive experience.

Once an offer is extended and accepted, there is a strong tendency to overestimate the individual's capabilities and believe they can achieve more than is realistically possible.

Beware of the honeymoon and savior syndromes, also discussed in this chapter. While positive progress is expected, excessive delegated responsibilities should raise caution. If there is an expectation for the new leader to be a savior, it can lead to disaster. Your role is to manage and lower the expectations others may have of your new leader. Don't let your ego cloud your judgment.

These syndromes can manifest much earlier than anticipated. Remain vigilant.

CHAPTER 5
COMMON MISTAKES

Even after sidestepping the pitfalls of the honeymoon and savior syndromes, other common challenges remain.

Knowing these risks is crucial. So, let's look at the fifteen most common mistakes. They are not in any particular order.

Fifteen Common Mistakes

Here are fifteen common points of failure to avoid.

1. Misalignment with Values or Strategy

This typical downfall occurs when a gap exists between the company's fundamental values, either expressed or implied, and those of the newly appointed leader. Whether glaring or subtle, overt or covert, a mismatch in values often proves insurmountable. Similarly, differing views on the company's strategic path can often derail an otherwise suitable match.

2. Failure to Achieve Early Wins

Leaders who cannot secure early wins or adequately address key challenges get into trouble. You have limited time to establish credibility. Execution is essential, but carefully choosing what to execute is vital for early success. This is why aiming for "quick wins" is a best practice. A quick win can be characterized as follows:

- Achievable: Something you are confident you can accomplish.
- Visible: Highly noticeable to key stakeholders.
- Agreed: Key stakeholders concur it's a necessary initiative.
- Timely: It can be completed in a several months or less and needs immediate attention.

A great example of a first "quick win" is your hundred-day onboarding plan. It's completely achievable, as you have full control over it. This plan is very noticeable to one of your key stakeholders—your manager. Onboarding experts universally agree on its necessity; it's considered a best practice. It's also timely—typically, this should be completed within your first thirty days in a new role. NOTE: Section 2 addresses this, and Section 3 provides an onboarding plan framework.

3. Excessive Focus on Execution

The converse of "failure to execute" is an excessive focus on execution, neglecting key stakeholder relationship building and strategy development. I've seen many well-meaning leaders achieve remarkable results in their first three months, only to encounter difficulties due to their failure to form effective relationships with those integral to their success. There exists a narrow window of opportunity to establish credibility.

The mistake here is the belief that significant immediate results will automatically create a favorable first impression. Consequently, leaders often overly concentrate on producing results, failing to build the relational bridges necessary to support their objectives and plans. By pushing too hard for results, it's easy to mistakenly trust the wrong individuals, receive inaccurate information, act upon it, and find yourself in a major predicament.

4. Inability to Say "No" or "Not Yet"

Newly appointed leaders often struggle to decline requests. It's challenging early on to say "no," especially when you're keen to please your key stakeholders. However, this can lead to significant issues. One client described this prevalent concern:

> "My boss gave me a long list of projects when I started, which I accepted without hesitation. I was overwhelmed before I knew it."

Mastering when to say "yes," "no," or "not now" is somewhat of an art, hence the book title. Aim to understand your key stakeholders' top priorities, focusing only on those tasks that will make the most impact. Prematurely saying "yes" before comprehending its implications can bring about significant headaches and tarnish your reputation if you fail to achieve the desired results.

5. Self-Esteem Challenges

It may surprise you that many leaders grapple with self-esteem issues, often concealed by a strong ego. These issues can surface early in a new leader's tenure, exhibited by a desire to please and prove oneself worthy of the role. One client detailed this common condition:

> "In retrospect, I was overly eager to prove their decision right. I tried to conquer everything and neglected to build the necessary relationships. Before long, I was clashing with some key people, leading to my premature exit."

This problem is closely tied to the "inability to say no" challenge. It's essential to have confidence in yourself and resist the urge to please everyone. As a leader, trust in your capabilities. There's no need to prove yourself; your position validates that others already believe in your suitability for the role.

6. Excessive Eagerness to Take Charge

Unbridled ambition can often derail a career. Post-termination, one client revealed:

> "I had been job hunting for so long that I was eager to have something to manage again. Once in charge, I made many decisions. It felt great until a few key decisions turned out wrong, causing my downfall. I failed to take time to build necessary bridges for success."

My observation is that the longer someone has been unemployed, the stronger this tendency is to charge in too forcefully, attempting too much too soon. While the thrill of finally leading an organization is invigorating, this excitement can prompt excessive rapid changes. Pace yourself and remember that every organization is unique and adapts to change at different speeds. Gauge what your organization can handle and moderate the pace of the individual and organizational changes you pursue until you're solidly established.

7. Inability to Adapt to the Culture

Another typical failure point is cultural adaptation. As one client experienced:

> "I lasted only three months because I didn't assess the culture and adjust my style. I was like an organ transplant rejected by the body. Next time, I'll slow down, fully understand the culture, and align my approach with the organization rather than expecting the reverse."

Some cultures are more entrenched than others. Numerous factors need consideration as you integrate into a new environment. These include your position in the organization and the influence you can exert, the degree of stakeholder support you possess or can swiftly secure, and the strength of the existing culture, along with its adaptability to change. Gaining an impartial understanding of the culture you're entering is essential to effectively facilitating change.

8. Misalignment with Manager

We previously discussed the significance of aligning with your manager and the organization's goals. In her exit interview after a brief nine-month tenure as a program manager, a client highlighted:

> "I didn't fully support the changes my manager wanted. This misalignment, which I hesitated to address, led me to push my own agenda rather than fully align with the organization's objectives. I failed to align better with various key players, and this was my undoing."

Achieving alignment is a solid first step—the science of onboarding. However, maintaining alignment throughout a relationship with your manager is more of an art. Situations often evolve, and today's alignment might not apply next month or next quarter. Regular check-ins with your manager to ensure continued alignment with organizational goals are irreplaceable.

9. Inadequate Planning

The written hundred-day plan is the gold standard. Every book on this subject tells you to make one. There's no good reason to bypass this critical step, even though I have clients who do just that. It will easily become your first significant "quick" win. Neglecting this opportunity is puzzling. One ousted leader shared:

> "Daniel suggested a written hundred-day plan, but I didn't see the need for a formal plan. I accomplished a lot in my first three months, had significant wins, and my team was pleased. However, my boss disagreed with my focus. The misalignment could've been avoided if I'd made a detailed plan and reviewed it with her. Next time, I'll follow the guidance you provided."

Your coach or mentor doesn't want to hear, "Next time, I'll listen." We want you to understand the risk, take action, and thrive. Sadly, this client was fired due to misalignments on key objectives.

10. Reluctance to Fire Perceived Poor Performers

During coaching, many new leaders express doubts about certain direct reports. Typically, proficient performance managers don't linger on this issue without decisive action. Here's a narrative I often hear from underperforming leaders:

> "I was advised to dismiss an individual as soon as I started. I thought I could improve their performance and didn't act until it was too late. My reputation suffered because I held on to someone I believed I could fix. Others perceived this as a major weakness. I viewed it as a chance to prove myself. I tried to be a hero, won the battle, but lost the war. The person I saved is still there. I am not."

From an outsider's perspective, it's easy to spot the "writing on the wall." The decision to terminate employment is never simple and is even more challenging when you're new. This falls under the "art" category, as there's no scientific formula for the right time to act. There are many factors to consider, but if your manager advises ending a relationship, it's generally wise to seriously consider this, swiftly determine your actions, and align on the course.

11. Overzealous Change Approach

A close cousin to Mistake 3: Excessive Focus on Execution, this is a typical career stumbling block, especially common among "Type A" leaders. A client explained this issue:

> "This has happened twice in a row, and I'm concerned about the impact on my resume. Two jobs in less than two years. It's clear I tend to rush. I can easily identify necessary changes, but I now understand the importance of winning over the people involved before initiating change. Without this, you might end up like me, on the outside, wondering what went wrong."

Leaders often step into new roles brimming with confidence, sharing high expectations of success with the organization. However, this joint vision can sometimes border on overconfidence, leading to missteps. Leaders might think, "I've done this before, and it's always been successful. I've never failed to integrate into a new organization." Yet even the most experienced leaders falter. It's wise to exercise caution until you're well settled and have sufficient data for informed decision-making.

Sharon's Story

Sharon engaged me as her coach during her first week in a new position. Her pace was so swift that it was hard for me to keep up. She was brimming with overconfidence. Does this sound familiar? This skilled leader became so absorbed in daily operations that she overlooked strategic planning for her integration into the organization. Despite my efforts to guide her, I couldn't slow Sharon down. A staunch supporter of women leaders shattering the glass ceiling, I was reluctant to do so. I did recommend she meet with her boss to ensure alignment and to assess if her intensity was excessive. However, Sharon didn't heed my advice. Five months in, she was let go.

It was disheartening to witness Sharon's relationship with her superior deteriorate while I stood on the sidelines. In retrospect, I should have insisted on spending more time with her. This event unfolded over two decades ago, and since then, I've improved at knowing when to step in. However, I am still challenged by clients who become so engrossed in tactical execution that they neglect strategic thinking and planning. Getting fired for failing in the process is one thing. Failing while you are using an experienced coach is another. Listen to your advisors, mentors, and/or coach.

12. Excessive Busyness

Leaders on the verge of failure often describe their situation similarly: "I'm swamped. It's like drinking from a fire hose." This signals missed fundamental practices. If you're excessively busy, you're likely not allotting time for preparation or seeking feedback and advice. This can be a damaging error.

When a leader appears too consumed for their own good, I'll use the "fire hose" analogy and inquire if they're experiencing that feeling. Those in trouble often respond, "No, it's more like drinking directly from the fire hydrant!"

I have heard these two phrases hundreds of times. Every time, my answer has always been, "Slow down; take time to plan your moves. Be strategic."

Be cautious not to overwhelm yourself. You're the only one who can manage your workload. Although it might seem impossible, I've never seen a leader unable to secure their manager's assistance for some operational breathing room. You can avoid feeling drowned in responsibilities by initiating this challenging conversation early in your tenure.

13. Avoidance of Constructive Conflict

Significant mistakes can be rectified if promptly recognized and addressed. At times, engaging in constructive conflict with a superior is necessary to clarify misunderstandings and align on common goals.

Often, a new leader exerts upward change, unaware of resistance at the top, while senior management applies downward pressure that hinders the new leader. This misalignment is often due to excessively polite communication at higher leadership levels, where cues can be subtle and challenging to interpret, especially in fresh relationships. This pattern is increasingly prevalent the more senior the role. Misunderstanding or failing to align with the organization's culture can exacerbate this issue, as the following story will demonstrate.

Bob's Story

Bob, the CEO of a six-billion-dollar public company, appointed John as president—his potential successor. As the executive coach to both, the board requested that I evaluate John's suitability for the CEO role. John was a great fit in all aspects except one: Bob's perception was that John lacked attention to detail.

Though John was meticulous, Bob, an engineer by training and a perfectionist, saw the company culture as intensely detail focused. Bob (also chairman of a very supportive board) had taken the company from founding through a highly successful IPO. Bob credited his success partly to deep immersion in the business's details. John overlooked a few deal details within his first sixty days, costing the company five million dollars. Bob never forgot this, and it marred John's chances of succeeding him. Unfortunately, I couldn't convince Bob and John to discuss this issue directly, leading to John's departure after eighteen months.

I felt especially bad for John, who was my first Fortune 500 CEO coaching engagement in 1987. He took me with him throughout the next twenty years and gave me a huge leg up in the world of coaching public company CEOs. However, I could never convince John to implement *The Art of Your Start* playbook, and as a result, his career was tarnished by continued terminations from top jobs. Go to school on him.

Performance feedback is crucial during the first twelve months in a new leadership role and beyond. Though superiors may hesitate to give constructive feedback to avoid offending a strong leader's ego, obtaining such feedback is vital for the leader's success. Sometimes, constructive conflict may be necessary to clarify differences and reestablish a positive working dynamic. As shown in John's case, avoiding these conversations will jeopardize your career. I will talk more about this and give a full playbook in Section 2, as well as resources in Section 3.

14. Conflict with a Manager

Constructive conflict is good. Destructive conflict is bad. Constructive conflict can bolster growth, but unresolved or destructive conflict can jeopardize your career. This principle becomes evident in the story of Beth and Jimmy.

Beth's Story

Beth, a public company CFO, sought my coaching shortly after hiring Jimmy, her new VP of Finance. Problems quickly emerged between the two. Jimmy, who was particularly assertive, had significantly different views on operational changes and challenged Beth's methods frequently. Beth, a methodical leader who had her way of getting things done, felt that Jimmy was rushing things. Conversely, Jimmy believed Beth was too slow in making necessary changes. The escalating disagreements between them were clear red flags. Let's delve deeper into their conflict, which provides an insightful lesson.

Jimmy was known for immediate, impactful changes, leading to substantial wins in his past roles. However, in his new position, this approach backfired, revealing a serious misjudgment about the pace and style of the organization.

Hired to evaluate Jimmy's situation, I quickly identified significant damage just a few months into his role. Confidential interviews with peers, subordinates, and superiors revealed a pattern of aggressive, hurried decision-making, which was alienating those around him. He urgently needed to correct his approach, but unfortunately, it was too late. Just eight weeks after I began coaching him, the company let him go.

Jimmy's downfall was largely due to his style. Beth sought cultural adaptability in Jimmy, who was mission driven to deliver remarkable results. Though his quick pace led to an organizational restructure within eight weeks, the team he was supposed to lead was exceptionally loyal to Beth, and his fast-paced, decisive, and assertively direct style didn't sit well with them. In my view, this talented finance VP's downfall was his failure to build a strong, trusting relationship with his manager. Had he invested time in understanding the culture and moved at a slower pace, as well as used an effective onboarding playbook (something we'll delve into in Section 2), he could have retained his position.

15. Failure to Meet Agreed Metrics

This common mistake needs no further elaboration. Not achieving the agreed metrics happens the least, which is telling. Just hitting the agreed performance metrics does not provide immunity from failure.

Summary

As we conclude Section 1, I encourage you to complete the following exercise:

Among this list of potential pitfalls, select four to seven that you think would most likely cause your downfall, should it happen. Now, rank order them, with 1 as the highest.

    ___ 1. Misalignment with Values or Strategy
    ___ 2. Failure to Achieve Early Wins
    ___ 3. Excessive Focus on Execution
    ___ 4. Inability to Say "No" or "Not Yet"
    ___ 5. Self-Esteem Challenges
    ___ 6. Excessive Eagerness to Take Charge
    ___ 7. Inability to Adapt to the Culture
    ___ 8. Misalignment with Manager
    ___ 9. Inadequate Planning
    ___ 10. Reluctance to Fire Perceived Poor Performers
    ___ 11. Overzealous Change Approach
    ___ 12. Excessive Busyness
    ___ 13. Avoidance of Constructive Conflict
    ___ 14. Conflict with a Manager
    ___ 15. Failure to Meet Agreed Metrics

I recommend the following steps:

1. Discuss this self-assessment with your advisors, mentors, and/or coach.
2. Create a list of actionable steps to avoid these missteps.
3. Revisit this list once a month for the first half year and self-assess progress.

The Manager's Corner: Common Mistakes

The loss from the unsuccessful integration of new leaders extends beyond financial and reputational costs. Examples include:

- Employee morale and productivity: A leadership transition that is poorly handled can create uncertainty and anxiety among employees, which can lower morale and productivity. Over time, this can lead to increased employee turnover.
- Strategic misalignment: A new leader who isn't properly integrated might fail to grasp the organization's strategic direction, causing disruptions and possibly steering the company off course.
- Operational disruption: Inefficient handovers and integration can lead to confusion about roles, responsibilities, and processes. This confusion can affect daily operations and customer satisfaction.
- Knowledge loss: When leaders leave or are not successfully integrated, valuable institutional knowledge and industry insights can be lost. This loss can negatively impact the organization's ability to make informed decisions.
- Innovation and growth: New leaders often bring fresh perspectives and ideas that can drive innovation and growth. However, unsuccessful integration can stifle these potential benefits.

Many of these failures can be prevented. Review the list of common failure points in this chapter and consider how you can support your new leader in avoiding them. Keep an open and honest conversation with your new leader about these possible pitfalls, and don't hesitate to share any red flags you observe.

Newly appointed leaders promoted from within your current company have an edge: they can receive feedback from familiar faces. If your leader is new to the organization, assist them in finding someone trustworthy to offer an impartial perspective on the company's cultural and organizational dynamics.

Also, strive to be a support system for your subordinate. Help your leader uncover their blind spots. This will equip you with the necessary information to prevent your new hire from being perceived as an "average," "poor," or "bad" choice by their colleagues, subordinates, or superiors.

You need to be aware of their performance and their perceived image in the organization. While they desire this feedback, they may not want to seem needy or insecure. Make it a priority to actively gather feedback early on and establish a safe space for them to receive it from you. Reassure them that you are acting in their best interest. You are.

CHAPTER 6

SECTION 1 CONCLUSION

The initial twelve months in a new leadership role are pivotal to your organizational success and future prospects. It's crucial to adopt a deliberate and strategic approach to assimilation and integration in your new role. The efforts required extend far beyond any onboarding procedures or reading materials provided. Understand that this is a year-long journey. Failure to acknowledge this can lead to complacency, causing you to overlook red flags indicating you're veering off course, potentially creating issues for you in your second year and beyond. Always keep your eye on the bigger picture. Play the long game.

Your initial year isn't just "business as usual." It's an ideal time to perfect your assimilation and integration strategy. Attaining excellence in this journey can have a profound and enduring effect on both your organization and your career trajectory.

Consult experienced advisors during your journey. Successful leaders know the importance of getting guidance from mentors, advisors, or coaches (or all three!) when handling the complexities of a new leadership role. Even minor tweaks can greatly impact your path, and the higher your position, the more precision you require. To borrow a golf metaphor, there's ample time for a player to prepare before teeing off, but once they start their swing, last-minute coaching is impossible. Having someone help you learn how and when to adjust your swing is incredibly beneficial. Just as in golf, in the leadership sphere, minor modifications can dramatically influence where you end up.

Moving forward, remember expectations may be high in certain areas and low in others. This paradox underscores the need to be observant, taking time to learn and absorb as much as possible. By leveraging the tools and resources in this book, you can confidently steer your new leadership role, excel in your duties, and leave a lasting mark on your organization.

Remember the saying, "Only the paranoid survive." This mantra, most notably linked to Andrew Grove, the former CEO of Intel, highlights the importance of situational awareness.

If Section 1 managed to instill even a sense of caution in you, my goal is accomplished. Not only do I want you to survive, I want you to flourish. This requires thoughtful consideration before making critical decisions. Again, no matter how seasoned a leader you are, your first year is not just "business as usual."

Now, some good news. Section 2 presents a tried-and-true framework for excelling at onboarding and assimilation. Coming up are the common success factors, best practices, and established processes to excel in your first year.

SECTION TWO

THE SOLUTION

Pyramid (bottom to top):
- Build Trust!
- Understand Needs!
- Involve Stakeholders!
- Listen to Concerns!
- Deliver Results!
- Serve with Excellence!

Section 1 identified the problem. I will offer you a comprehensive solution in the next two sections: Section 2, the playbook, and Section 3, resources for its implementation.

The solution for both the hired leader and the hiring manager is the same: a playbook for the first year. This necessitates a paradigm shift.

Change your perception of "onboarding" during the first month or quarter to include full assimilation and integration. You're in for a longer journey, so prepare with a solid plan.

My hope is that you will adopt this playbook as your own, expand it with your own ideas, and customize it as you see fit. May it serve you well throughout your career, and may it serve those you hire as you grow the next generation of top leaders.

CHAPTER 7
THE BUILDS™ PLAYBOOK

BUILDS™ is a clear, structured framework (playbook) for onboarding, assimilation, and integration that every organizational leader can use.

However, if you already think you have a plan, ask yourself:

- Is it mostly in your head?
- How good is it? Does it work? Is it a proven process?
- How many times have you successfully implemented it?
- Is it well structured?
- How easily reviewable is it?
- Can you share it with someone you hire to ensure a successful process for them?

You might have a playbook. If so, jot down thoughts on the following:

- Where did your playbook fall short?
- What strategies were successful?
- Which actions didn't work?
- How can you enhance your approach this time?

Whether you're a new leader, an experienced one, or a manager aiding a direct report, the BUILDS™ imperatives can amplify your success. This adaptable and efficient playbook enables leaders to monitor progress, pace appropriately, and adjust when needed. Consider adopting BUILDS™ as your ultimate leadership assimilation and integration playbook.

Most Playbooks Are Not Well Structured

The issue with many playbooks is that they are typically disorganized, lack a clear success framework, and haven't been committed to writing. What's likely needed is a more formal playbook. Regardless of your tenure, the six BUILDS™ imperatives can help drive greater success for yourself and those you hire.

Before we delve into the playbook, let me briefly explain the "why."

There are leaders, "habitual starters," who have begun numerous jobs. They're typically "short-termers," only lasting a year or two before moving on, willingly or otherwise. Despite their starting experience, they struggle to sustain roles. Their playbook, not geared for long-term success, proves ineffective.

Then we have seasoned leaders with decades of experience and numerous job transitions. Their playbook for assuming leadership roles is clear, built on best practices gleaned from hundreds of top leaders. However, only a few possess a written guide, with most relying on a mental playbook. Despite repeated successes, one wonders if written documentation could enhance performance by offering a ready reference for each new leadership transition. If you're confident in your playbook's solidity, feel free to skip to Section 3. It contains invaluable resources from stellar leaders who've mastered the nuances of starting new leadership roles.

Average leaders lie somewhere between novice and seasoned when it comes to onboarding, assimilation, and integration. Many only read half an onboarding book before starting a new role, struggle to articulate their playbook, and often wing it. Would a succinct, easy-to-remember guide improve their situation? If you identify with this group and aspire to excel beyond average, commit to finishing this book and consider implementing at least one recommendation from Section 3.

Last, we come to the probable reader—you, a high-potential, upwardly mobile leader. You're in the middle stages of leadership and have successfully navigated potential pitfalls, but you don't want to rely on luck. You understand that climbing the corporate ladder increases the stakes. Congratulations on treating the onboarding, assimilation, and integration process with the gravity it deserves.

Adopt the BUILDS™ Playbook as Your Own

The BUILDS™ acronym was devised in order to easily recall the six competencies crucial for mastering onboarding, assimilation, and integration. This mnemonic will aid in structuring your strategy for your first year and beyond.

BUILDS™ stands for six key imperatives:

- Build Trust!
- Understand Needs!
- Involve Stakeholders!
- Listen to Concerns!
- Deliver Results!
- Serve with Excellence!

Over the years, I've observed that successful leaders have a refined strategy for transitioning into a new role. This game plan provides direction, progress checkpoints, and guidance on pace and necessary adjustments. Successful leaders also follow a set of imperatives. To that end, you will notice that each BUILDS™ point is marked with an exclamation point. By embracing these rallying cries, you can get behind each one, steering you toward significant victories in your leadership journey.

Feel free to make this playbook truly yours by adapting and personalizing it. Throughout this section, I've left space for you to supplement these ideas with your own. My suggestions are by no means exhaustive, and I anticipate you'll come up with additional strategies to effectively execute "your" playbook. Make it personal and relevant to your own specific leadership journey. In other words, "Take the best, and leave the rest."

Remember Your Playbook

Before every match, the coach passionately urges her team, "Remember your playbook!" The team understands the message. They have a well-rehearsed set of plays to execute. Regardless of the sport, the goal is to have a strong offense and solid defense, score points, and win. Utilize these six imperatives to evaluate your monthly performance. Determine how well you're achieving assimilation and integration as a highly effective leader.

Your BUILDS™ playbook lays the groundwork for creating a potent organization and enjoying a successful tenure. Each letter signifies a vital competency to develop and sustain throughout your journey, helping you flourish in your leadership role.

Develop a method to keep this BUILDS™ playbook top of mind. Perhaps create a sticky note for your computer with the BUILDS™ diagram or any other approach that works for you.

Build Upon the Successes of Others

BUILDS™ consists of essential objectives and imperatives I've extracted from over three decades of observing successful leaders who excel at this process. My contribution is packaging this wisdom into a framework that's easy to recall, follow, and pass on to others you bring on board.

Each step builds upon the one before. They are separated into three phases.

THREE-PHASE PROCESS

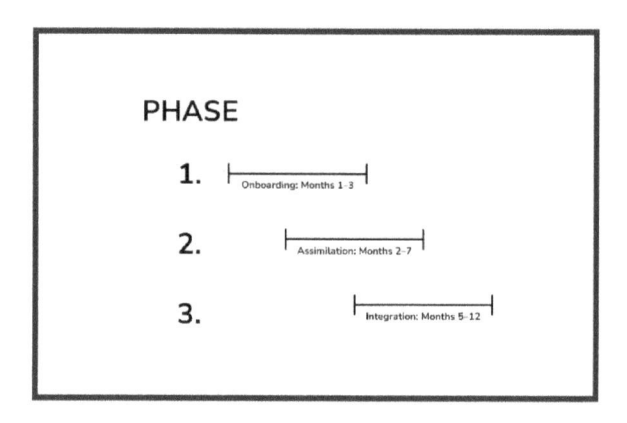

```
PHASE
  1.  |—Onboarding: Months 1-3—|
  2.        |—Assimilation: Months 2-7—|
  3.              |—Integration: Months 5-12—|
```

Below is a brief outline of each phase, along with general timelines. These timelines can vary based on different organizational cultures. Thus, defining the timeframe for each phase is more an art than a science. Trust your instincts, guided by the following phase descriptions.

Phase 1, onboarding, usually covers the initial one to three months. This is the time to get to know the organization, its culture, and your key stakeholders. It involves grasping the expectations of your role, building relationships, and gaining crucial knowledge and skills. Setting clear objectives and creating a robust foundation is key. The first three elements of the BUILDS™ model—Build Trust, Understand Needs, and Involve Stakeholders—are particularly crucial at this stage.

Phase 2, assimilation, generally kicks off in the second or third month and concludes around the fifth to seventh month. During this phase, the leader deepens their understanding of organizational dynamics, aligns with the team's objectives, and fortifies stakeholder relationships. It involves active team participation, collaborative efforts with colleagues, and effective utilization of their expertise. The assimilation phase aims to build credibility, trust, and a sense of belonging within the organization. It is also when you start working on yourself and securing bigger wins, corresponding with the BUILDS™ elements of "Listen to Concerns" and "Deliver Results."

Phase 3, integration, can initiate as early as the fourth or fifth month and stretches up to twelve months or beyond.

In certain organizations, you might still feel like the "new person" even after a year, merely beginning to be assimilated into the culture. Remember, this timeline heavily depends on the organization. This third phase aims at completely integrating the leader into the fabric of the organization. By the end of this process, the leader fully owns their role, embraces additional responsibilities, and has clearly proven their capacity to deliver results. They persist in nurturing relationships, empowering their team, and contributing toward the long-term success of the organization. Integration entails adjusting to the unique challenges of the organization, sustaining momentum, and positioning oneself as a crucial contributor and leader. The key to succeeding in Phase 3 lies in the last of the six critical imperatives of the BUILDS™ System: **Serve with Excellence!**

NOTE: As mentioned, Section 3 of this book offers invaluable resources tailored to each of these phases, organized in such a way that you can easily identify the resources most likely to be useful in your current phase.

By understanding and purposefully navigating each phase, leaders can effectively manage the transition, assert their influence, and optimize their contributions in their new role.

As we delve into these six imperatives, it's important to recognize how they work harmoniously together, each layer strengthening the other, ultimately culminating in the pinnacle of Serve with Excellence. Through this journey, you can and will achieve both personal and organizational excellence.

Take a Break

Let me pause here and mention the value of taking a strategic break, even if you don't feel you need one.

Integrating a thoughtfully planned one-week vacation during the three- to six-month mark of your onboarding process can prove to be an invaluable checkpoint. This pause serves as an opportunity for reflection on your progress thus far and allows you to recalibrate your approach moving forward. The timing of this break should be determined by the pace at which you are progressing through the phases. Typically, around the three- to four-month mark is ideal for taking a step back to evaluate your accomplishments, rejuvenate, and strategize for the next phase.

To make the most of your "break," follow these steps during your time off:

1. Reflect on your progress: Take time to review your original hundred-day plan. Assess what you've achieved and where you might have missed the mark. Celebrate your wins and identify areas that need further attention.
2. Analyze successes and failures: Pinpoint the factors that contributed to your victories and understand the reasons for any setbacks. This insight will be beneficial in helping you adjust your approach for the future.

3. Refine your hundred-day plan: Based on your self-reflection, tweak your original hundred-day plan. Develop a fresh set of objectives and action steps for the next quarter.
4. Strategize for your next quarter: Lay out your priorities for the upcoming three months, integrating ideas and suggestions from Phase 2 in Section 3. This strategy should be based on your successes and address any areas for improvement.
5. Share with your team: When you get back to work, communicate your insights, revised goals, and updated plan for the next quarter with your team. This open communication will reinforce trust and show your dedication to continuous improvement. Also, share your new ideas with your manager and get their input, ensuring you have full alignment.
6. Carry out the refined plan: Execute flawlessly to plan.
7. Keep open communication: Continually engage with your team and stakeholders. Regular feedback sessions will ensure you stay aligned with expectations and the broader goals of the organization.

By using this structured approach to reflection and planning, you're laying the foundation for greater success in your leadership role. The insights you gain during your break will empower you to be more strategic, enabling you to correct your course as needed and "build" on your successes. It will facilitate your continuous growth and achievement in your role by giving you time to regroup, replan, and re-energize.

NOTE: You'll notice that going forward, Section 2 intentionally includes space for your ideas and insights. I suggest getting a physical copy of this book to use the provided blank spaces or margins to enrich this playbook with your unique perspectives and experiences. This enables you to craft a personalized guide catering to your specific needs and objectives, enhancing its professional development value.

CHAPTER 8 — BUILD TRUST!

Build Trust!

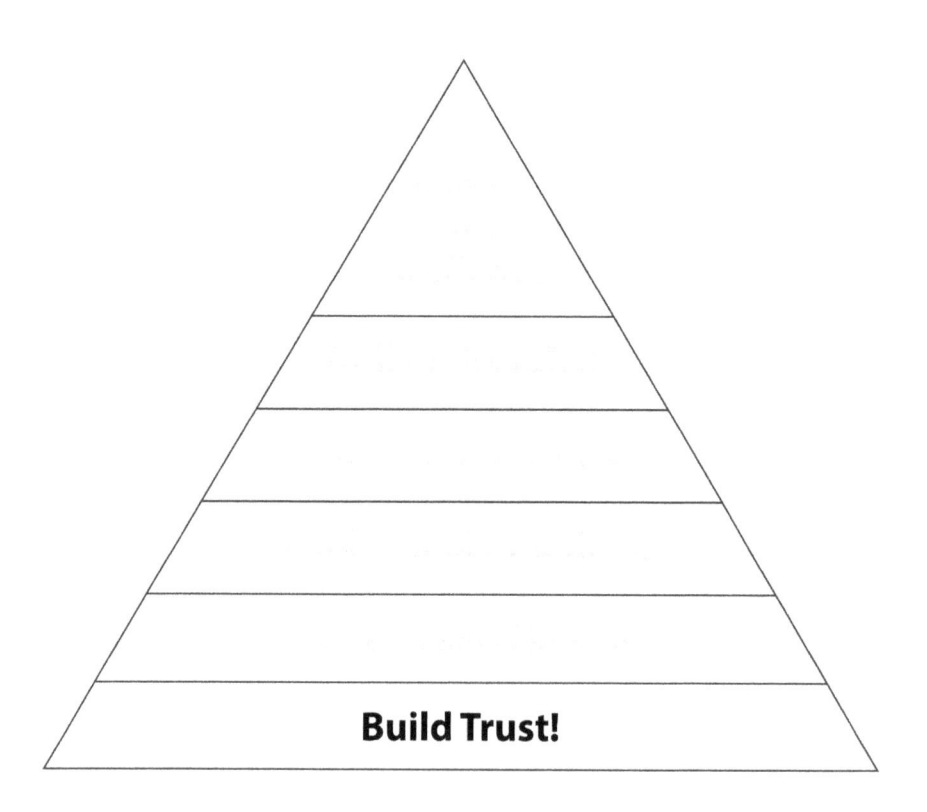

Intentionally Build Trust

As you transition into a new role, your primary goal should be to cultivate trust with key stakeholders. While multiple strategies can aid in this pursuit, the crux of success fundamentally lies in forging and maintaining high-trust relationships. Quality relationships founded in trust form the foundation for achieving your goals. However, consider this as merely the first step. It's critical to sustain, nurture, and strengthen these bonds over time. Trust building is a continuous process. Even after years in your role, there's always the potential to broaden your influence through further trust building.

Go Slow

Though it may seem contradictory to the sense of urgency you feel when assuming a new role, the saying "Slow is smooth, and smooth is fast" is very relevant. The objective is to build robust, high-trust relationships, a process that simply cannot be rushed. It demands concentrated effort and patience. By becoming fixated on achieving immediate results or ticking off project milestones, you risk undermining the opportunity to lay a strong groundwork for this crucial mandate.

Starting a new leadership role can often demand immediate focus on effectively managing opportunities and challenges. The pressure from higher-ups and colleagues to deliver quick results can be intense, and it's quite likely that you yourself have set high expectations, keen on providing concrete proof of your beneficial influence on the organization. Trust, an element that is tough to quantify, can be easily sidelined in the pursuit of outcomes that are more readily measurable.

Securing notable victories can ignite positive momentum, but early missteps can occur just as quickly. Curb the instinct to rush. Building relationships takes time and varies among individuals. While hitting targets matters, nurturing trustworthy ties with key stakeholders is vital for lasting success.

Suggested Actions
1. Compile a detailed list of key stakeholders.
2. Enlist your manager's help to expand the list and obtain background data on each person.

3. Prioritize the list into very high, high, medium, and low-medium categories.
4. Investigate each stakeholder on LinkedIn pre-meeting and mention your findings during discussions.
5. Document discussions and maintain a written profile for each stakeholder.
6. Regularly update these profiles, noting personal and professional insights.
7. Consider further actions, like seeking collaboration opportunities, addressing stakeholders' concerns, and tracking meeting action items.

List other actions that come to mind.

-
-
-

Gain Alignment with Your Manager

Your immediate manager is one of your key stakeholders, and their support is essential. If you're just starting, discuss your "first thirty days" playbook with them, seeking their endorsement for the following:

1. Establishing high-trust relationships with key stakeholders.
2. Comprehending the needs of all stakeholders: superiors, customers, direct reports, and peers.
3. Crafting a hundred-day plan.
4. Submitting a draft plan to your manager by week three's end.
5. Discussing the draft with your manager in week four.
6. Incorporating proposed revisions.
7. Executing the plan starting from week five.

This approach enables expectation alignment and trust building while setting the stage for your first significant quick win—an effective onboarding plan matching your manager's expectations. If you're beyond your initial thirty days, some suggestions may not apply, but consider retaining them for future reference and as you onboard new hires. Just as a reminder, read this book with bifocal vision—focus on immediate relevance, but also note insights pertinent to onboarding, assimilating, and integrating future leaders.

Suggested Actions
1. Arrange consistent check-ins with your manager to maintain alignment during onboarding. Aim for a first draft of your plan by the close of week three.
2. Solicit feedback from your manager and other key stakeholders to modify your plan as needed. Finalize the plan by the end of week four.
3. Develop an action plan for each onboarding step, specifying timelines and accountable individuals.
4. Participate in pertinent meetings or events to understand the organization's culture, values, and objectives better.
5. Identify a mentor or reliable colleague to guide and support you as you acclimate to your new role.

    List other actions that come to mind.
-
-
-

Embrace Reality

In any scenario, there are three realities: your perception, the other person's perception, and the objective reality of events. Ideally, these three align, but that's seldom the case. As a leader, your role is to foster accurate perceptions, both in yourself and others, promoting alignment and trust.

This is particularly paramount in terms of how others perceive you as a leader. Building trust hinges on an accurate, positive perception of you and your actions. Therefore, it's crucial to understand how others view you and work to align their perception with your intended leadership style and objectives. To accomplish this, regularly seek feedback, actively listen to others' perspectives, and be open to making necessary adjustments. Strive for transparent, authentic communication, setting clear expectations, and honoring commitments. By doing this, you can align everyone on a shared understanding and consequently build trust.

Remember, perception shapes reality, and trust building relies on your ability to accurately perceive how you are being received as a leader in your new role.

Suggested Actions
1. Regularly request feedback from superiors, peers, direct reports, and key stakeholders.
2. Actively listen to others' viewpoints, avoiding defensiveness or dismissiveness.
3. Communicate transparently and openly, setting clear expectations and fulfilling commitments.
4. Strive to understand others' perception of you as a leader, working to align it with your intended leadership style and goals.
5. Make necessary adjustments based on feedback; be willing to acknowledge mistakes and implement corrective actions.
6. Establish a routine plan to assess and address any disparities between your desired image and others' perceptions.

7. Seek guidance from an advisor, coach, or mentor to refine your leadership perception.
8. Gauge how you're perceived by others by keenly observing their body language.

List other actions that come to mind.

-
-
-

Manage Perceptions

As mentioned above, trust building requires self-assessment of your leadership style and comprehension of others' perceptions. Using tools like DISC-based behavioral assessments can help deepen your understanding of your behavioral tendencies and give you greater insight into how you may be coming across to others.

Each person has a preferred behavioral style, and it is vital to comprehend and adapt to those preferences accordingly. Recognizing others' styles is a skill that can be learned with the assistance of numerous available resources. This knowledge offers valuable insights about your team, enabling you to grasp their key behavioral drivers. Armed with this understanding, you can make informed decisions and take appropriate actions. Recognizing common or unique aspects you share with your key stakeholders is particularly beneficial.

To obtain an optimal early perspective, solicit assistance from various sources, such as mentors or trusted advisors who are well-versed in leadership assimilation and invested in your success. They should possess high emotional intelligence, offer candid feedback, and aid in elevating your EQ. Ensure you have at least one person who routinely observes you and provides unbiased feedback on your interactions with others.

You will find an in-depth explanation of the DISC in Section 3.

Suggested Actions
1. Review previously taken behavioral assessments.
2. Complete a DISC Behavioral Preference Indicator assessment to deepen your understanding of your behavioral tendencies and preferences. Refer to Section 3 for further details.
3. Have your direct reports complete the DISC assessment so you can understand their preferences and adjust your leadership style accordingly, adapting your style to better meet their needs.
4. Request your manager or leadership team (or board of directors, if you're a CEO) to undertake the DISC assessment. This will enhance your understanding of their preferences and facilitate trust building.
5. In your first year of assimilation and integration, engage a mentor, coach, or advisor to obtain a fresh perspective and feedback on your leadership approach.

List other actions that come to mind.

-
-
-

Refreshing your knowledge of behavioral sciences will stimulate your awareness of varied behavior patterns. Numerous resources are available, each providing insight into the diverse ways individuals tend to behave.

While understanding your own behavioral style is valuable, it's even more crucial to recognize and adapt to the styles of others. Familiarize yourself with a system for identifying different styles, helping you understand your natural chemistry with stakeholders. Discerning others' styles is a learned skill that warrants your attention.

Encouraging your team to complete a behavioral preference indicator profile will provide invaluable insights. By understanding your team's behavioral drives, you gain a glimpse into their actions, thinking patterns, feelings, and decision-making processes. That's why adopting a "listen and learn" approach in your initial few months is so essential.

Avoid Unforced Errors

Another crucial element in building trust with your new team is avoiding what might be termed "unforced errors." Often, new leaders make easily avoidable mistakes, primarily due to being overwhelmed by a barrage of information and responsibilities.

Over one-fifth of new leaders leave or are let go during their first year. To avoid this fate, it's crucial to periodically step back from daily tasks and seek objective feedback on your performance. I highly recommend requesting monthly feedback from your superior during your first quarter. Arrange sincere, in-depth discussions where you actively solicit their perspective. Ask, "In your view, how can I further improve my performance?" and genuinely listen to their response. This builds trust with your manager and opens the door for the feedback you need.

You only get one opportunity to make your first hundred days count. Savvy leaders seize this chance to build a reputation for effectiveness. Those who fail to foster positive impressions miss out on the chance to gain a significant edge. It's essential to manage initial perceptions, whether they're fair or not. Evident weaknesses, a lack of authoritative presence, or inadequate self-assurance all project an undesirable image. Sometimes, team members might hesitate to follow a leader who doesn't fit their expectations. One accomplished leader outlined this strategy as follows:

"I strive to avoid being pigeonholed by my colleagues or superiors. Once you're labeled, it's incredibly difficult to shed that image. I don't want to be prematurely branded as being too extreme or too mild in a particular way. Instead, I aim to take a step back and understand the culture, both the informal and formal channels of communication, identify the key influencers, and truly grasp the core values of the organization—not just the ones presented in the mission statement."

To achieve this, strategize every major action you take in the early stages meticulously. This is not the time to relax or resort to ways operated in a previous role, where you had been well integrated.

Suggested Actions
1. Ask your manager for feedback monthly.
2. Establish an environment in which your manager feels comfortable providing candid feedback.
3. Modify your strategy based on the feedback received.

Consider other potential actions that could improve your performance. List them here.

-
-
-

Take Periodic Assessments

During the initial one hundred days, regular evaluations can prove highly beneficial. These assessments can range from extensive leadership appraisals to brief moments of introspection. At the beginning of your tenure, your schedule is usually somewhat more flexible, allowing you to dedicate a few hours each month to strategic evaluation. A coach, mentor, or HR partner can assist you with conducting an assessment tailored to your specific situation. Refer to Section 3 for several great assessments you can take.

Suggested Actions
1. Take the Unleashing Leadership Excellence Assessment (Section 3).
2. Explore other assessments provided by your people and culture / HR department.
3. Execute an informal 360-degree assessment by soliciting feedback from key stakeholders.
4. Dedicate some time to evaluate your progress in building relationships. Identify any that need to be fortified and schedule one-on-one meetings as needed.

   List other actions that come to mind.
-
-
-

Avoid Trust Derailers

Certain factors can hinder the development of productive, enduring relationships. Let's call these potential obstacles "trust derailers." They include:

1. Fumbling your initial introduction
2. Portraying an unauthentic or insincere persona
3. Prioritizing tasks over people

4. Dominating discussions
5. Failing to actively listen and understand
6. Showing signs of impatience
7. Overlooking or disregarding the sentiments shared
8. Exhibiting a lack of humility
9. Exuding a know-it-all attitude, steering with ego, or indulging in self-praise

Focus on making a positive first impression by prioritizing others' needs over yours. This approach will help build mutual trust.

Establish a positive impression by allocating ample time in your schedule to develop and strengthen relationships with key stakeholders. Take pleasure in learning about the persons, not just their roles. Move beyond surface-level interaction and embrace authenticity. Your openness will act like a welcoming signal, drawing others toward you and establishing believability, likeability, and trust (BLT).

BLT serves as the staple nourishment for successful leaders. Feed your relationships with BLT to foster positive interactions. Refer to "Relationship-Building Tactics" in Section 3 for a complete playbook on executing your initial sets of stakeholder meetings.

Establishing trust forms the primary building block of your playbook. Authenticity and genuine interest in forming connections form the vital components of successful initial interactions. Multiple paths lead to trust building, and your task is to decipher the unique code for each individual you encounter. If you're deliberate and concentrate on attaining this crucial imperative, it will lay the robust foundation upon which all else stands.

Suggested Actions
1. Evaluate the compilation of "trust derailers" and implement

necessary remedial measures.
2. Complete "Relationship-Building Tactics" (found in Section 3).
3. Embrace the concept of BLT; notice when it is absent and strive to attain it with all key stakeholders.
4. Review your roster of stakeholders and assess the level of BLT with each one (your best subjective estimation will do), and focus on enhancing your scores over time.

List other actions that come to mind.

-
-
-

Expand Your *Build Trust* Playbook

I've presented several trust-building strategies in this section. However, I'm sure you also have your own unique ideas for fostering trust. What might those be? I encourage you to create a list. For each idea, write a brief explanation about its nature and your approach to it. Then, formulate a series of actions you can take to implement these trust-building methods. Remember, Build Trust is a fundamental cornerstone of successful leadership, no matter where you are in the process.

Topic:
Method:
Actions to take:

-
-
-

The Manager's Corner: *Build Trust!*

It's important not to rush your new leader into action. Adopting a patient approach and allowing them to proceed at a steady pace initially will yield better outcomes in the long term. Support your new hire in dedicating ample time to establishing robust, high-trust relationships with vital stakeholders. I shared this proverb in this chapter: "Slow is smooth, and smooth is fast."

Building trust takes time. As the foundation upon which everything else is built, this process involves much more than just the initial meetings. Therefore, you should prompt your leader to schedule multiple relationship-building meetings early on. In Section 3, there is a resource called "Relationship-Building Tactics," intended for your leader's use. I suggest you review it with them.

Your relationship-building efforts aim to sidestep low-trust relationship pitfalls. Support your leader proactively, removing barriers to scheduling key stakeholder meetings. This fosters a necessary environment of trust and collaboration. One meeting is generally not sufficient; I recommend finding reasons for repeated meetings. Only then will your new hire be able to achieve this first imperative.

Establishing these relationship foundations is a time investment. As you know, these relationships are crucial.

CHAPTER 9 UNDERSTAND NEEDS!

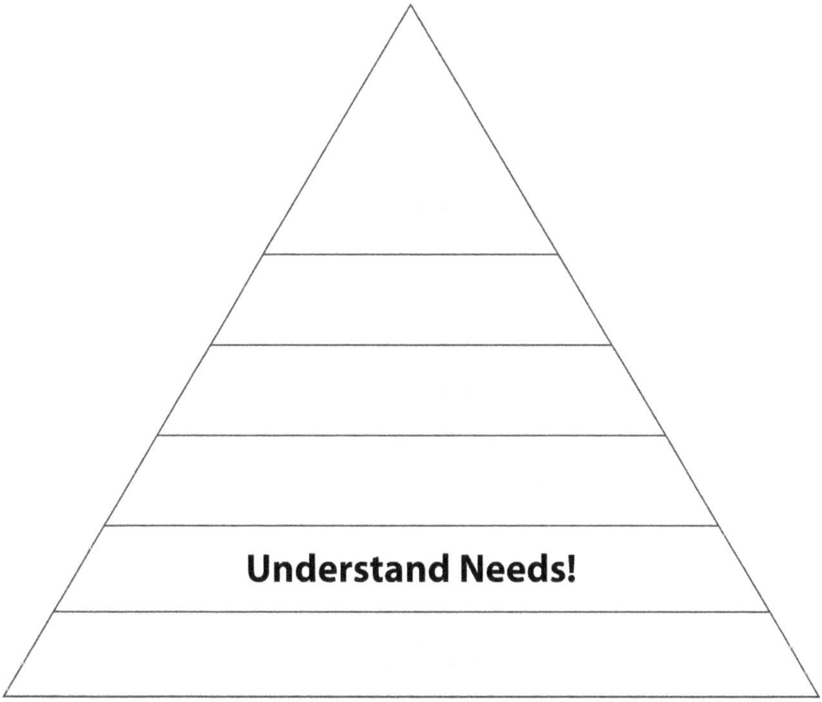

Intentionally Understand Needs

Your second major imperative or objective, based upon and then running parallel to trust building, is understanding needs. Clearly, you need to discern the needs of your direct reports, peers, boss, board, shareholders, marketplace, and beyond. Yet, the "how" might not be immediately clear. Achieving this requires an exceptional level of intentionality.

Following is a playbook for better understanding needs.

Listen and Learn

Regardless of how much of an expert you are, you still need to assess needs to confirm your assumptions. Perception is key. If you appear to have all the answers before you've truly listened and learned, you've made a leadership misstep. While it's especially important to avoid this perception early on, you will have to maintain your reputation throughout your tenure. The day you assume you have all the answers and no longer listen to others' needs marks the beginning of your decline as an influential, effective leader. In essence: great leaders always listen.

When asked about your change plans during the initial thirty to sixty days, I recommend responding with, "I'm currently in the phase of listening and learning." You can add, "At the moment, I aim to understand your needs and those of the organization." This approach is next to impossible to fault, even by those who might perceive you as a threat. It provides the best results and puts you in control. You'll discover much more by listening and learning rather than offering preliminary thoughts on potential solutions or action plans. By asking questions, you maintain more control than by making statements you might regret later as you gain further insights.

Utilizing the "listening and learning" approach is ideal during your initial months in your new role. The timeframe will hinge on the pace of your organization—adapt accordingly. Beyond this period, it's anticipated you'll have formulated a perspective and an action plan. In due course, you'll crystallize your intentions regarding actions, changes, and those who will be affected. However, during this preliminary stage, it's prudent to predominantly share your thoughts with your immediate manager (or the board if you're the CEO), exercising caution and limiting the extent of sharing with others. Projecting yourself as a humble, eager learner can foster an environment where people feel comfortable expressing their genuine thoughts and feelings about the organization.

Focus on "your organization," not the organization at large, if you are not the CEO. When posing questions about the challenges your team and the organization in your domain are experiencing, concentrate on the areas you can control. If you're a senior leader, such as the CEO, COO, CFO, CMO, etc., the whole organization may very well be your concern, but otherwise, stay focused on what's within your reach. An end-to-end organizational assessment and diagnosis is rarely your job. For your first stakeholder meetings, consider a structured approach. You'll find a useful playbook in Section 3.

Suggested Actions
1. Commit the company's vision, mission, core values, and key objectives to memory.
2. Quickly learn the names of key stakeholders and as many others as possible.
3. Initiate a listening tour, keeping personal opinions to a minimum and remaining in a "listen and learn" mode for the first month or two.
4. Position yourself as a receptive leader; genuinely absorb what is shared and show that you've listened through your actions.
5. Don't fall into the trap of being the know-it-all; maintain your habit of listening and learning even as you become more familiar with your role, adhering to Stephen Covey's wise approach: "Seek first to understand, then to be understood."
6. Initiate individual, team, and organizational assessments to gain unbiased feedback.

List other actions that come to mind.

-
-
-

Conduct Interviews

Carrying out interviews early in your role is an excellent strategy for obtaining a thorough evaluation of the people in your direct organization. For example, holding skip-level meetings with employees who directly report to your subordinates is a standard, ongoing best practice.

It's important to make others comfortable enough to share honestly rather than feel like they're being interviewed. Strive to create a relaxed and conversational atmosphere. This exchange should be a dialogue, not merely a barrage of questions. Your key objectives are first, to establish a high-trust relationship, and second, to carry out an efficient assessment. A natural give-and-take conversation is most useful to accomplish this.

During your first few months, you might wonder, "How can it be a conversation if I can't share all my insightful ideas? After all, I've done my research and have concepts I'd like to discuss." Here, it's crucial to strike a balance. You might be too fresh in the role to share your opinions or test your ideas. Stay in the assessment phase. Your ego may not like this, as you'll feel compelled to offer some of your input. My recommendation: Check your ego at the door. Maintain a diagnostic stance.

An effective way to do this is by utilizing "active listening." It involves reflecting on what you hear from the other person, and paraphrasing back what you heard. Be careful not to parrot their words, as this may come off as mechanical and insincere. Instead, be authentic, show genuine interest in what they have to say, and repeat back in your own words what you are hearing. Regardless of their position in the hierarchy, everyone has valuable insights to offer. By leaning into the conversation and employing active listening, you project both intellectual AND emotional intelligence. You will find more information on this in Section 3.

Many new leaders are so engrossed in their duties that they neglect the individuals involved. Even worse, they may acknowledge the importance of their team but claim they're "too busy" to fully engage with them. However, in those initial weeks and months, there's no excuse for being too busy for your colleagues. They are essential to your long-term success. As you know, without them, you can't reach your goals.

Suggested Actions
1. Arrange additional informational conversations with key stakeholders.
2. Carry out an effective assessment, ensuring people don't feel like they're being interrogated.
3. Hone your active listening skills.
4. Maintain your priority of building trust at the forefront of your interactions.
5. Schedule skip-level interviews every quarter or so to better understand your direct reports, their performance, and team morale.
6. Think about using a SWOT (Strengths, Weaknesses, Opportunities, Threats) approach for more formal assessments.

List other actions that come to mind.
-
-
-

Pressure Test Your Diagnosis

If you were to enter a doctor's office, proclaim, "I'm not feeling well," and instantly receive a bottle of antibiotics, it would indicate a case of medical negligence. A thorough examination should be conducted before diagnosing your condition and suggesting a recovery plan. You'd expect the doctor to consider your symptoms and measure your temperature and blood pressure, among other diagnostic steps. Prescribing treatment without adequate diagnosis is malpractice. Similarly, during your initial three to six months in a new role, various diagnostic assessments need to be performed. Your early one-on-one and team meetings are integral to this process, but there is plenty more you can do.

Let's hypothetically say you've carried out an effective assessment, have a good grasp of the situation, and have a perfect plan to improve the organization. It's still important not to jump the gun by prematurely sharing your diagnosis. You may feel the urge to demonstrate your competence and insight, letting your ego take the lead. This results in overhasty statements that may later prove to be inaccurate. First impressions are lasting, and prematurely sharing your analysis is a quick way to falter and lose credibility. It's best to hold on to your early assessments and conclusions for a while.

Suggested Actions
1. Carry out a comprehensive evaluation of your direct reports, your organization, and the projects and initiatives under your purview.
2. Keep your preliminary assessments to yourself and a trusted advisor or two while you test your hypothesis.
3. Validate your assumptions and conclusions with a trustworthy confidante before openly presenting conclusions. This can prevent potential inaccuracies and protect your credibility.

List other actions that come to mind.

-
-
-

Expand Your *Understand Needs* Playbook

These are just a few ideas for this imperative. You likely have more thoughts about understanding the needs of your organization. Make a list and elaborate on each idea, describing what it means and how you will accomplish it. Then, create prioritized action steps to improve your ability to validate these needs.

Topic:
Method:
Actions to take:

-
-
-

The Manager's Corner: *Understand Needs!*

Support your direct report in performing a comprehensive evaluation of the people and organization they've been assigned to manage. Transparently communicate your insights regarding the personnel, departments, projects, and any other relevant aspects to aid your leader in familiarizing themselves with their role and responsibilities, giving them the benefit of your wisdom and experience.

Review the suggested actions in this chapter, and add your own as needed. These are only recommendations. I trust that you have a keen understanding of what your leader needs to do in order to perform an effective assessment and truly Understand Needs.

CHAPTER 10
INVOLVE STAKEHOLDERS!

Involve Stakeholders!

Intentionally Involve Stakeholders

Consider the compass points: north, south, east, and west. They represent four main stakeholder categories. North includes your manager, their manager, and so on, up to the board and shareholders. South represents your direct reports and their direct reports, extending to frontline employees, consultants, and contractors. East signifies

Customer Compass diagram: North — Leader, CEO, Board, Investors; East — External Customers; South — Staff, Direct Reports; West — Peers, Colleagues, Other Departments.

customers, partners, and external alliances. West stands for direct and indirect peers. All are important, but prioritizing is essential. Determining when and how to engage with each vector is both an art and a science.

Following is a playbook for involving stakeholders:

Identify Key Stakeholders

Key stakeholders are just that—key—to your success.

Your progressive success in this role, your tenure within this organization, your long-term career, and the organization's peak performance all now hinge on two crucial imperatives: built trust and understood needs. It's indeed puzzling why leaders often underestimate the importance of building high-trust relationships with critical constituents and fully understanding their needs. Common excuses include:

- "I don't have time; I'm too occupied with my day-to-day tasks."
- "That person is unreachable; I can't secure a spot on their calendar."
- "I don't particularly like them and would rather avoid engagement."
- "They just don't understand the real problems here."

- "I have the solution and a clear mandate for change. This is not really necessary."

There's no end to the list of excuses one can conjure up. However, they remain just that: excuses. Your key stakeholders need to play an active part in your job, just as you need to be involved in theirs. While this isn't new information, it's worth emphasizing for several important reasons:

- Engaging key stakeholders effectively from the outset lays the groundwork for future success.
- Neglecting to build effective bridges may leave you isolated and exposed.
- Most organizational cultures gauge your leadership abilities based on your skill in involving others.
- Unless you build a strong foundation of trust and a shared understanding of needs, you will be unable to do your job.

It is worth the investment of time and energy to go out of your way to accomplish these imperatives as you now engage in the third building block: Involve Stakeholders.

Suggested Actions
1. Construct a prioritized, rank-ordered list of significant stakeholders.
2. Devise a strategy for cultivating robust relationships with each one you will need to involve in executing your job.
3. Implement your strategy through effective collaboration.
4. Formulate a plan for maintaining long-term engagement with each stakeholder; execute this plan.

5. Detect any excuses for not accomplishing the above and address them.

   List other actions that come to mind.

-
-
-

Identify and Cultivate Allies

Allies are individuals with whom you've established trustful relationships. They back your assimilation and integration process and subsequent performance. They run the gamut from subtle supporters to vocal champions.

From the outset, it's crucial to start forming alliances. Early on, getting unbiased feedback can be challenging due to your newness. Face-to-face meetings are irreplaceable for creating strategic alliances, as virtual meetings have limitations. In the beginning, people will understand your need to meet key individuals in person. Plan a "world tour" early in your role. Visit people where they work or invite them to your office—do whatever is necessary to have in-person interactions if possible.

A word of caution: While many will seek to befriend you, keep in mind that some may have competing, hidden, or even negative agendas. Exercise discernment and watch for signs that either build or erode trust. Not everyone will be your ally. Some may have a tainted reputation, and you could experience "guilt by association" if you get too close. There's no exact formula for this—you must rely on your judgment. This is the "art" in your "start."

In the early days, exercise patience in your decision-making. Refrain from acting on limited information from a single source.

Cross-check your observations with key stakeholders and navigate your relationships with allies thoughtfully. Proceed with considered caution, as some might lay traps for you, while others could unintentionally set you up for failure.

Suggested Actions
1. Identify potential allies within the organization; cultivate and strengthen those relationships.
2. Pressure test your allies for authenticity, genuine backing, and real support.
3. Reciprocate where, when, and as often as appropriate.
4. Beware of insincere allies or those with conflicting objectives or competing agendas.
5. Triangulate and cross-check data for reliability.

List other actions that come to mind.
-
-
-

Understand the Culture

Recall the Jimmy and Beth scenario from Section 1. Do you think Jimmy would have kept his job if he understood the culture? My opinion is that he would still have been dismissed. Why? He failed to adjust his pace of change to match Beth's comfort level. He was determined to force the culture to align with his own expectations.

Avoid trying to shape the culture to your preferences without full alignment from key stakeholders. That's why establishing allies in your first one hundred days is so crucial. Many small aspects of an organization's culture can create stumbling blocks.

Seeking help along the way is vital to success. Rely on trusted colleagues and your manager to help understand the organization's culture and values. Additionally, a neutral third party like an advisor, mentor, or coach can provide the impartial feedback necessary to identify and avoid common pitfalls.

As a quick aside, I have mentioned advisors, mentors, and a coach many times now. There is a full playbook in Section 3 for gaining a mentor. Be sure to read it and seek out several.

Many failures originate from cultural clashes. A significant portion of a leader's pre-employment interview revolves around cultural compatibility. You were likely asked, "Will you fit into our culture? Can you thrive here? Will the organization accept your leadership style?" These questions persist well into your tenure. Long after you've been hired, they remain in the minds of key stakeholders. You are constantly being evaluated for "cultural fit" throughout your first year.

Suggested Actions
1. Comprehend and embrace the culture before attempting to alter it.
2. Seek help from your allies, whether internal or external, to enhance your understanding.
3. Share your observations with a reliable person, such as a coach, mentor, or advisor.
4. If your manager has been with the organization for over a year, rely on them to help you understand the culture's nuances.
5. Understand that different sectors of the organization may have unique "subcultures" that need careful consideration.
6. Secure complete alignment from key stakeholders for any proposed changes.

List other actions that come to mind.

-
-
-

Embrace the Organization's Core Values

Allies are key to helping you grasp the organization's fundamental values. Following that, it's your responsibility to uphold them. Frequently, the stated core values are the ones that senior leaders aspire to rather than the ones actually practiced. Use your observational skills and depend on your allies to discern the true core values reflected in the collective actions of the organization. The "art" lies in championing both the stated and the actual values.

This discussion brings to mind an experience with Chad, a first-time CFO, who enlisted my services to assist him in transitioning into a new organization. Let me share with you our conversation 120 days into his tenure.

Chad's Story

"Chad, have you encountered any challenges yet? Given it's your first time in the CFO role, I'm somewhat surprised by all the positive updates. Is there anything in your onboarding process, four months in, that you're finding difficult?"

"No, everything's been excellent! The transition has been smoother than I anticipated."

"Let me ask you something. Have you identified the organization's core values? CEOs typically have a strong passion for these."

"I think I've read them somewhere, but I'm unsure of the specifics."

"I recommend you identify them and then discuss them with your boss. Determine which ones are valued most and assist in promoting them within your operation."

"That sounds like a great idea!"

As a leader, Chad should have already identified his organization's core values. However, being new to a senior leadership role, he overlooked this crucial aspect. That's a glaring warning signal. For Chad, the core values were secondary, but for the CEO, they were central. The quickest route to forging a solid, high-trust bond with a superior is identifying their primary concerns and embracing them as your own.

In our subsequent coaching session, Chad mentioned that he had a discussion with the CEO about the organization's core values. It appeared one of the CEO's main frustrations was the lack of emphasis placed on these values by his direct reports. Seizing this opportunity, Chad initiated several actions to promote the company's core values within his organization. Before long, he was highlighting them at a company-wide meeting and quickly became the CEO's preferred change agent.

At the time of this writing, Chad has a very rewarding career at that company, largely due to this powerful relationship.

Suggested Actions
1. Identify both the official and the implicit core values of the organization and commit them to memory.
2. Determine which of those core values apply to your department.
3. Create a set of core values specifically for your department that are in line with the core values of the overall organization.
4. Live out those core values—embody them, exude them, and have your team embrace them.

   List other actions that come to mind.
-
-
-

Maintain a Lasting Positive Impression

Your goal extends beyond a remarkable *first* impression; it's about leaving a *lasting* positive impact on your manager, key stakeholders, and all team members. The optimal way to achieve this is to kick off exceptionally strong in your initial year. Take note, "strong" doesn't imply "fast," "overly direct," "demanding," or "self-serving." Read "Serve with Excellence!" and all of Section 3 to understand fully what this means.

Establishing a powerful, positive impression lays the foundation for a continued and lasting legacy.

Now, let's quickly review our building blocks so far.

Build Trust: If you're perpetually overwhelmed and constantly in a rush, there's no room to construct efficient, trust-based relationships. Consequently, you'll overlook essential cues on your journey. While some may seem trivial, ignoring significant ones is risky. Noticing these cues will circumvent substantial blunders.

Understand Needs: If your focus is solely centered on your solutions, concepts, aspirations, and anticipations, you'll overlook the importance of active listening. Furthermore, without high-trust relationships, you're unlikely to receive accurate information even if you're attentive to others' input.

Involve Stakeholders: If your initial aim isn't to understand before being understood, stakeholders might not support your success and could even facilitate your failure. Building vital alliances, both internally and externally, will assist you in understanding how to adeptly navigate the frequently complex dynamics of organizational relationships and culture.

Achieving these three imperatives will lay a sturdy ground for mastering the next imperative: Listen to Concerns.

Suggested Actions

1. Understand the perceptions that others hold of you. Recognize that these may not match your self-perception, but as a leader, you try to discover the actual reality, which can be different from both yours and theirs. (Yes, this is indeed an art.)
2. Strive to build high-trust relationships, remembering that they form a crucial foundation for your integration to the organization.
3. Consistently remain in evaluation mode, given that situations are always changing and evolving. Stay up to date with the organization's shifting priorities and ensure alignment with key stakeholders.
4. Persistently build allies throughout the organization because, without them, your leadership will be less effective. Contemplate this: A leader without allies is no leader at all.

List other actions that come to mind.

-
-
-

Expand Your *Involve Stakeholders* Playbook

Formulate your own ideas on how to engage stakeholders effectively. Make a list and provide a brief explanation of each idea and how it can be implemented. Finally, develop a set of actionable steps to incorporate these strategies into your stakeholder involvement approach.

Topic:
Method:
Actions to take:

-

-
-

The Manager's Corner: *Involve Stakeholders!*

As your leader expands their influence, it is crucial for them to cultivate allies who can and will support the execution of their playbook. As a manager of this leader, your role in helping and supporting them as they build alliances with key stakeholders is essential. As you know, your success in your own role is closely tied to the achievements of your leader. Being a reliable and supportive ally, you contribute heavily to their overall success.

CHAPTER 11 LISTEN TO CONCERNS!

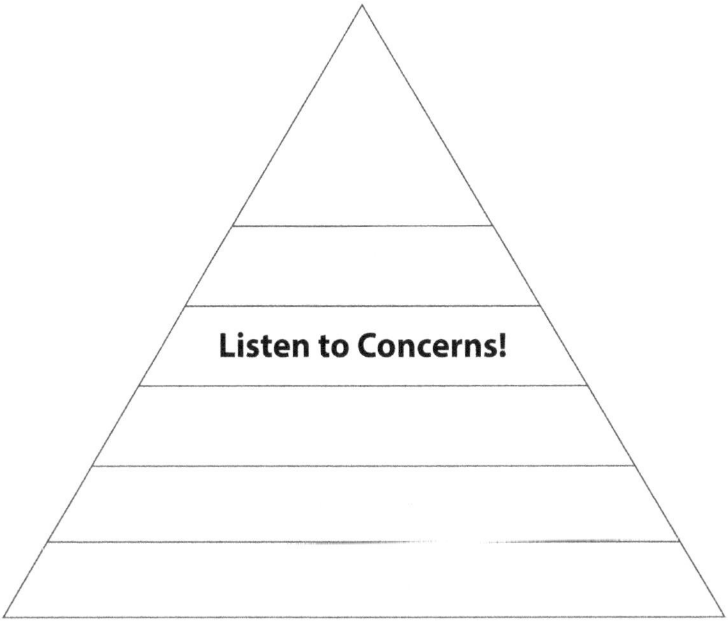

Intentionally Listen to Concerns

Awareness of areas of concern is essential for you to do your job. Failing to recognize and address these concerns can lead to significant problems. As the saying goes, "What you don't know can hurt you. Ignorance is not bliss." Some potential areas of concern may involve:

1. You
2. Your team

3. Your manager
4. Your department
5. Your organization

Active listening is essential in every situation. It involves truly hearing what is being said, understanding the underlying message, and taking appropriate action. This competency is vital, and your initial approach of listening and learning will continue to benefit you throughout your first year and beyond. Great leaders consistently demonstrate exceptional listening skills and remain open to constructive feedback without shutting down potential sources.

Let's break down these five categories of concerns:

Listen to Concerns about You

Active and attentive listening enables you to recognize any concerns regarding yourself.

Maintaining an objective perspective on your performance is crucial throughout your tenure. It's easy to lose objectivity during the busy first six months, and sometimes, the initial positive reception can extend beyond a year. However, I've observed instances where leaders were hailed as organizational saviors for an extended period, only to face setbacks in their second year. To ensure objectivity, actively listen to your key stakeholders to pick up on subtle cues that may indicate concerns about your performance.

These concerns will fall into one of the following five categories of competency:

1. Character: Who you are on the inside, your core qualities, and your alignment with the culture.
2. Execution: Getting results, making things happen, and achieving organizational objectives.

3. Relationship: Getting along with others, your behavioral style, and emotional intelligence.
4. Management: Managing people, managing performance, and managing projects and initiatives.
5. Leadership: Influencing others, building culture, casting vision, and instilling core values.

I have identified twelve competencies for each of these five categories of competency. See Section 3 for the complete list and some exercises you can do to help remove potential blind spots.

Embrace fearlessness when evaluating your own performance. Take proactive measures to address any actual or perceived performance issues. Section 3 also suggests a qualitative 360-degree assessment (interview based—not an electronic survey), which can be highly beneficial around the six-month mark in a new role. Subsequently, I suggest having one every two years thereafter. This assessment provides a comprehensive understanding of your perceived performance from the key stakeholders.

Suggested Actions
1. Seek regular performance feedback from your manager, ideally every quarter.
2. Establish a safe environment for receiving feedback by avoiding defensiveness and refraining from making excuses.
3. Show appreciation to anyone providing constructive feedback, refraining from reacting negatively. This will encourage open communication and ensure that individuals feel comfortable sharing, without regretting their decision. When you do get constructive feedback, simply say, "Thank you for the feedback. I will look at this and take positive actions." Do not make excuses, give context, or try to minimize the feedback in any way. Otherwise,

you will shut down future feedback and eliminate a crucial source of highly valuable information.
4. Maintain open communication with your manager, actively seeking areas for personal growth and development. Avoid settling for generic praise and dig deeper for specific opportunities to improve.
5. Take advantage of available assessments to uncover strengths, weaknesses, and blind spots. The more self-awareness you gain, the better equipped you'll be. Consider the sixty-competency leadership assessment mentioned in Section 3.
6. Embrace opportunities for a qualitative 360-degree interview-based assessment to gather valuable insights from multiple perspectives.

List other actions that come to mind.

-
-
-

Listen to Concerns about Your Team

Be receptive to concerns raised by leaders from other areas regarding your team. Avoid dismissing them without consideration, as there may be valid points worth examining. Take a self-reflective and non-defensive approach to assess the situation. Communicate to others that you have heard their input and are actively taking steps to evaluate the issues. Keep stakeholders informed about your progress and the insights you gather. Remember that promptly addressing perception issues is essential. The same script applies here as in the above paragraph: Simply thank the person for the feedback. Treat it as the precious gift that it is.

Creating a safe space for colleagues and direct reports to express concerns enables you to gather crucial information for making necessary changes. Conducting a comprehensive assessment of your team's people, processes, and infrastructure is a top priority in the initial stages and should be an ongoing endeavor.

Addressing genuine problems and distinguishing them from imagined ones can be challenging. It is an art rather than a science. Rely on your instincts, advisors, and the strong foundation of trust you have established to gain accurate insight into whether larger organizational issues need to be addressed.

Suggested Actions

1. Maintain an open mind and refrain from any and all defensiveness. Your ego is not your amigo. Humility rules the day.
2. Conduct thorough investigations before making decisions to avoid knee-jerk reactions.
3. Consider feedback from multiple sources, taking into account the credibility and relevance of each source, and then triangulate the input.
4. Seek advice from trusted advisors and allies to gain valuable perspectives.
5. Keep key stakeholders informed throughout the investigation process and appropriately involve them in decision-making regarding actions you plan on taking before you take them.

List other actions that come to mind.

-
-
-

Listen to Concerns about Your Manager

One of the quickest ways to get fired is by throwing your manager under the bus.

As a leader, it is essential to refrain from this unless you are aware of a criminal or ethical concern. In such cases, follow proper channels. Otherwise, avoid speaking negatively about your manager and discourage gossip or political maneuvering from others who may try to provoke you into making this mistake. Handle these sensitive matters skillfully and approach your manager when necessary with the negative feedback you are hearing.

When faced with attempts to engage in character assassination, use this elevator speech: "I have a personal policy of never speaking negatively about anyone." This statement effectively shuts down negative gossip. If there are genuine issues, address them privately with your manager and aim to help them understand the problems without revealing specific sources. Navigating this delicate dance is a crucial skill to master. Instinct is something you refine over time, and it is shaped by your experience, so learn to rely on your gut. It will be an effective guide for you as you grow to the next level. The best leaders have good instincts, and with intentional cultivation, you will harness this power.

Suggested Actions
1. Refrain from engaging in negative discussions or gossip about your manager or anyone else.
2. Approach your manager directly with any constructive feedback when appropriate.
3. Practice discretion and prioritize confidentiality, especially if you have made a commitment to do so.
4. Cultivate your instincts and refine them over time. Learn to trust your gut.

List other actions that come to mind.

-
-
-

Listen to Concerns about Your Department

Develop a strong identification with your manager and the organization they lead, prioritizing their goals and objectives over those of your department and team.

As a leader, it is essential to adopt a mindset that extends beyond your current role. Aim to identify with the level above your position. For instance, if you are a first-line manager, envision yourself in the office of the second-line manager. If you are a second-line manager, see yourself in the office of the VP, and so on. By adopting this perspective, you can align your goals and actions with the broader vision of the organization. This approach will prevent issues that arise when leaders fail to identify mainly with the leadership team on which they sit, and not the one comprised of their direct reports.

Leaders at every level often prioritize the protection of their teams while providing lesser support to their broader departments or divisions. This pattern can be observed even among CEOs, who may focus on safeguarding their direct reports without fully embracing a shareholder perspective. Unless everyone makes a conscious effort to identify with the group one or two levels above them, this inclination tends to prevail throughout the organization. By cultivating awareness of this dynamic, leaders can bridge the gap and align their actions with the larger organizational perspective. In his national bestseller, *The Advantage*, my colleague Patrick Lencioni spells out his concept of the "first team." Your "first team" is the team you sit on. That is where your loyalty lies, not first to your team of direct reports.

By adopting the proper identity, you avoid excessive protectiveness toward your team and become a champion for your manager and your peers. Share constructive feedback about your manager's organization (your department) with them to assist in enhancing its management. Foster a collaborative approach for improved organizational effectiveness. In Section 3, you'll discover some great ideas to employ regarding this topic.

Suggested Actions
1. Read "The Advantage" by Patrick Lencioni as a playbook for building a high-performance team and department. Pay special attention to Patrick's "first team" concept. It is a winning strategy.
2. Prioritize the leadership team that you sit on as your "first team."
3. Listen attentively to concerns about your department, refraining from defensiveness.
4. Provide constructive feedback to your manager and support them in their role. The concept of "leading up" will help you. It is fleshed out in Section 3.

List other actions that come to mind.
-
-
-

Listen to Concerns about Your Organization

The same comments apply not only to your department but also to the overall organization in which you are employed. Silos and conflicts between departments, such as sales and finance or sales and marketing, hinder organizational performance. As a top leader, strive to be a bridge builder and avoid being a silo creator. Fostering collaboration and breaking down barriers between teams will lead to overall organizational success. In the following suggested actions, there is a great playbook to help you achieve this.

Suggested Actions
1. Read "*Silos, Politics and Turf Wars*" by Patrick Lencioni as a guide to breaking down silos and fostering better communication, collaboration, and teaming across departments and the organization.
2. Listen attentively to concerns raised about your organization, particularly from customers and key stakeholders.
3. Adopt a policy of constructive and diplomatic engagement, avoiding blaming or undermining other organizations within your entity. Stay away from destructive politics.
4. Share constructive feedback with your manager and support them in improving their performance.
5. Lead up (like "managing up," but a more accurate description of the behavior and required skill set to do it effectively). Section 3 explains how.

List other actions that come to mind.
-
-
-

Listen to Concerns You Have

When faced with concerns about a direct report, follow this playbook for effective management. First, listen to your own instincts and trust your judgment. Second, consider the input of others who have objective insights into the person's performance. Third, thoroughly assess the situation and make a decision. Anyone who remains in your organization after your initial ninety days becomes your responsibility, as if you personally hired them. During this limited timeframe, utilize your playbook to build trust, assess needs, involve stakeholders, listen to concerns, and ultimately determine whether they should stay or leave. Delaying action can result in credibility loss or outright failure in your role.

Larry's Story

Larry is a current client I had a call with this morning. He is a C-suite executive in a PE-owned, one-billion-dollar company. He is new, in his first six months, and he has a lot more influence than he realizes. There are people on the team who are not performing. Larry is an overly relationship-oriented person who shies away from giving constructive feedback. The advice I gave him is the advice I will give you: Be bold. Be courageous. If giving constructive feedback is not your natural tendency because you lean more toward the DISC's high I, S, or C scales, you need to consciously move into the high D quadrant. (See Section 3 for a detailed explanation if you are not familiar with the DISC.) In order to get there, you may need to take what feels like ten steps (but may actually be four). By the end, it might feel like you have taken twenty. It is normal and natural to feel out of your comfort zone when giving constructive feedback. But taking these steps is a must if you are going to be effective.

Larry's story is not finished. He will take the steps. How many, I don't know. Larry's four steps may feel like thirty, and he may not get to where he needs to be, possibly limiting his effectiveness. Only time will tell.

For a very detailed explanation of the DISC, see Section 3.

Suggested Actions
1. Evaluate your team's performance.
2. Determine the appropriate course of action within a reasonable

timeframe, typically between your first thirty to ninety days in the role. However, be mindful of individual circumstances and avoid being overly prescriptive. It is crucial to exercise careful judgment, as retaining underperforming team members can signal ineffective leadership.
3. Strive to strike a balance between impulsive terminations and prolonged procrastination.
4. Become a student of the DISC; learn your behavioral style, and those of others. Take the steps necessary to adapt your style to the needs of the performance management situations you face.

List other actions that come to mind.

-
-
-

Expand Your *Listen to Concerns* Playbook

What are some other concerns that require your attention? Beyond the surface of this imperative, it is crucial to listen to customers, partners, and the market. Consider creating a list of these potential areas of concern, followed by a brief explanation of each. Additionally, develop a set of actions to guide you in effectively and actively listening to these concerns. Your "listening and learning" posture will continue to serve you and the organization well beyond your critical first year.

Topic:
Method:
Actions to take:

-
-
-

The Manager's Corner: *Listen to Concerns!*

As your new leader gains their footing and assimilates and integrates into the organization, it is important to support them in maintaining a "listen and learn" mindset. Remember that this process is a year-long endeavor. Often, there is a tendency to relax after the initial few months of onboarding, just as the honeymoon period fades and challenges arise. Keep in mind that the new leader is still navigating the complexities of the organization and will benefit from your assistance. Stay mindful of their newness and provide the necessary support to overcome barriers, obstacles, and roadblocks they may encounter.

Developing a mentor/mentee relationship with your leader is highly beneficial. Refer to "Valuable Resources" in Section 3 for a guide on how to find a mentor. If you do not have one, it might be a good idea to seek one or more mentors for yourself. That could include asking your direct manager to mentor you. Section 3 has a complete playbook and script for achieving this.

If you are the CEO, you may consider working with an "active and supportive" board member. A retired CEO, or CEO coach, could also be a valuable asset.

CHAPTER 12
DELIVER RESULTS!

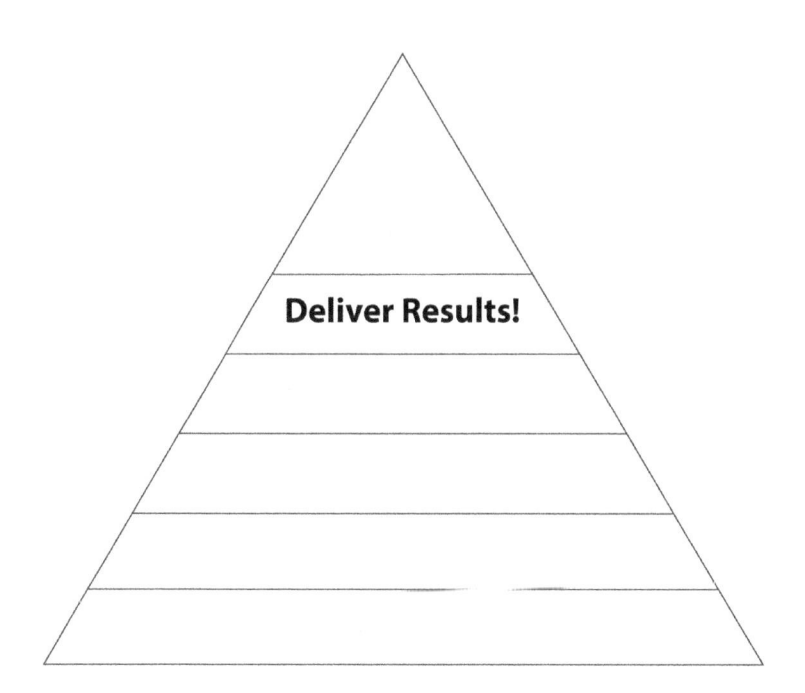

Deliver Results!

Intentionally Deliver the "Right" Results

Achieving the desired results is undoubtedly important, and it may seem obvious to be intentional about it. However, the key lies in the "how" of getting the "right" results and ensuring they align with the organization's strategic objectives.

It is crucial to consider the approach taken to achieve results, as it cannot be a matter of "results at all costs" or merely the "appearance of results." Both extremes on this continuum are considered failures. Striking the right balance and focusing on strategic and meaningful results is paramount for long-term success.

Driving results has important factors to consider. Here are three that come to mind:

1. Achieving the right results in alignment with your manager's directives and key stakeholders' objectives. To avoid falling short, you must prioritize results that are aligned with the organization's priorities.
2. Delivering results within the agreed-upon timeframe. Moving too fast or too slow can have negative consequences. Consider the organization's culture, expectations, and capacity for change when determining the appropriate pace.
3. Balancing desired results with maintaining relationships. It is crucial to achieve results that everyone wants while ensuring that relationships are not compromised. Strive to find a balance where outcomes are attained without detrimental effects on relationships.

Many leaders who achieve exceptional results still ultimately lose their jobs. Postmortems I've conducted with managers indicate that while these individuals were successful in driving outcomes, they did not effectively bring the organization along with them, or the cost of the results was too high in terms of relational capital. These issues can affect CEOs, C-suite executives, and everyone else.

"Smoke-and-mirror" results are problematic. Here are a few examples:

- Reorganizing a department solely for the sake of appearances, without addressing the pressing priorities, can create an illusion

of progress. This brings to mind the "three envelopes" joke I will relay in a moment.
- Taking on a seemingly impossible project and allocating significant resources may come across as results being achieved. However, without the necessary organizational support, even heroic efforts may not lead to the desired outcome of project completion.
- Saving an employee no one else wants to retain may give the impression of getting results. However, if the motivation behind this action is more about personal ego and demonstrating the ability to rescue someone rather than fulfilling the organization's needs, it will not serve you or the organization.

These examples don't involve deliberate deception. You're genuinely striving for the organization's benefit. However, your decisions may not always be wise, leading to initiatives that seem productive initially, but fail to yield clear victories in the end.

Three Envelopes

A new CEO takes over at a struggling company and finds three numbered envelopes left in his desk by his predecessor with a note: "Open Envelope #1 when you run into problems."

A few months in, the company hits a crisis. The CEO opens the first envelope: "Blame your predecessor. When this stops working, open Envelope #2."

It works, and the company recovers. However, another crisis occurs months later. He opens the second envelope: "Reorganize. When this stops working, open Envelope #3."

After reorganization, things improve again. But eventually, another crisis happens. He opens the third envelope, expecting another nugget of wisdom. Instead, the note reads: "Prepare three envelopes."

In summary, we need to combine "deliver" and "results" with words like "strategic," "agreed-to," "aligned," or "supported by your manager." Be thoughtful about your commitments, ensuring that any initiative undertaken can be completed to widespread approval.

There are several actions I recommend:

1. Achieve results in a manner that aligns with your organization's methods.
2. Avoid reorganizing for the sake of reorganizing. Avoid the "three-envelope" syndrome.
3. Recognize that every organization is unique. Adapt your "results orientation" to fit within the culture, with the full approval and alignment of your manager and key stakeholders.
4. Ensure that you are positioned for success by bringing all key stakeholders and the organization along with you if and when you do a reorganization.

List other actions that come to mind.

-
-
-

Track Your Results

I encourage you to maintain a mental tally of your significant achievements, accessible at a moment's notice without the need to refer to written notes. The most effective way to do this is by keeping a journal of the results you've accomplished during your first year. Begin this journal on your first day and continue it for the entire twelve months. Document every significant win. Each time you add an achievement, review your past entries. Date each entry to maintain a timeline of accomplishments.

This list will prove useful more often than you might expect, in instances like:
- When you're seeking a raise or promotion
- During preparation for or in the midst of performance reviews
- When responding to criticisms regarding your performance not meeting expectations

You alone are accountable for monitoring your results. Without this tracking, you may lack the necessary data to convincingly advocate for yourself or defend your actions. In Section 3, there is a chapter on the Leadership Development Plan, which will help you track your progress.

Suggested Actions
1. Establish an electronic (ideally) or paper-based results journal.
2. Record all your achievements.
3. Consider maintaining this journal throughout your entire first year.
4. Create a Leadership Development Plan.

List other actions that come to mind.
-
-
-

Measure Your Results

Some of the thinking of Dr. Deming, a respected statistician and the pioneer of Total Quality Management (TQM), is often summarized as, "You can't manage what you can't measure." This principle is also echoed in such sayings as, "What gets measured gets done," and "What gets measured gets managed."

Applying appropriate measurement to a task, project, or initiative enhances the likelihood of achieving the intended outcome.

Effective leaders are adept at tracking progress. However, it's crucial to apply the "right" amount of measurement. There exists a spectrum, with those who measure too little on one end and those who measure excessively on the other. Mastering the art of how, when, where, and by whom to measure is crucial. While entire books exist on this subject, the takeaway is to become proficient in measuring results and avoid either extreme.

Suggested Actions
1. Regularly monitor progress and share updates with key stakeholders at a suitable frequency (avoiding over- or under-reporting).
2. Develop a comprehensive system for tracking project outcomes, including milestones and metrics, with clear "definition of done" statements (DoD) for all.
3. Establish a weekly scorecard for measurable elements; consistently have your team track progress and score these metrics.

It will also be beneficial to read a couple of books on the subject of results measurement. Here are a few ideas:

1. *Measure What Matters* by John Doerr: This book emphasizes the Objectives and Key Results (OKR) model, which Google and other major companies use to set and achieve audacious goals.
2. *The Balanced Scorecard: Translating Strategy into Action* by Robert S. Kaplan and David P. Norton: This classic management book presents a holistic approach to measuring company performance beyond the financial bottom line.
3. *The 4 Disciplines of Execution: Achieving Your Wildly Important Goals* by Sean Covey, Chris McChesney, and Jim Huling: This

book provides a simple, proven formula for achieving important strategic goals.
4. *Radical Focus: Achieving Your Most Important Goals with Objectives and Key Results* by Christina Wodtke: This practical guide on using OKRs is told through a story, which makes it more relatable and easier to understand.
5. *Traction* by Gino Wickman: Though not strictly about setting goals, this book provides valuable insights on a comprehensive operating system and is useful in guiding goal-setting processes.

Each book has its unique perspective on goal setting and measurement. Depending on your specific needs, one or more of these could be a good fit for you.

List other actions that come to mind.

-
-
-

Ask for Guidance

Your ego is not your amigo. You've heard me say that before.

Requesting help may seem like a sign of weakness, but it's quite the opposite. It's a sign of strength and wisdom, particularly during your first year and most notably during your initial few calendar quarters.

Let me guide you through a vital shift in perspective. Change your thought process from "I'm too busy to seek help now" to "This is *the* best time to do so." Transform the mindset of "I know exactly what to do" to "I *must* seek assistance from those I trust."

Executive Hangman

Here's a fun exercise I designed decades ago to make this point: Hangman for Leaders™. Draw the traditional hangman diagram with three blank lines underneath, representing a three-letter word. Say, "This is the most powerful three-letter word in the English language, and it's the secret to successful assimilation and integration." Note that you can replace "onboarding" with other relevant terms.

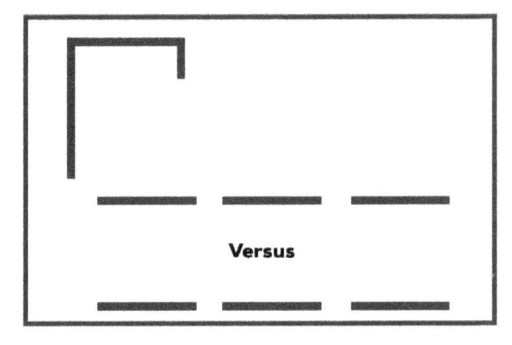

Explain that the game is identical to the classic one—with one exception. Say, "It is a rule I know, that you don't." Without further explanation, mention that they'll get a head, body, two arms, and two legs only—no fingers or toes! Then, invite them to start. They can guess either full words or individual letters. Usually, the excitement to solve the problem overtakes curiosity about the unknown "rule." They will likely fail, and get "hung."

Then, conduct Round Two: Solve for the next word. You explain that this word also has three letters and destroys your ability to employ the first word, which is a key principle to being a successful leader.

When I conduct this exercise, I add another layer at the beginning of Round Two: "Remember, there is a rule that I know that you don't know. Are you ready to begin? Let's play!" It's extremely rare for anyone to ask about the rule.

Note each incorrect answer beside the hangman diagram and add a body part until the hangman is complete. It's uncommon for anyone to solve the problem. Try and see if you can.

Now that I've piqued your curiosity, let's explore some crucial questions to ask yourself:

1. Am I prioritizing appropriately?
2. Do my initiatives align with organizational objectives, core vision, and mission?
3. Am I targeting the correct results to pursue? Do I have top-down support for these goals?
4. Am I asking others for help?

What else can you ask? Compile a list of additional questions that can help guide you in delivering exceptional results.

-
-
-

Here is my last "ask" of you. Did you think to ask what the rule was that I know that you don't? Well, here is the rule: "If you ask for help with anything, anytime during the game, I am to give it to you, whatever you ask."

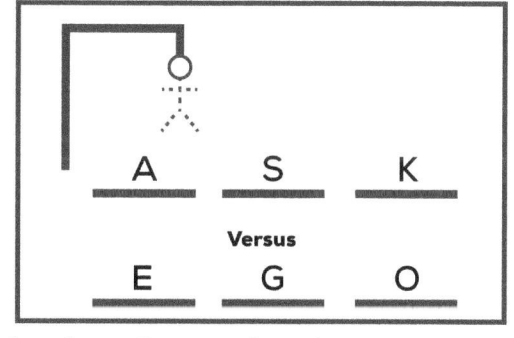

Even armed with that information, hundreds of groups I have played this leadership development game with over the past three decades still insisted on figuring out the second word without asking for help. This includes groups of powerful, well-accomplished CEOs and C-suite executives. Sometimes, they have the biggest egos and want to solve the "problem" without my help, even after completing the first round and determining the hidden rule and the first word: "Ask." This is a profound learning that will hopefully inform your leadership for the rest of your career. I call this the Ask Principle™, and it applies equally well to your personal life.

Here is the game, solved in two moves:

Step 1: Ask: "What is the rule?" Answer: "The rule is if you ASK for help, you will get it."

Step 2: Employ the Ask Principle™ and ask for help. Ask, "What is the word?"

Obtain an Assessment at the Six-Month Mark

In Section 3, you'll find a detailed protocol for evaluating your soft skills. I highly recommend that you follow it, identify your key strengths and weaknesses, and eliminate any blind spots. It may be tempting to postpone this until you're more established in the role, in phase 3 of our three-phase model (1. Onboarding; 2. Assimilation; 3. Integration). If your memory needs refreshing, reference the diagram earlier in this book for the approximate timelines for each phase.

There is no exact date I can give you as to when to start doing this introspection on yourself. Sometimes it happens in the first few months, while other times it happens in the several after that. However, my experience suggests doing this earlier enhances your awareness of key challenges you may have to address regarding your leadership skill set.

At the six-month point, consider a qualitative (interview-based) 360-degree assessment. Consult with your HR department to see if they offer this service. If you're working with a coach, they almost always provide this assessment. Receiving feedback early in your tenure allows for timely course corrections to meet or exceed the expectations of your manager and key stakeholders. Commit to taking this action, regardless of how busy you are at the six-month mark.

By the end of your first year, your fate in the role is often set. Many leaders are asked to leave organizations around the eighteen- or twenty-four-month mark based on decisions made during their first year. I've seen talented leaders blindsided by this outcome, utterly unaware of its possibility. Typically, those who are let go express surprise, claim they saw no warning signs, and believe they were performing exceptionally. Don't let this happen to you. Some are identified as high potential. This is the desired outcome of all this work.

Suggested Actions
1. Seek objective feedback through a qualitative 360-degree assessment at your six-month employment anniversary, and then every one or two years subsequently.
2. If a qualitative 360 isn't available, opt for a quantitative (survey-based) assessment.
3. Employ the Ask Principle™ throughout your journey, and remove any blind spots you may have.
4. Complete the assessments in Section 3, particularly the Unleashing Leadership Excellence Assessment.

List other actions that come to mind.
-
-
-

Create a Leadership Development Plan

In my leadership coaching methodology, we follow four phases. They are:

1. Orientation to Leveraging Your Leadership Coach
2. Assessment of Strengths, Weaknesses, and Blind Spots
3. Goal Setting and Creating a Leadership Development Plan (LDP)
4. Self-Coaching, Coach the Coach, and Developing Direct

Reports

I share this to highlight Phase 2, Assimilation, which provides the necessary data to craft an effective LDP in Phase 3. For more details on these topics and a sample of the LDP tool, refer to Section 3.

To set this plan in motion, begin with a self-assessment. Evaluate your skills and choose to focus on your personal strengths and weaknesses that are most pertinent to your current situation.

Once you have an honest self-appraisal, you can set targeted goals. Using these, develop a Leadership Development Plan (LDP) and establish a clear route to achieve it. The LDP will comprise comprehensive developmental objectives. The plan follows these simple steps:

1. Identify the highest-priority developmental objectives.
2. Strike a balance between leveraging strengths and addressing weaknesses.
3. Clearly articulate the goal statement and formulate a SMART (Specific, Measurable, Achievable, Relevant, Time-bound) goal.
4. Prioritize the plan, focusing specifically on your unique needs.
5. Develop behavioral and cognitive metrics to convert this into a tangible action plan.
6. Record positive accomplishments.
7. Share the plan, entirely or partially, with your manager at crucial junctures, as appropriate.

There are multiple methods to create an LDP. This is just my approach.

Without intending to be overly prescriptive, your LDP goals should:

- Span six to twelve months (intrinsic change takes time)
- Concentrate on improving your leadership soft skills
- Be comprised of several goals that leverage your strengths, several addressing your top weaknesses, and one dedicated to the development of your direct reports

Ideally, you should start your role with a clear understanding of areas needing development. You have a brief window to seize the strategic advantage that typically presents itself here. If you have a well-structured LDP before you start or within your first thirty days, it's a significant advantage. However, you can develop one anytime during your tenure. If you don't have one right now and you are just starting, focus on the onboarding and assimilation process. As soon as you are firmly established, start working on your own and others' leadership development.

I often coach leaders who have been in their roles for years. We begin with a qualitative 360-degree assessment completed during the first thirty- to forty-five days, then use the data to finalize an LDP within a few weeks. You can do this yourself or with the help of a mentor, advisor, coach, or potentially your manager.

I use the word "potentially" because:

1. Many may lack the necessary skill set.
2. It can be time-consuming, and they might not have the needed time.
3. You may prefer maintaining a certain level of privacy, choosing to achieve some of your developmental goals before sharing your LDP with others.

Suggested Actions
1. Start developing a Leadership Development Plan (LDP).
2. Review this plan at least once a month.
3. Identify four to seven strengths that can be more effectively used, are relevant to your role, and can enhance other strengths.
4. Seek assistance in creating the LDP from a mentor, coach, advisor, or manager.
5. Identify your top four to seven weaknesses that could obstruct your performance in your current role. Ensure these are highly relevant to your situation and not merely theoretical.
6. Select a few from each category that are the most critical.
7. Finalize your LDP.
8. Incorporate an item in your LDP specifically dedicated to the development of your direct reports.

NOTE: As a reminder, Section 3 has a chapter on this for you, including an example of an LDP.

List other actions that come to mind.

-
-
-

Gain Continued Wins

Three to six months into your role, you have:

- Established a strong foundation of trustful relationships (Build Trust)
- Performed an exhaustive evaluation of your organization's challenges (Understand Needs)
- Engaged vital stakeholders who are now committed to your success (Involve Stakeholders)

- Heard stakeholders concerns and addressed them with suitable actions (Listen to Concerns)

You're now in the Deliver Results phase, orchestrating and achieving significant initiatives. Though you have been working to deliver results from day one, now you are in full execution mode. You're targeting and securing major wins in three vital areas: people, projects, and processes. Your initial hundred-day plan has been executed flawlessly, and you're now setting goals and yielding results on a quarter-by-quarter basis.

A word about "quarter-by-quarter" is worth mentioning here. I recommend you have a one-day offsite, as close to the beginning of your organization's quarter close as possible, after you have all results and metrics from the previous quarter. The offsite should involve a three-hour postmortem on the quarter you just completed and a five-hour look-forward planning for how you are going to execute the new quarter you are just beginning.

As you delve into a rigorous execution phase, you recognize that correct actions boost success while missteps tarnish the positive reputation you've built. Despite pushing hard, you remain wary, aware that the latter half of your first year is often the most challenging. The initial grace period is over, and the surge in activity heightens your visibility. Before things escalate, consider revisiting one of the recommended books from Section 3.

As you may remember, *The Art of Your Start* is intended to address gaps in the existing literature. It serves as a companion resource that encourages you to explore other books mentioned in this section and the next. If you find yourself too occupied to do so, it's a sign that you're too busy, and this should serve as a warning to reassess your time and priorities.

Suggested Actions
1. Aim for bigger wins, but always mitigate risks. Prudence is key in your first year.
2. Be mindful of your brand reputation; avoid impulsive actions and take only calculated risks. It does you no good to take on an initiative that is seen as a failure. Be "in it to win it," each and every time. That does not mean avoiding hard challenges; it means that if you take something on, you must deliver positive results.
3. Develop a quarterly cadence of looking back, learning from the previous quarter, and looking forward, to ensure you and your team will achieve the necessary insights and desired results.
4. Utilize the resources in Section 3.
5. Find resources to help tackle operational issues, including selecting an appropriate book from the reading list. Whatever you do, don't stop reading.
6. When in doubt, ask for help. (Employ the "Ask" principle.)

List other actions that come to mind.
-
-
-

Expand Your *Deliver Results* Playbook

What I have provided are a few practical suggestions that align with this critical imperative. Certainly, you have additional strategies for delivering effective results. What might they be? Jot them down. Elaborate on each by describing what it entails and how you implement it. Next, generate a series of actions you can undertake to apply these strategies as you strive to deliver impactful results.

Topic:
Method:
Actions to take:

-
-
-

The Manager's Corner: *Deliver Results!*

This chapter stands out as one of the most vital parts of the BUILDS™ playbook. If you can, thoroughly read it. The successful delivery of results is just as crucial for you as it is for your new leader and the rest of your team.

Specifically, the following recommendations should be considered at this juncture:

1. Assist your leader in tracking and measuring outcomes; strive for detailed precision by utilizing a weekly tactical scorecard and a set of prioritized quarterly objectives with explicit milestones and deadlines.
2. Implement the Ask Principle™ by asking your leader how you can provide assistance. Understand that most leaders strive for self-sufficiency and will hesitate to seek your advice or assistance, fearing it may be perceived as a sign of weakness. Foster a safe environment where your leader feels comfortable seeking your input.
3. Support your leader in receiving unbiased feedback at their six-month point through a 360-degree assessment. If you've never undergone one yourself, you might consider leading by example. Partially or completely share your report with your leader, thus

motivating them to discuss their results with you.
4. Construct a supportive atmosphere where your leader is at ease discussing development opportunities. Regularly address these points in your one-on-one meetings, asking about their progress and celebrating achievements.
5. Assist your leader in formulating a Leadership Development Plan. Refer to this chapter and Section 3 for more insights about this powerful tool. Revisit this plan quarterly during one-on-one meetings and acknowledge areas where they've made progress. Consider yourself a coach to your leader, aiding them in advancing to the next level of functional effectiveness.
6. Support and encourage your leader in establishing a quarterly cadence of one-day offsites for reflection and planning with their team. You may want to sit in. You also may want to have these yourself if you are not already doing so.
7. Support your leader in choosing and studying exceptional books, articles, or whitepapers that are related to operational performance and directly applicable to their current work.
8. Acquaint yourself with all the tools and resources contained in Section 3.

CHAPTER 13
SERVE WITH EXCELLENCE!

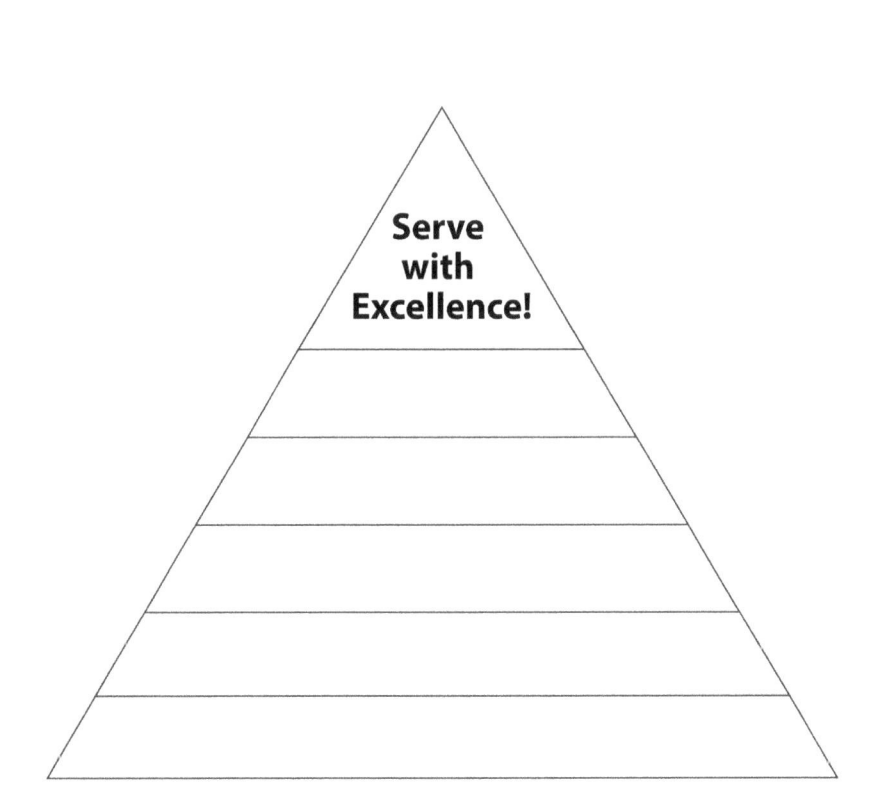

Serve with Excellence!

Intentionally Serve with Excellence

Exceptional leaders perceive their role as a commitment to serving others. This approach is not incidental; it's very deliberate, grounded in a profound sense of duty toward the team and organization. Their concern transcends mere engagement; they are driven by an ardent desire to fulfill this responsibility with unparalleled distinction.

Superiors, in observing such leaders, quickly discern this fundamental trait and, consequently, often extend greater autonomy to those they perceive to be devotedly serving them and others. This trust instills in them an inherent desire to support these leaders, either consciously or subconsciously, and cultivates robust and positive working relationships.

Similarly, peers of such extraordinary leaders find themselves being served, consequently lowering their typical defenses. This encourages improved cooperation, fosters effective teamwork, and fortifies trust. Leaders committed to delivering exceptional service motivate others to reciprocate, thereby generating a virtuous cycle of mutual service that is self-perpetuating.

Subordinates typically relish the opportunity to work under such exemplary leaders. Feeling cared for and valued stimulates their drive to work more diligently and efficiently. If these individuals are leaders in their own right, a synergistic dynamic is kindled as they observe and experience exceptional leadership.

Regardless of where we look, the appreciation for leaders who serve others, underscored by a zealous pursuit of excellence, is evident. Irrespective of your existing leadership prowess, your influence can only be enhanced if you embrace and embody this principle of serving others with distinction. It is essential, however, that this mindset is consistently reflected in your actions, illustrating unequivocally your commitment to serving your stakeholders.

If this portrayal resonates with you, strive to align your words and actions, sending a strong, powerful message that you are a leader who envisions your role as one of service rather than being served. In turn, you are likely to witness an expansion of your organizational influence, and your reputation as an altruistic leader who genuinely cares about bettering yourself and the lives of others will flourish.

Suggested Actions
1. Embark on a journey of leadership study to comprehend more deeply the essence of being a "leading leader" and ardently pursue becoming one.
2. Explore the servant leadership philosophy. Evaluate its alignment with your personal convictions and determine which facets of this leadership style you will incorporate. Section 3 provides an explanation of this leadership method.
3. Engage with your mentor, advisor, or coach to help you navigate this concept.
4. If this leadership ethos accurately encapsulates your vision of leadership, it is crucial to effectively communicate this to your key stakeholders. Understanding your leadership philosophy will foster alignment and cooperation.
5. Regularly conduct self-assessments to ensure you are living up to your commitment to servant leadership. Reflect on your actions and decisions, asking yourself if they truly serve the best interests of your team, and organization.
6. Invite and genuinely consider feedback from your team. Servant leadership is centered on serving others, and there is no better way to understand your team's needs than by listening to their feedback.
7. Establish clear goals and visions in line with the servant leadership ethos. Aligning your team's efforts with the organization's mission will not only serve the organization but also facilitate the personal growth and development of your team members.

List other actions that come to mind.

-
-
-

Be a Servant-Leader

Servant leadership is a leadership philosophy that emphasizes the leader's role as a servant first and a leader second. It is rooted in the idea that leaders exist to serve their followers rather than the other way around. This approach to leadership has been popularized by influential thinkers such as Robert Greenleaf, who first coined the term "servant leadership" in his 1970 essay, "The Servant as Leader."

At its core, servant leadership is about focusing on the needs and interests of others and helping them grow and develop to their fullest potential. This can involve practices such as active listening, empathy, and empowering others to make decisions and take ownership of their work. Servant-leaders also prioritize building strong relationships based on trust, respect, and collaboration.

Adopting a servant leadership approach can have numerous benefits for you and your organization. It can lead to higher levels of employee engagement, productivity, and job satisfaction, as well as stronger team cohesion and more effective decision-making. In addition, servant leadership can help you foster a culture of continuous learning and development, as you encourage your followers to take risks, learn from failures, and seek out new growth opportunities.

By taking these actions, you can become a servant-leader who is passionate about serving others with excellence. Becoming a servant-leader is a journey, not a destination. It takes time, effort, and commitment to develop the skills and mindset needed to serve others effectively. Embracing this approach to leadership will create an overly positive impact in your organization and make a meaningful difference in the lives of those you serve.

There is more to learn about this topic in "Phase 3: Resources for Serve with Excellence" in Section 3, which directly supports this chapter.

Suggested Actions
1. Cultivate a servant mindset: Concentrate on understanding and addressing the needs and aspirations of others, helping them evolve to reach their peak potential. Practice empathy, active listening, and compassion in all your interactions. Strive to comprehend others' unique challenges and goals.
2. Lead by example: Set the standard, exhibiting the behaviors and values you wish to inspire in others. Demonstrate an unwavering work ethic, treat others with dignity and kindness, maintain transparency in communication, and embrace accountability for your actions, acknowledging your errors openly.
3. Promote collaboration and teamwork: Prioritize establishing relationships rooted in trust, respect, and collaboration. Create avenues for teamwork, motivating your team to collaborate in pursuit of common objectives. Cultivate an environment that encourages open dialogue, constructive criticism, and mutual support.
4. Empower and trust: Enable your team members to take charge of their work, developing a sense of ownership and confidence in decision-making. Encourage them to embrace new challenges, explore innovative ideas, and take informed risks. Provide the necessary resources and support for them to succeed while also granting them the freedom to learn from their mistakes.
5. Champion continuous learning and development: Commit to ongoing learning and development for both yourself and your team. Seek opportunities to acquire new skills and knowledge, and motivate your team to follow suit. Offer your coaching and mentorship to aid them in refining their skills and attaining their full potential.

List other actions that come to mind.

-
-
-

Give Others Your Very Best

To genuinely embody Serve with Excellence, you must be your optimal self. Effectively serving others requires you to be in a state of personal excellence. This involves having a lucid understanding of your strengths and weaknesses and the readiness to reveal and address your blind spots. This requires consistent self-reflection and evaluation to identify potential avenues for improvement and personal development. Refer to Section 3 for practical tools to assist you.

Evaluating strengths entails identifying your unique talents, capabilities, and proficiencies that position you for leadership success. These are where you deliver significant impact and maximum value to your team and organization. Acknowledging weaknesses involves understanding areas where you may encounter difficulties or require extra assistance. This might involve skill deficiencies, recurring mistakes, or overlooked areas.

Removing your blind spots gives you a broader perspective, circumvents invalid assumptions or biases, and enhances your ability to serve others effectively. This demands humility, receptivity to feedback, and a willingness to be coachable.

Engaging in leadership assessments can offer profound insights into your leadership style and highlight areas for development. Various assessment types exist, ranging from personality tests, 360-degree feedback mechanisms, emotional intelligence assessments, and more. Assessment instruments provide invaluable insights into your strengths and weaknesses, and remove blind spots.

Enhancing your ability to influence others is a crucial facet of servant leadership. This involves honing robust communication and relationship-building skills and cultivating ability to inspire and motivate others toward a common vision or objective. Through the assessment of strengths, recognition of weaknesses, and blind spot removal, you can comprehend your unique leadership style and activate the skills and mindset necessary to serve others with excellence.

The Serve with Excellence imperative demands ongoing self-reflection, assessment, and personal growth. By relentlessly pursuing the best version of yourself, you will have a profound impact in the lives of those you serve and evolve into a more effective servant-leader.

Suggested Actions

1. Undertake a personal SWOT analysis: This helps evaluate your strengths, weaknesses, opportunities, and threats. Reflect on your experiences to identify key abilities and areas for improvement.
2. Seek others' feedback: Collect from colleagues, mentors, or friends regarding your leadership style and performance. Embrace constructive criticism and act upon areas needing improvement.
3. Take leadership assessments: Utilize personality tests, emotional intelligence assessments, and 360-degree feedback to glean insights into your leadership style, strengths, and areas for improvement.
4. Create a personal development plan: Based on your SWOT analysis, feedback, and assessment results, draft a plan outlining specific goals, strategies, and timelines for improving your capabilities. Regularly review and revise this plan with a coach or mentor to monitor progress.
5. Commit to continuous learning: Embrace ongoing development to be the best version of yourself. Attend industry events, read relevant books, and engage with podcasts and online courses to keep abreast of trends and widen your skill set.

List other actions that come to mind.

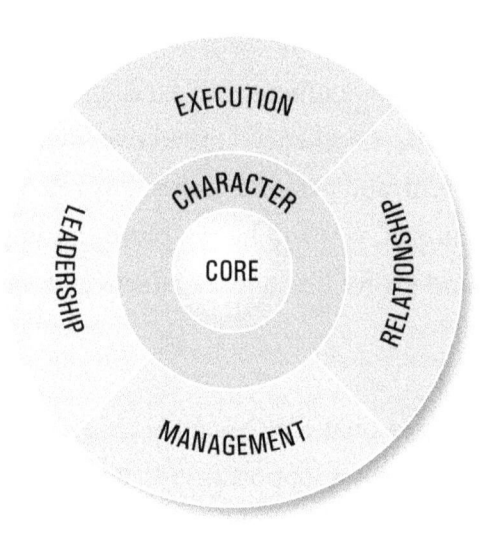

-
-
-

Use Every Opportunity to Grow

Top leaders must possess a balanced skill set and excel in all aspects of leadership. There are four critical areas I've identified that all leaders must master. These "quadrants of competency" are Execution, Relationship, Management, and Leadership.

Lack of proficiency in any of these categories limits your leadership and your ability to reach the next level in your career. In addition, there's a fifth category, which I refer to as Character. This set of competencies surrounds your core, like a rim on a tire. Regardless of how well-rounded and sturdy the tire is, a defective rim will hinder your ability to become a great leader and succeed in your role. You can't afford a flat tire, but you certainly don't want a bent or warped rim.

Combined, I call these Critical Categories of Competency™. Much more on this in Section 3, coming up right now. Hang in there; you are in the home stretch. We'll also discuss your core, which is akin to an axle in this metaphor.

Suggested Actions
1. Complete the Unleashing Leadership Excellence Assessment.
2. Regularly assess yourself to gain and maintain an accurate view of your strengths and weaknesses and remove blind spots.

   List other actions that come to mind.

-
-
-

Expand Your *Serve with Excellence* Playbook

You have several actions that fit into the "S" category in your BUILDS™ playbook. I am sure you have additional ideas of ways to serve with excellence. What are they? Make a list. Flesh out a paragraph on each, explaining what it is and how you do it. Then, come up with a set of actions for you to employ as you become a great servant-leader.

Topic:
Method:
Actions to take:

-
-
-

The Manager's Corner: *Serve with Excellence!*

As a leader, you are instrumental in guiding your team to serve with excellence and develop as servant-leaders. Here's how you can support them:

1. Establish precise expectations: It's crucial to set clear standards for your team and elucidate what embodying servant leadership means within your organization. Ensure your direct reports understand your organization's values, mission, and vision, and guide them to reflect these principles in their daily tasks.
2. Deliver regular feedback and coaching: Consistent feedback and coaching helps your team identify improvement areas and hone the requisite skills to serve with excellence. Offer constructive feedback and celebrate success.
3. Promote professional development: Urge your team to seize professional growth opportunities, such as attending workshops, enrolling in seminars, or seeking additional training or education. This empowers them to gain new skills, broaden their knowledge, and amplify their capacity to serve others with excellence.
4. Cultivate a collaborative culture: To serve with excellence, a collaborative and team-oriented culture is essential. Motivate your team to collaborate toward shared goals, champion open communication and constructive feedback, and acknowledge and reward team efforts.
5. Lead by example: Emulate the behaviors and values you wish to see in your team. Exhibit a strong dedication to Serve with Excellence by passionately serving your team members and being a role model for expected behaviors.

Through these initiatives, your team will become more effective leaders who serve others with excellence. This results in increased employee engagement, job satisfaction, and organizational performance and creates a positive and productive work environment. Assist your team in tracking and measuring results and maintain a detailed weekly scorecard and a quarterly set of prioritized objectives with explicit milestones and deadlines. Incorporate Serve with Excellence as one of your expectations and provide regular feedback on progress.

CHAPTER 14

SECTION TWO CONCLUSION

To the Leader

Congratulations. If you have made it this far in *Art of Your Start*, you are a dedicated leader who is serious about excellent assimilation and integration into your leadership role.

In conclusion, Section 2 of *Art of Your Start* has provided you with valuable insights, strategies, and best practices to ensure your successful transition and integration during your first year. Your dedication to learning and growing is commendable and will set you apart from the majority of other leaders who have not invested this time. Keep up the good work.

You now have a comprehensive framework, or playbook, for your first year and beyond. Please customize it to your unique needs.

Your BUILDS™ playbook has six key imperatives:

- **B**uild Trust!
- **U**nderstand Needs!
- **I**nvolve Stakeholders!
- **L**isten to Concerns!
- **D**eliver Results!
- **S**erve with Excellence!

Each is foundational, built on the work of the previous step. You may want to take a picture of this diagram and keep it in front of you during your first year, just as a reminder of where you are currently and where you are headed.

```
              /\
             /  \
            / Serve \
           /  with   \
          / Excellence! \
         /──────────────\
        /  Deliver Results! \
       /─────────────────────\
      /   Listen to Concerns!  \
     /──────────────────────────\
    /    Involve Stakeholders!    \
   /──────────────────────────────\
  /     Understand Needs!           \
 /──────────────────────────────────\
/        Build Trust!                 \
────────────────────────────────────────
```

Embrace this new journey with confidence, knowing that you are now better prepared to face the many challenges and opportunities that invariably come with leadership in a new role.

As you grow, remember your learning journey doesn't end here. Keep seeking new knowledge, mentorship, and resources to further enhance your leadership skills and abilities. Surround yourself with a supportive network, and never shy away from asking for feedback.

Great leaders aren't born overnight. They're shaped through continuous learning, self-reflection, and persistence. Stay true to your values, remain adaptable, and always strive for excellence. With the right mindset, you will undoubtedly become the exceptional leader you aspire to be.

To the Manager

This concludes Section 2.

As a manager to a newly inducted leader in their first year, you've embarked on a pivotal journey, cultivating success and growth for your team. In fostering the assimilation, integration, and development of your leader, you're setting the groundwork for effective leadership, cohesive teamwork, and remarkable organizational performance.

Recognize the importance of offering guidance, support, and mentorship during the early stages of your new leader's tenure. This defining period will shape their leadership style, relationship with the team, and ability to realize organizational goals. Whether you're a board member aiding a new CEO or a manager nurturing a direct report, your intentional effort in this process will yield substantial organizational rewards, no matter what the level.

Promote continuous learning and feedback for your new leader, encouraging openness to novel ideas and viewpoints. This nurtures a culture of relentless growth and development, benefiting not only them but the entire team. Facilitate collaboration and ensure open channels of communication for a smooth, successful transition.

Your supervisory role is key to crafting an environment where your leader can flourish. Serve as a beacon of support and guidance, assisting them through the challenges associated with their role. Celebrate their achievements and openly address areas that require improvement. Curiously, the higher the leadership position, the less constructive feedback given. Prevent this oddity for your leader, as high-potential leaders thrive on constructive criticism. Ensure it's provided.

Ultimately, your investment in your leader's assimilation, integration, and development will yield a high-performing, engaged, and motivated team. Your dedication to fostering robust leadership will drive your organization's sustained growth and success.

SECTION THREE

VALUABLE RESOURCES

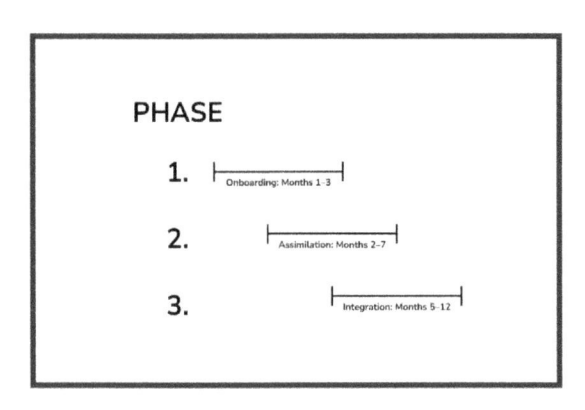

```
PHASE
  1.  |—Onboarding: Months 1-3—|
  2.        |—Assimilation: Months 2-7—|
  3.              |—Integration: Months 5-12—|
```

In Section 3, I will provide a diverse array of resources and expert systems specifically designed to help leaders like you thrive during your first year.

This section is divided up into parts and supports each area of Section 2, as follows:

Phase 1: Resources for Build Trust, Understand Needs, and Involve Stakeholders.

Phase 2: Resources for Listen to Concerns and Deliver Results.

Phase 3: Resources for Serve with Excellence.

PHASE 1
RESOURCES FOR BUILD TRUST, UNDERSTAND NEEDS, AND INVOLVE STAKEHOLDERS

The chapters in this subsection provide expert systems for the first three of the six key imperatives discussed in Section 2.

The transition into a new leadership position can be both exciting and challenging, with countless opportunities for personal and professional growth. However, navigating this journey without the right resources is very difficult. This section equips you with necessary tools, knowledge, and support systems, ensuring your success.

Throughout "Valuable Resources," I will introduce expert systems, encompassing various aspects of leadership development. Each system is carefully curated and tailored to address the unique challenges faced during that period, ensuring you have the most relevant and practical guidance at your fingertips.

I'll also explore the benefits of mentorship, networking, and professional development programs, highlighting how these can further enhance your leadership skills and contribute to your overall success. Moreover, I will share inspirational stories and real-life examples from seasoned leaders, offering valuable insights and lessons that can be applied to your own journey.

As you delve into this section, be proactive by integrating these assessments and expert systems into your first year. I've arranged these resources in an order that will align with your execution of the six BUILDS™ imperatives. However, feel free to use them as you best see fit.

CHAPTER 15
RECOMMENDED READING

The following is a curated list of outstanding books and articles by esteemed colleagues who have also specialized in onboarding, assimilation, and integration. While their work is not directly referenced or footnoted within this book, it is important to acknowledge their contributions. My intention in creating this original work, *The Art of Your Start*, has been to complement and build upon the exceptional foundation laid by my colleagues.

Identifying and addressing the gaps and missing links in existing literature is my goal, providing a comprehensive guide to navigating your first year. Many books and articles focus only on the first three months. My experience has shown that crucial transitions and potential terminations often occur at the six-, nine-, and twelve-month marks and beyond. As such, I have chosen to emphasize the importance of the entire first year.

Following are books I've assigned clients over the past two decades, during numerous onboarding, assimilation, and integration engagements. They appear in the order of when I started assigning them:

1. Ciampa, Dan, and Michael Watkins. *Right from the Start*. Boston, MA: Harvard Business School Press, 1999. This book is a classic and ideally suited for C-suite executives. This comprehensive guide

focuses on the critical initial months and offers practical advice on managing change, building a team, and setting direction. With real-life examples, research-backed insights, and deep C-level operational advice, this guide helps new executives make an impact from day one. Since its publication in 1999, I have personally advised hundreds of CEOs and executives to read and follow this great playbook.

2. Watkins, Michael D. *The First 90 Days*. Boston, MA: Harvard Business School Press, 2003. Another classic from Watkins, this book serves as a valuable resource for leaders in lower-level roles. It is a practical guide that helps new leaders successfully navigate their first three months in a new role, offering strategies for accelerated learning, building alliances, and driving early wins. It is about half the length of *Right from the Start* and hence is much more popular with first-and second-line managers.

3. Bradt, George B., Jayme A. Check, and Jorge E. Pedraza. *The New Leader's 100-Day Action Plan*. Hoboken, NY: John Wiley & Sons, 2009. Written by experts in the onboarding field, this book offers many tools and resources useful for the new organizational leader. It provides a structured approach for the first hundred days, focusing on strategic planning, team building, and effective communication to establish credibility and achieve early success.

By combining the insights from *The Art of Your Start* with any of the preceding works, you will gain a holistic understanding of your journey as a new leader. Together, these resources will equip you with the knowledge and strategies needed to ensure a successful and fulfilling first year in your new role.

For Those Responsible for Onboarding, Assimilation, and Integration

There are many useful articles and white papers available to you, besides my book and the aforementioned. Those from SHRM Foundation (Society for Human Resource Management) and HBR (Harvard Business Review) are particularly credible and useful.

The Manager's Corner: *Recommended Reading*

Understanding the importance of onboarding, assimilation, and integration is crucial for both new leaders and their managers in ensuring a smooth transition. By seeking out and utilizing high-quality resources, both parties gain valuable insights and strategies which help navigate challenges and opportunities arising during this consequential phase.

I firmly believe that the first year, rather than just the initial few months, represents the most critical period in a new leadership role. Consequently, it is essential for all stakeholders to maintain ongoing intentionality and invest energy in fostering a supportive and successful environment throughout this crucial period.

Engaging with these resources allows leaders to develop essential skills, foster productive relationships, and lay the groundwork for long-term success. Simultaneously, managers and organizations can learn how to better support and facilitate the growth of their newly acquired leaders.

CHAPTER 16
RELATIONSHIP-BUILDING TACTICS

Your First Few Weeks

As you embark on your new role, your initial interactions with key stakeholders offer a wealth of vital information which help you establish trust. Capturing and reviewing this information is crucial for building strong relationships and making a great impression. During your first meetings, there are four key quadrants of information to explore with stakeholders. This chapter will detail each quadrant, enabling effective navigation of these conversations and laying the foundation for successful working relationships.

Connecting the Pieces

I've developed a tool, Connecting the Pieces, to assist in gathering and organizing valuable personal and professional insights about key stakeholders. By keeping good notes on each individual you interact with, you'll be better prepared to form deeper connections and appreciate the unique viewpoints of colleagues.

You can use a spreadsheet, a slide deck, or a specialized note-taking application to organize yourself. Although the tool I recommend is a slide deck, select any system that fits your needs. I have my clients build a PowerPoint to use as a flashcard system so they can quickly review and commit to memory the critical details gleaned from initial interactions.

The objective is to have a handy and effective way to compile and revisit your notes, allowing you to swiftly assimilate information and insights you've collected about your stakeholders. This strategy will illustrate to key stakeholders that you have listened and remembered what they shared, enabling you to establish relationships faster and make a strong initial impression.

Instructions
1. Identify key stakeholders and hold informational interviews with them, gaining insight into the four vectors identified below.
2. Review your notes on a regular basis until you have mostly committed this information to memory.
3. Add to your notes as you gain additional information on each stakeholder.

Four Key Quadrants to Explore
Organize the information you gather into the following four areas:

1. Personal background: This includes details about their lives outside of work—their family, interests, and hobbies. By understanding their personal experiences, you can establish a more meaningful connection with them and better appreciate their unique personal life situation.
2. Business background: This encompasses their professional experience, skills, expertise, and career trajectory. By learning about their professional journey, you will better understand their approach to work, their strengths, and areas where they might need support.
3. Issues they are facing: By identifying the challenges and obstacles your stakeholders are currently grappling with, you can gain

insight into their priorities and concerns. This understanding will help you offer relevant support, guidance, or resources to address these issues effectively.

4. How you and your execution of your role can help them: Based on the insights gained from the first three areas, identify opportunities where your leadership and the execution of your role can positively impact your stakeholders. Demonstrating your commitment to their success and addressing their concerns will build trust and accelerate a positive working relationship.

By systematically gathering and organizing information in these four areas, you will develop a comprehensive understanding of your key stakeholders, giving you the opportunity to effectively tailor your leadership approach and better support their needs.

I suggest using pen and paper to take written notes during your stakeholder meetings rather than relying on a computer or electronic device. This approach allows you to make a stronger interpersonal connection. At the end of each day, transfer your notes into a digital format or a well-organized system, so you can easily update and access them as your relationship with each stakeholder develops. Make it a habit to review your notes regularly over the coming months, as this will help you better understand your stakeholders and improve your ability to support them.

Following is a further elaboration of each of the four quadrants.

Explore Their Personal Background

When starting an individual meeting, take some time to learn about your colleague as a person and their life outside of work. Details like the names of their significant other, children, or close friends at work are important. Understanding where they live, how long they've lived there, and what brought them to their current residence is also valuable. Though there is a strong tendency for both parties to dive into work-related discussions prematurely, avoid rushing past their personal background if you discern an openness to go there.

To break the ice, engage in a reciprocal exchange by sharing information about yourself as well. An excellent first question might be: "Where are you based, and how long have you been there?" Or: "Where are you originally from?" After they respond, share your own situation. Next, you may ask something like, "What brought you to where you are now?" That's a great open-ended question that's easy to answer and may offer great insight into who they are as a person and what kind of decisions they've made to be where they are today. Then, you should share your answer to the same question. This back-and-forth will keep the meeting conversational instead of feeling like an interview, which is exactly what you want. In today's work-from-anywhere world, the answers might be quite interesting. The next question could be, "Do you have a family?" This question allows the other person to share what they're comfortable discussing without being overly intrusive.

It's important to avoid probing too deeply into their personal lives. You'll likely be able to gauge how open or reserved someone is, so in all cases, follow your instincts. Focus on creating a comfortable and open conversation that allows both parties to learn about each other. Only explore areas your stakeholder is comfortable talking about, and stay within your organization's HR guidelines. Some ideas of what to remember about them personally include:

- Spouse or significant other's name and children's names, ages, and interests.
- Favorite vacation destinations, locations of second homes, or dream travel spots.
- Hobbies and personal interests, including creative outlets, or volunteer work.

- Favorite sports, including teams they support or sports they participate in
- Favorite foods, restaurants, or types of cuisine; any dietary preferences or restrictions
- Educational background, including alma mater and degrees
- Shared connections or acquaintances, whether through friends, family, or professional networks
- Influential books, movies, or TV shows they enjoy or find meaningful
- Memorable life experiences, such as significant achievements, travel adventures, or personal milestones
- Anything else you can discover that will help you connect on a personal level and build rapport

By collecting and understanding these personal details about your key stakeholders, you accelerate a strong connection and foster more trust in a shorter period of time.

Explore Their Business Background

Before meeting with a key stakeholder, review their LinkedIn profile. Going into the meeting unprepared can leave a negative first impression.

As you delve into their background, asking about their current role and tenure is a safe opening. For instance, you could ask, "What led you to join this organization?" This question serves as a smooth transition from personal topics to professional ones. After hearing their response, share your own reasons for joining the organization. A natural follow-up might be, "How long have you been in this role?" Then, asking, "How do you like it?" can elicit valuable and revealing insights. Their feelings about their role could range anywhere from great enjoyment to strong dislike. Which aspects do they appreciate most? Which ones do they enjoy least? This is valuable information.

Learn about their job history in a conversational manner that doesn't feel like an interrogation. Give them the opportunity to share their background in their own words. Let them know you've already read their LinkedIn profile and mention a specific aspect to demonstrate your familiarity. Then, actively listen to their story. This personal exchange demonstrates your genuine interest in their experiences. As they tell you about their background, you will gain valuable information that will be useful down the road. Failing to ask early on can make it awkward to inquire later, when they may question your motives. As a new team member, it's natural for you to be curious about their background and experiences.

When sharing your own background, keep it brief, avoid boasting, and don't try to impress. Maintain a matter-of-fact tone and consciously shift the focus back to them to continue building rapport and understanding. Have a balanced conversation, but avoid talking too much about yourself.

During this conversation, practice active listening without conveying any judgment. Refrain from agreeing or disagreeing; your primary goal is to understand them better and make them feel heard. Steer clear of expressing too much enthusiasm for the organization, as this might discourage candid responses, causing you to miss out on uncovering their true feelings about certain aspects of their role, organization, or the company as a whole.

Additionally, unless you are the CEO, be cautious about spending too much time discussing the organization. Focus primarily on their area of responsibility and yours. When talking about team members' roles and tenure, use your judgment when deciding whether to take notes. If they share negative opinions, it's best not to write those down in front of the stakeholder. Instead, record those thoughts during a break between meetings.

Scheduling back-to-back meetings with no breaks is not recommended, as you need time to complete your notes. Without adequate breaks, the quality of your notes will suffer. It's advisable to schedule some buffer time to allow for note-taking and reflection. If that is not possible, take at least a five-minute break between meetings to collect your thoughts and enhance your notes.

Some areas to explore include:

- Education: Ask about college, grad school, degree(s), and any additional certifications or professional development courses this person has completed.
- Professional history: Study their LinkedIn profile and take notes on their work experience, roles, and accomplishments.
- History with the company: Find out how long they have worked here, roles held, promotions, and their noteworthy achievements.
- Reasons for joining the company: Explore their motivations for choosing this organization, what attracted them to their current role, and any expectations they had.
- Reasons for staying with the company: Discuss factors that have contributed to their continued commitment, such as personal growth, team dynamics, company culture, or opportunities for advancement.
- Greatest successes achieved: Learn about their proudest accomplishments within the company, as well as any challenges they overcame in achieving these milestones.
- Professional goals and aspirations: Gain insight into their short-term and long-term career objectives and how they envision their future within the organization.

- Leadership style and values: Understand their approach to managing and collaborating with others, including their preferred communication styles, decision-making processes, and guiding principles.
- Areas for growth or improvement: Identify any skills or competencies they wish to develop or strengthen and explore potential opportunities for mentorship, training, or support.

By gathering and understanding this business background information, you can better tailor your leadership approach, align with your stakeholders' professional goals, and foster a positive relationship.

Identify Issues that Involve Your Role and Organization

Encourage stakeholders to share insights on issues related to your role and organization. Ask open-ended questions like, "What are the problems you see that I need to address?" This will allow your colleague to discuss various topics, including other people in your organization, as well as operational and systemic issues that require attention. Follow-up questions can include: "What has been tried before to resolve these problems?" "What has worked?" "What hasn't been successful?" and "What has failed?" Seek their opinion on the necessary corrective actions and their observations on past successes and failures.

The conversation may naturally progress to discussing your predecessor's performance. At this point, you might want to offer confidentiality and ask questions like: "What did they do well?" "Where was their performance suboptimal?" "What pitfalls did they encounter that I should avoid?" "What advice could you offer me to be more successful?" Maintain a neutral stance when hearing about issues they perceive with your role, predecessor, or the organization, and remember to thank them for their feedback.

Initiate discussions to uncover both major and minor issues by asking open-ended questions. You'll likely encounter various opinions about past successes and failures, as well as potential solutions. Exercise caution and refrain from sharing your insights and opinions too early in your tenure, as you may later regret that once you gather more information from other sources.

Some key areas to explore may include:

- Challenges this person perceives within your organization
- Broader issues they see affecting the company as a whole
- Specific obstacles they face in their day-to-day work

By understanding the different perspectives on key issues, you will better assess the overall situation and determine the most effective strategies for addressing these challenges.

Explore How You Can Help

Discover how you can help your stakeholders by asking thoughtful questions such as, "If I excel in my role, how will it positively impact your organization?" Aim to understand the connection between your role and theirs, as well as the support they may need from you and your team. Another helpful question might be, "What kind of assistance do you require from me and my team?" This question emphasizes your genuine interest in serving them and making a positive impact in their areas of responsibility.

Remember, "No one cares how much you know until they know how much you care." It's crucial to be genuinely interested in being of service to your superiors, peers, direct reports, and customers. The most effective leaders truly desire to serve everyone in their professional orbit.

To ensure you cover all the bases, prepare a list of insightful questions in advance. This will help you navigate the conversation and gather valuable information that can guide your actions.

Using the Ask Principle™ (asking smart, thoughtful, open-ended questions), some great areas to explore might be:

- Ask: "What can I do to make your job easier?" This question demonstrates your willingness to support them and collaborate effectively.
- Ask: "How is my role going to help yours?" By understanding their expectations of your role, you can better align your efforts and work together toward common goals.
- Ask: "What are your needs from my role?" Gaining insight into their specific requirements will enable you to tailor your approach to meet their needs.
- Ask: "How can we improve communication and collaboration between our teams?" This question can help identify any gaps or barriers that may be hindering effective teamwork.
- Ask: "Do you need any resources or support from me or my team?" Offering assistance can strengthen your working relationship and ensure they have the necessary tools for success.
- Ask: "What are the key performance indicators (KPIs) or metrics that matter most to you in relation to my role?" Understanding their priorities will help you focus your efforts and make data-driven decisions. Note: Some use Objectives and Key Results (OKRs).
- Ask: "Are there any upcoming projects or initiatives where my expertise could be valuable?" Identifying areas where your skills and knowledge can promote collaboration and contribute to shared success is crucial. However, exercise caution and avoid

immediately volunteering to take on any specific project. Instead, focus on understanding the stakeholder's needs and expectations, which will enable you to provide tailored support and build strong working relationships.

- Ask: "How can I help you develop your skills or advance your career?" When speaking to your direct reports, this question will show your commitment to their professional growth and development.

By actively engaging with your stakeholders and asking thoughtful questions, you better understand their needs and expectations and will begin laying the foundation for a successful relationship.

The Manager's Corner: Relationship-Building Tactics

Speed read the contents of this chapter.

As you can see, there is an extensive amount of information your new leader needs to gather and retain during initial stakeholder meetings. Though you undoubtedly have numerous expectations and projects lined up for this leader, it is essential that you allow them the time required for multiple meetings with their key stakeholders BEFORE full-on execution. Overloading your leader early on puts them at a significant disadvantage. The ideal time for exploratory meetings is within the first thirty to sixty days of their role.

Be patient as your leader engages in effective relationship building. This investment will pay dividends in the long run, as it sets the foundation for better communication, teamwork, and problem-solving within the organization.

CHAPTER 17
STAKEHOLDER MEETING TACTICS

Initial Team Meetings

As you begin your new leadership role, it's crucial to meet with your key team members as soon as possible. While it's essential to get acquainted, build trust, and understand their expectations, be aware that everyone has their own agendas, whether conscious or unconscious. For the time being, it's important to explore their perspectives while keeping your own thoughts and plans to yourself. Though this approach may seem uncomfortable, there are many valid reasons for it.

Fully understanding individuals' agendas takes time and careful observation. Some people may not even be aware of their biases and agendas, while others may deliberately conceal them. Over several months, by actively listening and observing, you can discern these biases and potentially conflicting agendas. The sooner you identify and navigate potential conflicts, the better.

To uncover people's agendas, prepare a strategy for your initial meetings. Develop a list of questions in advance to guide your conversations. Asking the right questions will enable you to gather more information than will sharing your own ideas and plans. Everyone expects the new leader to have lots of questions, so it'll be easy to slip these "agenda-revealing" questions into your first few interactions. It's important to listen and learn before proposing any specific course of action, as arriving with a predetermined plan may raise suspicion and hinder your ability to build trust. Keep your plans to yourself. After all, you're brand new. How can you possibly know what to do before you listen and learn? Adopt "I'm here as to listen and learn" as your mantra.

Set the Right Tone for Stakeholder Team Meetings

In addition to your one-on-one meetings, another way of getting to know people is through team meetings with your peers and direct reports.

Establishing the appropriate tone for these meetings is vital for building trust and fostering effective communication. Create a relaxed and informal atmosphere, allowing everyone to feel comfortable and open. As the meetings progress, gradually shift the focus toward more business-related discussions.

If you lean too heavily on structure, the meetings may feel rigid and impersonal, giving the impression that you prioritize tasks over people. On the other hand, if the meetings lack structure, you may appear disorganized and lacking focus. Striking the right balance is key to creating a positive and productive environment.

To achieve this delicate balance, consider participants' preferences, expectations, and communication styles. When you planned your onboarding process, you may have already gathered insights into your colleagues' behavioral styles. This knowledge will help you tailor your approach, making meetings more engaging and effective.

Encourage dialogue by asking open-ended questions and actively listening to opinions and concerns. This will demonstrate your commitment to understanding different perspectives and collaborating on ideas and solutions.

Additionally, set clear objectives for each meeting and ensure everyone understands the goals you aim to achieve. This will provide a sense of purpose and direction while still maintaining an open and inclusive atmosphere.

By carefully navigating the tone and structure of stakeholder meetings, you'll cultivate an environment of trust, open communication, and collaboration, laying the foundation for a successful working relationship.

Your behavioral style definitely impacts your approach to individual and team meetings. I recommend you become "DISC literate" by completing the DISC behavioral assessment and administering it to your direct reports. Check with your HR partner to see if DISC profiles are available for your peers and superiors. A review of them would be most helpful. In the next chapter, I will talk about this assessment and provide you with a people-reading system I developed based on the DISC, which will help you quickly determine others' behavioral styles without having to give them the DISC assessment (although I recommend giving it to them regardless). Note: See me if you need a source for these valuable assessments.

Note-Taking During Stakeholder Meetings

From my experience, I've noticed many leaders don't take enough (or any) notes during their initial meetings with stakeholders. Several factors contribute to this. Some individuals may rely on their strong memory. However, not taking notes could give off an impression of disinterest or superiority. As a newcomer, taking notes demonstrates your attention and engagement with the information shared.

If your reason for not taking notes is a lack of interest, it's imperative to adjust your attitude. No matter your skills or experience, failing to engage your stakeholders leads to detrimental outcomes.

At times, initial stakeholder meetings are organized back-to-back in the early days of onboarding, aiming to familiarize you quickly. This can be overwhelming, hindering real-time note-taking. You might plan to recap at the end of the day, but this approach causes you to forget or miss crucial details and opportunities to show appreciation for your colleagues' insights.

Take notes during each meeting, capturing the conversation as it transpires. This will aid your retention of vital information and communicate your intent of understanding and valuing your team members' viewpoints.

You will not cover everything in a single meeting. Coordinate another meeting while you're still together. Directly scheduling is efficient, bypassing the potentially weeks-long process of scheduling through assistants. Strike while the opportunity is present to ensure timely calendaring.

The Manager's Corner: Stakeholder Meeting Tactics

You play a critical role in supporting your new leaders during the crucial early stages of their tenure. One of the most important aspects of this support involves facilitating individual and team meetings with their stakeholders. These interactions provide an opportunity for relationship building, open communication, and fostering a positive and collaborative work environment.

Effective note-taking is another critical skill that new leaders should develop, as it helps them retain valuable information gleaned from these meetings. Encourage your leader to choose a suitable note-taking method and retrieval system for easy access to the information gathered. This system will serve as a useful resource as they navigate their new role and work on projects with their team.

A powerful tool that managers can introduce to their new leaders and teams is the DISC behavioral profile. This assessment provides valuable insights into an individual's communication and working style, allowing for better collaboration and understanding among team members. As your leader and their team members complete the DISC profile, the results will significantly accelerate and enhance their working relationships.

In addition to administering the DISC profile to your leader, you should also complete the assessment yourself and obtain a comparative report with your leader. This report enables both parties to accelerate the development of a positive working relationship, as you will gain insights into how to better interface with each other. By understanding respective communication styles, you and your leader will collaborate more effectively and make better decisions together.

CHAPTER 18
STRUCTURE FOR A HUNDRED-DAY PLAN

Reasons for Creating a Hundred-Day Plan

In the preceding chapter, we highlighted the significance of stakeholder meetings during your initial onboarding process. As we delve into this chapter about your hundred-day plan, the importance of those stakeholder meetings will become increasingly clear.

The development and presentation of a hundred-day plan is a significant early milestone in your tenure. You'll craft this plan during your initial thirty days.

The ensuing one hundred days are pivotal, laying the groundwork for your future success. A well-executed plan is crucial, serving as your first "early win" and playing a key role in your assimilation and integration as a new leader.

The hundred-day plan is your chance to leave an indelible mark. It articulates your vision, introducing your leadership style and key priorities. It generates confidence with your manager and team, promoting a transparent and constructive vision.

Your hundred-day plan is a strategic tool to anticipate and address potential hurdles that may surface during this transitional phase. By proactively identifying challenges, you exhibit your problem-solving acumen and earn greater trust from everyone.

In the course of crafting your plan, involve your manager. This joint effort aligns objectives, priorities, and timelines, laying a solid foundation for a strong working relationship. It creates a shared understanding of your goals and allows for valuable feedback on your strategy. This living document reflects your commitment to open communication and heightens your plan's potential for success. It also sets a precedent for a collaborative approach, which is vital for creating a supportive, results-oriented partnership. I recommend your manager receives this plan within three weeks of your start date. And then, I suggest you engage in a back-and-forth revision process, finalizing it by your thirty-first day.

Use your plan to track your progress. With clearly defined milestones, you can assess your performance and make necessary adjustments. Each milestone reached enhances your credibility among your team and stakeholders, generating momentum.

This plan is more than just a roadmap—it's your first significant achievement. By investing in a thoughtfully designed and detailed plan, you're laying the groundwork for your first early win.

Structure of the Hundred-Day Plan

As you create your plan, follow this outline. It will guide you through the process, with detailed information for each slide in your presentation.

Creating your hundred-day plan in a slide program enhances its presentation and equips you to share it with a larger audience. Here is slide-by-slide content for your hundred-day onboarding plan.

Slide 1: Title Slide: Use your company's standard slide presentation template with the company logo and other branding elements. Make the title clear and concise, indicating this is your hundred-day onboarding plan. Ask marketing for a well-branded slide template.

Slide 2: Index Slide: Depending on the length of your plan, you may want to have an index for ease of navigation.

Slide 3: Initial Observations – Strengths: Stay focused on your area of responsibility and your organization, though you may also want to highlight the great working relationships you have observed with other areas of the organization.

Slide 4: Initial Observations – Weaknesses: Stay focused on your area of responsibility. However, you may want to diplomatically call out other stakeholder groups that are causing performance issues in your department or division.

Slide 5: Initial Observations – Opportunities and Threats: You may or may not have enough information to do this slide. I would consider it optional, but nice to have.

Slide 6: Executive Summary of Hundred-Day Plan: Offer a high-level overview of your plan, organized by month. This snapshot allows your audience to grasp the overall structure and progression of your onboarding plan and quickly understand your intentions. Outline key objectives, priorities, and timelines. This high-level snapshot sets the stage for the rest of your presentation and helps your audience gain a clear picture of your roadmap.

Slide 7: Detailed Hundred-Day Plan: Include a comprehensive slide with detailed information on your objectives, priorities, and action steps. This slide, while dense, provides essential context for your plan. Clearly define your short-term (thirty days), medium-term (sixty days), and long-term (one hundred days) goals, ensuring they align with the organization's strategic priorities. Incorporate clear, measurable objectives for tracking progress. Review this with your manager at the end of each thirty days, and adjust as warranted.

Slide 8: Month One Plan: Outline key objectives for your first month.

Slide 9: Month Two Plan: Focus on early "quick wins" during your second month. What are some low-hanging fruit that you can pick off? Ideally, these projects have strong key stakeholder support, showcase your leadership, don't consume too much of your time, and can be delivered within thirty to sixty days.

Slide 10: Month Three Plan: Although you may have limited visibility into your third month, allocate space in your plan for a review with your manager. Get help in fleshing out what your third month will look like. Have a review with your manager at the end of months one, two, and three. Bake this into your plan.

Slide 11: Gantt Chart: Showcase your timeline and dependencies with a Gantt chart. This powerful visualization tool allows you to track progress and identify potential bottlenecks, making it an indispensable part of your plan. This will help you analyze all that you are promising, and usually results in better planning, under-promising, and giving you the room to over-deliver on results. If you are taking on too many projects, the Gantt chart will quickly pinpoint this.

Slide 12: Appendix: Compile any additional slides that you might need during your presentation in an appendix. These resources can serve as useful reference points during discussions or Q&A sessions. This approach is a clever way of including all the supporting data while keeping the presentation concise and focused.

Ideas for the Appendix

Following are ideas for additional slides:

- Personal Vision and Values: Your leadership philosophy, personal values, and the guiding principles that will shape your approach to

your new role. This slide establishes your leadership identity and lays the groundwork for the expectations you'll set for yourself and your team.
- SWOT Analysis: You may have had time to conduct a thorough SWOT (Strengths, Weaknesses, Opportunities, and Threats) analysis of the organization, department, or team you're joining. This evaluation will help you understand the current landscape and identify areas where you can make an immediate impact, but it may be too extensive to feature in the main part of the presentation. In that case, you may prefer to include only one slide regarding your findings in your main presentation, called "Initial Observations."
- Stakeholder Mapping: Identify key stakeholders both inside and outside the organization, including your team members, peers, managers, clients, and partners. Outline your plan for engaging with each stakeholder group to build relationships, understand expectations, and foster collaboration.
- Details of a Major Key Initiative: High amounts of detail should go in the appendix. Explain the primary initiatives and projects you'll undertake during the main part of your presentation and how these initiatives align with your goals and objectives. Provide a high-level action plan, including resources, timelines, and anticipated challenges. Heavy details on initiatives should go in the appendix.
- Milestones and Metrics: Set measurable milestones to track your progress and quantify success. Define key performance indicators (KPIs) for each goal and objective, and establish a system for monitoring and reporting on these metrics. You may or may not have time to develop this information. If you do, depending on the time available and desired level of detail, it can go in either the main body or the appendix.

- Communication Plan: A comprehensive communication plan to keep your team, stakeholders, and manager informed about your progress. It outlines the frequency and format of updates, and establishes channels for feedback and collaboration.
- Continuous Improvement and Reflection: End your presentation with a commitment to continuous improvement and reflection. Explain how you'll regularly review and adjust your plan as needed, learn from your experiences, and adapt your leadership approach to achieve your goals.

Find Examples of Onboarding Plans

Browse the internet to find examples of leadership onboarding plans. Here are some search terms and websites to help guide your research.

Search Terms:
1. Leadership onboarding plan examples
2. Executive onboarding plan templates
3. 100-day onboarding plan for leaders
4. New manager onboarding checklist
5. Onboarding strategies for executives

Websites:
1. Harvard Business Review (hbr.org): Look for articles on leadership onboarding and executive transitions.
2. Forbes (forbes.com): Search for articles on executive onboarding and leadership development.
3. LinkedIn (linkedin.com): Use the platform to find professionals who have shared their onboarding experiences or resources.
4. Society for Human Resource Management (shrm.org): Look for

resources and templates related to leadership onboarding and management transitions.
5. CCL (ccl.org): The Center for Creative Leadership has resources on leadership development, including onboarding.

By using these search terms and exploring the suggested websites, you should be able to find a variety of leadership onboarding plans, templates, and resources to assist you. I collect great plans from clients, and can share these with you with their permission.

Summary

Design an amazing hundred-day plan. It is your first quick win, and it will be a major hit if you put the time and energy into making it spectacular.

Take the time to research and learn from the best onboarding plans available. By incorporating ideas from others' successes, you can develop a robust, innovative, and effective hundred-day onboarding plan that sets you apart.

Set your manager's expectations for doing this plan. Emphasize the importance of reviewing your hundred-day plan with them. Stress the benefits of ensuring alignment, gaining valuable feedback, and fostering a collaborative working relationship.

By following this structure and providing detailed content for each slide, your hundred-day onboarding plan will be well-rounded, comprehensive, and poised to set you on a path toward greater success.

The Manager's Corner: *Structure for a Hundred-Day Plan*

As the manager of the newly appointed leader, it is highly advisable to request that they develop a comprehensive hundred-day plan within the first three weeks of assuming their role. It should be due at the end of their third week. Review and edit this in a working session with your leader sometime early in the fourth week. Then, have them send you a final version to review, edit further, and approve.

This exercise holds immense value in fostering strategic thinking and goal setting, enabling the leader to establish a clear roadmap for their early days. By outlining specific objectives, milestones, and action steps, your leader can effectively prioritize their tasks, align their efforts with organizational goals, and showcase their proactive approach to their responsibilities.

The hundred-day plan serves as a framework for accountability, facilitates open communication between you and your leader, and lays the groundwork for a successful transition into their new role. I recommend you review this plan with them monthly at the end of their second, third, and fourth months in the role. During these reviews, you can assess their progress, provide guidance, and suggest any adjustments you deem warranted.

CHAPTER 19
THE DISC BEHAVIORAL ASSESSMENT

As we have previously discussed, you will do three main things during your first thirty days:

1. Build Trust! Establish high-trust relationships.
2. Understand Needs! Listen and learn, ask questions, and assess the people and organization.
3. Create a hundred-day plan.

Administering the DISC assessment during this time can be very helpful in accomplishing priorities one and two. If you employ it early enough in your tenure, it will also help inform your hundred-day plan.

About the DISC

The DISC assessment is a tool that helps individuals gain insights into their behavioral style preferences. The DISC assessment provides a snapshot of one's current behavioral style, which can change over time due to various factors such as experience, age, and roles held.

The DISC assessment provides a comprehensive analysis of behavioral style preferences. This valuable information can be leveraged to develop effective strategies in both personal and professional settings. Understanding behavioral tendencies enhances communication, improves teamwork, and accelerates development of positive, productive relationships.

Gaining insights into behavioral preferences can identify areas for improvement and help capitalize on strengths. For instance, the assessment can help with understanding how one responds to different situations, interacts with others, and approaches tasks. Armed with this knowledge, we can adapt our behavior to different situations and communicate more effectively with others.

Overall, completing the DISC assessment can lead to increased self-awareness and personal growth, as well as improved outcomes.

DISC Validation

The copyright to the DISC assessment was lost in the 1970s, resulting in a proliferation of poorly designed and inaccurate assessments flooding the market. Therefore, it's crucial to choose a DISC assessment that has been validated and has a proven track record of providing valuable insights. The DISC assessment I use has been validated over the past forty-plus years by millions of users, and I have personally administered it since I began leadership coaching in 1987.

Using a validated DISC assessment ensures that the information you receive is reliable and can be used to make informed decisions. As the saying goes, "Garbage in, garbage out." By using a reliable assessment, you can gain useful information about your behavioral tendencies, which can lead to personal and professional growth. Write me if you need a recommended provider.

Four Quadrants of the DISC

The DISC assessment categorizes behavioral tendencies into four quadrants, each representing a distinct and observable behavioral style. These four styles are Dominant (D), Influencing (I), Steady (S), and Cautious (C).

It's worth noting that the four quadrants are not meant to label individuals, but rather provide insights into behavioral tendencies. By understanding our preferences, we can adapt our behavior to better suit different situations and communicate more effectively with others. Here is the one I've created:

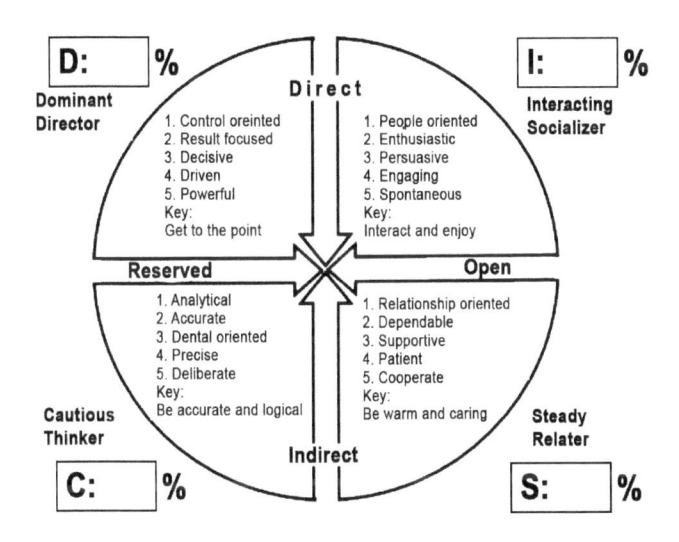

```
D: [  ]%                  Direct                    I: [  ]%
Dominant                                             Interacting
Director    1. Control oreinted  | 1. People oriented   Socializer
            2. Result focused    | 2. Enthusiastic
            3. Decisive          | 3. Persuasive
            4. Driven            | 4. Engaging
            5. Powerful          | 5. Spontaneous
            Key:                 | Key:
            Get to the point     | Interact and enjoy
         Reserved                            Open
            1. Analytical        | 1. Relationship oriented
            2. Accurate          | 2. Dependable
            3. Dental oriented   | 3. Supportive
            4. Precise           | 4. Patient
            5. Deliberate        | 5. Cooperate
            Key:                 | Key:
Cautious    Be accurate and logical | Be warm and caring   Steady
Thinker                                               Relater
C: [  ]%                 Indirect                    S: [  ]%
```

Overall, the four quadrants of the DISC model provide a useful framework for gaining insights into behavioral tendencies.

After conducting extensive research with experts in the behavioral sciences, I developed this model several decades ago. The four styles I identified are called:

- Dominant Director, characterized by take-charge tendencies, with a propensity to drive oneself and direct others.
- Interacting Socializer, characterized by being interaction oriented, upbeat, positive, social, and outgoing.
- Steady Relater, characterized by being steady, stable, and deeply relational, with a strong team orientation.

- Cautious Thinker, characterized by being analytical, accurate, and precise, with a high level of attention to detail.
See the associated diagram, which gives further detail.

These four preferred ways of being are interrelated. Different coaches and assessments may use varying models or terminologies to describe the same behavioral styles. However, what matters most is the accuracy and reliability of the assessment utilized and the fact that there are clearly four easily identifiable quadrants of human behavior. Regardless of the nomenclature, the core concept remains—understanding our behavioral tendencies drives personal and professional growth within ourselves and in relationships with others.

Individuals are not purely one style but rather a unique combination of all four. Each individual has varying preferences from each of the four quadrants, which is an essential understanding that decreases the negative tendency to label people. I came to this belief in the late 1980s when most of my peers were, in fact, using this tool to label people, which I saw as a gross misuse of the instrument. Consultants and trainers were going so far as to make name tags and desk placards with the letters "D," "I," "S," or "C." Clearly, one letter does not even begin to accurately explain a person's behavioral preferences. The research I conducted back then has led to the development of many rich reporting tools, which can provide a comprehensive analysis of an individual's behavioral style. This model helps explain that our unique combination of behavioral tendencies is made up of a certain percentage of all four styles.

Behavioral Adaptability

The DISC assessment can be a valuable tool to increase your behavioral adaptability. By understanding and adapting to different behavioral tendencies, you can communicate more effectively, collaborate more efficiently, and ultimately achieve better outcomes in your personal and professional life.

As the following diagram suggests, some leaders are very willing to adapt their behavioral style to better meet others' needs. In fact, some are so willing that this hinders their effectiveness as a leader. Generally speaking, however, the best leaders are more willing than not to adjust how they behave to work better with others. Some leaders are not willing to adapt their style at all, and we would say these individuals are inflexible in their behaviors. In my experience, these leaders are much less effective at leading others.

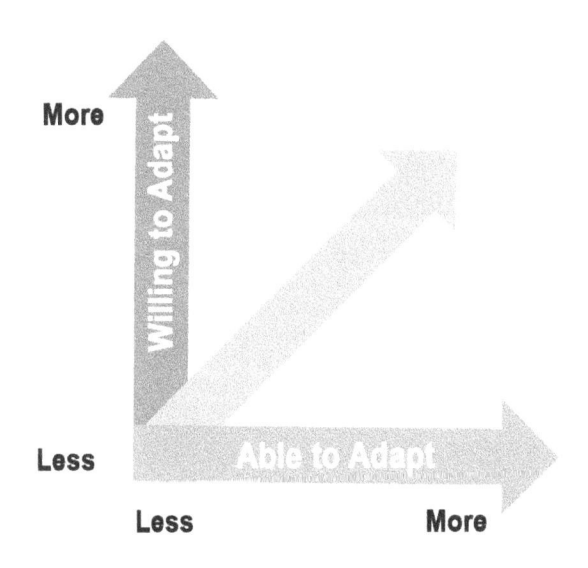

Some leaders have a high ability to adapt their style to meet others' needs. If this describes you, it is very likely you studied the behavioral sciences somewhere along the way, completed various behavioral assessments, consciously worked at trying out different behaviors with different types of people, and noticed you got better results due to your efforts.

The best leaders have both a high willingness AND high ability to adapt their behavioral style to better meet others' needs. This diagram shows the ideal path for great leaders (the center arrow). Where do you fall on these two indices? Where is there area for improvement? Increasing your flexibility (willingness to adapt) and your versatility (ability to adapt) will almost always make you a better organizational leader, because people tend to more closely follow those who speak their behavioral "language."

Here is a saying worth remembering:

High willingness to adapt PLUS high ability to adapt EQUALS maximum adaptability and better leadership results.

To reach your full leadership potential, you need maximum adaptability. Not understanding your behavioral tendencies weakens your ability to effectively adapt your style to the needs of others. Effective leaders can develop or improve positive relationships in much less time than would normally be needed through the use of the behavioral sciences. Most highly effective leaders are unconsciously or consciously adept at identifying and adapting their leadership style to the behavioral styles of the people with whom they work.

In my experience, every leader exhibits varying degrees or percentages of intensity in the four behavioral styles. It's important to recognize that every leader's behavior is typically a blend of all four styles. However, there is usually one style the leader favors more than the others, which we call the primary behavioral style. Additionally, individuals usually have a second preferred way of behaving, which we refer to as their secondary style.

Keys to Each Styles

Understanding your primary and secondary behavioral styles can provide valuable insights into your tendencies and preferences and those of others. This allows you to leverage your strengths and adapt your behavior to different situations, leading to better outcomes.

Each primary behavioral style has what I call a "key" to successful interaction with that style. These keys are essential to understanding how to tailor your approach to different individuals. As depicted in the preceeding DISC diagram, here are the four keys, one for each primary style:

- D: Get to the point. Individuals with a dominant style prefer clear and concise communication that focuses on the bottom line.
- I: Interact and enjoy. Individuals with an influential style thrive on interaction and enjoy socializing and building relationships.
- S: Be warm and caring. Individuals with a steady style prioritize warmth and caring in their interactions and value teamwork and collaboration.
- C: Be accurate and logical. Individuals with a cautious style value accuracy and logic and appreciate data-driven communication and decision-making.

Understanding these keys can help you better understand where others are coming from and adapt your leadership style to better meet the demands of a given person or situation. By leveraging your knowledge of the DISC assessment and its keys, you can improve communication and build stronger relationships.

DISC FAQs

Following are some DISC FAQs that may answer some questions that you have.

Q: What does the DISC measure?

A: DISC measures our preferred behaviors, categorizing them into four primary styles to help us understand our tendencies and preferences.

Q: How can I complete the DISC test?

A: The DISC assessment isn't a test but an assessment, usually taking fifteen to twenty minutes. After completion, you receive a report detailing your primary and secondary behavioral styles and strategies for using these strengths.

Q: Should I answer the DISC assessment questions based on my behavior at work or in general?

A: When answering DISC questions, focus on your work behavior. This will provide insights into your professional approach to tasks, communication, and interactions.

Q: What results can I expect from the DISC assessment?

A: The DISC assessment provides an overview of your behavioral style, highlighting your primary and secondary tendencies, and providing strategies for leveraging your strengths and adapting your behaviors.

Q: How can I validate the accuracy of the DISC assessment?

A: To validate the DISC's accuracy, share the results with people who know you well. This can provide additional perspectives, remove blind spots, and increase understanding of your behavioral tendencies.

Q: What exercises do you recommend to further validate my DISC report?

A: To further validate your DISC report, annotate it, highlighting areas you agree or disagree with. Sharing this with trusted individuals for feedback will provide additional insights.

Q: Can I use the DISC assessment for hiring purposes?

A: The DISC is not a competency predictor and should not be used solely for hiring decisions. Doing so also creates potential legal risks. However, it can give insights into the preferred work styles and behaviors of final candidates. Consult HR for guidelines.

Q: What is the best behavioral style for a leader?

A: There's no "best" DISC style for leaders. Success in leadership depends on factors beyond behavioral styles, such as communication skills, decision-making abilities, and emotional intelligence.

Q: What is the difference between the DISC and the Myers-Briggs Type Indicator (MBTI)?

A: DISC and MBTI differ in their focus. DISC measures observable behavior, while MBTI assesses core personality traits. Both should be used alongside other methods for a comprehensive understanding of an individual.

Q: What will my DISC assessment report tell me about how to better work with others?

A: DISC provides insights into your behavior and strategies for relating to people with different behavioral preferences. It suggests methods for resolving conflicts and enhancing collaboration.

Q: What are the applications for using the DISC assessment in the workplace?

A: DISC can be used in coaching sessions, leadership training programs, and team-building activities. It helps to improve communication, collaboration, and teamwork.

Q: What is the most important application of the DISC assessment?

A: The primary application of DISC is to improve personal and professional relationships, communication, teamwork, and behavioral adaptability.

Q: Which DISC do you think is the most accurate, and which do you recommend?

A: The Wiley DiSC assessment is a highly respected tool, providing a nuanced view of an individual's behavioral tendencies and personalized reports for improved communication and collaboration.

Q: How does the Wiley DiSC report address various intensities of behavior?

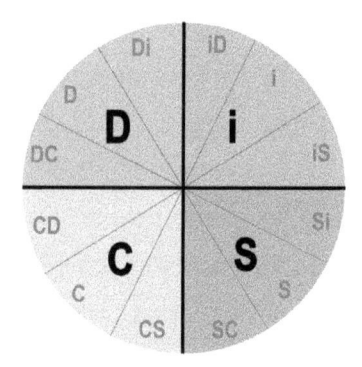

A: The Wiley DiSC assessment represents an individual's preferred behavioral style on a circular diagram. The plotted point's position indicates the intensity in each behavioral dimension, with strategies provided to enhance communication and collaboration.

Projecting Our Behavioral Style onto Others

We all tend to project our own behavioral style onto others and view the world through our own filters. We often prefer our own style and rationalize the world through its filter, which can limit our ability to fully understand and appreciate others. This tendency can lead to frustration with others' behavior and make it difficult to develop effective relationships and build high-performing teams.

By understanding your behavioral style and identifying and understanding the styles of others, you will become more accepting of different styles and perspectives. Through this process, you'll gain valuable insights into how others operate behaviorally. By recognizing and respecting different behavioral styles, you will build stronger relationships and create more inclusive and productive environments.

Value of Style Diversification on Teams

The value of style diversification on teams cannot be overstated. Each behavioral style brings its unique perspective and strengths to the workplace. Teams composed of individuals with the same narrow behavioral style might work well together, but they may also approach problems in a similar way, leading to a lack of diversity of thought and suboptimal results. This phenomenon is commonly known as "group behavioral think."

On the other hand, a team that encompasses a diversity of styles can have a greater diversity of thought, which can lead to peak team performance if everyone is given an opportunity to be heard. By embracing different perspectives, teams can come up with more creative and innovative solutions to complex problems. Individuals with different styles challenge each other's assumptions and encourage each other to think more critically, leading to better outcomes.

This leads me to a saying worth remembering: "If the only tool you have is a hammer, then every problem you see is a nail." Leaders who have a good understanding of their behavioral style are much better able to identify the styles of others. As you grow in your understanding and ability to control your own style, you may become more willing and able to adapt your style to meet the needs of others. Demonstrating adaptability is a powerful approach that will lead to your increased influence and success.

In summary, the value of style diversification on teams is clear. By embracing different perspectives and approaches, teams can achieve greater success and build more productive, inclusive work environments.

Identifying the Styles of Others: A Quick Guide

While having the DISC results of others can be useful, it's not always possible. Therefore, being able to quickly identify styles solely through observation is a valuable skill. Here are some quick tips to help you do so:

- D and I styles tend to be direct in their approach, with confident body language and assertive communication. They tend to use bold gestures and make direct eye contact.
- S and C styles tend to be less direct in their approach, with a more reserved body language and communication style. They often avoid direct eye contact and use less assertive verbal and body language.
- D and C styles are task oriented and focused on achieving results. They may prioritize efficiency and task completion over nurturing relationships.
- I and S styles are more people oriented and prioritize growing positive relationships over achieving tasks or results.

While these tips can help you make a quick assessment, it's important to keep in mind that everyone is unique and may not fit neatly into one style. To get a more accurate assessment, you must continue to use the power of observation over time.

An Observation-Only-Based DISC Assessment

Following is an assessment I created that will give you a fairly accurate read on the behavioral style of others without you having to administer an electronic assessment. It is solely based on observation and could conceivably be ascertained after just one video or in-person meeting.

Instructions: Answer as many of these ten questions as you can for each of your direct reports. You can also do this for your manager or peers. Create a spreadsheet and put these questions vertically in Column

A; in Column B, going horizontally, list each of your direct reports. Insert the letter corresponding to your observation of each individual. Tally up the totals and get a percentage of the four styles for each. Share this with your advisor, mentor, and/or coach.

Observation 1: Speaking style and tone of voice. Does this person try to control and direct the conversation and have a bold, forceful, or assertive tone (D), speak rapidly with great enthusiasm and have an upbeat, enthusiastic, and energetic tone (I), have a calm, soft, and friendly approach with a calming, empathetic, and reassuring tone (S), or tend to cut off small talk and get to the facts and task at hand with an unemotional and cautious tone (C)?

Observation 2: Listening style. Does this person often interrupt and respond quickly with direct and to-the-point comments (D), show active listening through verbal and nonverbal cues such as nodding, agreeing, and offering praise or affirmation (I), listen attentively and patiently, providing a supportive and empathetic ear (S), or carefully listen to and analyze information, often asking clarifying questions to fully understand the situation before responding (C)?

Observation 3: Questioning style. When asking questions, does this person ask direct and to-the-point questions that drive toward immediate actions or solutions (D), ask open-ended and exploratory questions, often focusing on feelings and experiences (I), ask questions in a supportive and empathetic manner, seeking to understand the other person's perspective (S), or ask precise and analytical questions, seeking specific details and data (C)?

Observation 4: Body language. Does the person have confident and dominant body language (D), open and expressive body language (I), relaxed and non-threatening body language (S), or reserved and controlled body language (C)?

Observation 5: Pace of speech. Does the person speak quickly and decisively (D), at a fast and energetic pace (I), at a slower and more measured pace (S), or with a deliberate and precise pace (C)?

Observation 6: Use of gestures. Does this person use large, expansive gestures and move around a lot (D), gesture excitedly with their hands or use other animated body language (I), maintain soft and friendly intermittent eye contact (S), or have more reserved and very controlled gestures and look away when talking (C)?

Observation 7: Decision-making style. Does the person make decisions quickly and decisively (D), based on intuition and feelings (I), with consideration for the team and the impact on relationships (S), or based on logic and data (C)?

Observation 8: Response to conflict. Does the person confront conflict head-on (D), seek to avoid conflict and maintain harmony (I), diplomatically, carefully, and patiently work to avoid conflict (S), or avoid most conflict, and carefully weigh all sides before making a decision (C)?

Observation 9: Social style. Does the person seek to dominate social situations (D), actively and articulately engage with others and make new connections (I), establish deeper and more meaningful relationships in a reserved but friendly way (S), or maintain a reserved and formal demeanor without interrupting or intruding (C)?

Observation 10: Approach to tasks. Does the person focus on achieving results swiftly and draw quick, decisive conclusions (D), prioritize innovation and creativity and have a spontaneous, upbeat, and enthusiastic attitude (I), establish and maintain strong relationships and complete tasks while being cooperative and systematic (S), or meticulously follow established procedures and respond slowly, cautiously, and thoughtfully (C)?

If possible, administer the DISC instrument, and chart the actual results. Where were your surprises? Where did you get it right, and where were your blind spots?

This exercise and the subsequent observations can help you identify someone's primary and secondary behavioral styles. Keep in mind that individuals can exhibit characteristics of multiple styles. It is also important to remember that this is not a substitute for a formal DISC assessment, which provides a more comprehensive and accurate understanding of someone's behavioral preferences.

Summary

Understanding your behavior and how you come across to others is an important step in the process of growing your leadership chops. The results of an accurate (many are not—beware) assessment will change over time, and as your type of work changes.

To increase your behavioral literacy, I recommend you complete a DISC-based assessment every three to five years.

The Manager's Corner: *The DISC Behavioral Assessment*

The DISC is one of the most useful tools in your toolbox and that of your direct reports. Become familiar with this powerful assessment if you are not already. If the DISC is new to you, I recommend you take it yourself and share your results with your manager and your direct reports. It is guaranteed to build stronger relationships. I recommend you also administer this to all your direct reports. It is a great team-building and development tool.

Be aware that the copyright to this amazing tool was lost in the late seventies. As a result, there is a plethora of similar tools on the market, all calling themselves by different names. The fact is that the four quadrants that the DISC identifies are the same across many seemingly different assessments. I recommend using the DISC by Wiley Publishing (they spell theirs DiSC), as it is one of the best and heavily validated. There is more information about this in the Q&A section of this chapter. See the last question: "Which DISC do you think is the most accurate, and which do you recommend?"

CHAPTER 20
GAINING MENTORSHIP

Ask for Help

It's natural to feel hesitant to ask for help. You may worry that you'll expose your weaknesses or reveal the challenges you face to others. However, seeking help is not a sign of weakness—it's a sign of strength.

Early in your tenure, you may not want to share issues you have with anyone but your manager. Even there, you may not feel safe doing so until more time elapses. This is where a mentor, advisor, or coach can be incredibly valuable. This provides a safe and confidential space for you to discuss your concerns, explore your ideas, and receive feedback.

Having a neutral sounding board, you will gain the confidence you need to make informed decisions and take calculated risks. A mentor, advisor, or coach offers an outside perspective on the organization and its culture, which can be incredibly valuable for you as you get acclimated. One of the key benefits is the opportunity for confidential and tailored one-on-one help. However, you have to be willing to invest in these relationships. It's important to note that not all mentors, advisors, or coaches are created equal. When seeking help, look for professionals who have relevant experience and expertise, as well as a style that aligns with your learning style and personality.

Seeking help is essential for success during your first year in a new leadership role. A mentor, advisor, or coach will provide valuable support, guidance, and developmental opportunities that will help you navigate the challenges of your role with confidence and skill. So, don't hesitate to ask for help—it's a sign of strength, not weakness.

Decide to Gain Mentorship

Every leader, whether junior or seasoned, can benefit from having one or several mentors. This chapter will guide you through the process of finding and gaining a mentor who can help you achieve your personal and professional goals. If you get nothing else from this book, my hope is that you'll at least gain a mentor or two. If you have one already, then another may be in order.

It's natural to feel reluctant or intimidated about approaching someone to be your mentor. However, the rewards of mentorship can be substantial, providing guidance, support, and a fresh perspective on your challenges. The good news is that mentors are often willing to share their time and expertise without any charge.

The first step is to identify someone whose work you admire and respect. Look for individuals who have experience, knowledge, and insights that can be valuable to your career. This could be someone in your organization or industry, or someone outside of your present network.

Once you've identified a potential mentor, you'll need to craft a message that introduces yourself and expresses your interest in their mentorship. I'll provide some scripts here you can use, depending on the audience.

Overcome Reluctance to Ask for Mentorship

You may understand the value of mentorship, but asking for it is a significant obstacle. Most potential mentors are receptive to such requests. It is up to you to initiate the conversation. Let's explore possible reasons for reluctance, ways to overcome these barriers, and how to ask for mentorship that gets results.

1. Overcoming Your Pride and Ego

One common reason you may be hesitant to seek mentorship is your pride. The idea of asking for help may seem uncomfortable or awkward due to your ego and the need to maintain an image of self-sufficiency. Recognize that seeking guidance is not a sign of weakness but rather an opportunity for growth and development. Embrace humility and acknowledge the value that a mentor can bring to your professional journey.

2. Building Courage

Gathering the courage to ask for mentorship can be challenging, but it's a crucial step in establishing a fruitful mentoring relationship. Remind yourself of the potential benefits of having a mentor, such as gaining new insights, learning from their experiences, and enhancing your professional network. Use these positive outcomes as motivation to take the leap and initiate the conversation.

3. Lacking an Effective Framework

When asking for mentorship, it's important to present your request in a way that makes it easy for the potential mentor to accept. Avoid putting undue pressure on them by directly asking, "Would you be my mentor?" Instead, try a more nuanced approach that acknowledges their time constraints and expertise. Consider using a request like, "I greatly admire your experience in [specific area], and I believe your guidance would be incredibly valuable to me as I navigate [specific challenge or goal]. Would you be open to having a conversation about how we might collaborate or engage in a mentoring relationship?"

4. Not Wanting to Impose

You may be reluctant to ask, for fear of imposing. Get over it! Show appreciation for the potential mentor's time and expertise by expressing gratitude for their willingness to consider your request. Make it clear that you understand the commitment involved and are prepared to be an engaged and dedicated mentee. Many are waiting for someone to ask, and they are grateful when you do.

5. Concern about Time

To make the mentoring relationship more appealing and manageable, consider suggesting a flexible structure. This may include setting up regular meetings, establishing clear goals and expectations, or being open to various communication methods, such as phone calls, emails, or video conferences. By offering flexibility, you make it easier for the potential mentor to commit to supporting you.

In conclusion, asking for mentorship can be a daunting task, but it's an essential step in fostering professional growth and development. By overcoming your pride and ego, building courage, crafting an effective request, demonstrating respect and gratitude, and creating a flexible mentoring relationship, you can increase your chances of securing a mentor who can guide and support you on your professional journey.

Script for Gaining a Mentor

The following is a great script for enlisting someone to mentor you:

Hi [Potential Mentor's Name],

I hope this message finds you well.

I have been following your work in [field or industry], and I'm impressed by your accomplishments and the impact you have made. I'm reaching out to see if you would be open to the idea of mentoring me from time to time in the areas of _____, _____, and _____ [areas of expertise they have that you need].

As a(n) [junior/emerging/mid-career/senior] leader, I'm looking for guidance and support to help me navigate the challenges and opportunities that lie ahead in my role as [title] at [company]. I believe that your experience and insights would be invaluable, and I would be honored to have you mentor me occasionally in these areas.

I understand that your time is valuable and limited, and I'm willing to be flexible and sensitive with scheduling and communication. If you're open to the idea, I would love to discuss this further. Can we schedule a quick 10- to 15-minute call to explore possibilities?

Thank you for your time and consideration. I look forward to hearing from you.

Best regards,
[Your Name]

By using a personalized script like this, you can show potential mentors that you've done your research, are serious about your career, and are willing to invest time and energy into a mentoring relationship. Remember, the key to gaining a mentor is to be authentic, respectful, and willing to learn.

When seeking a mentor, it's important to be specific about what you're asking for and how much time you're requesting. One effective approach is to keep your request short and to the point, using the principle of threes. This involves asking for guidance in three specific areas. For example, ask, "Would you be willing to mentor me from time to time in the areas of X, Y, and Z?" By limiting your request to three areas, you're making it clear that you're not asking for an overwhelming amount of time or expertise.

It's also important to be respectful of your potential mentor's time. You can use phrases like "from time to time" to indicate that you understand their busy schedule and are willing to work around it. If you can show that you value their time and expertise, you're more likely to gain their agreement to take you on as a mentee.

This approach is highly effective for gaining a mentor in any scenario, not only during assimilation and integration. Try it out. You'll be surprised how well this script works and how easily you'll get a "Yes, I would be happy to."

Mentorship can come from different sources. A varied cadre of trusted advisors is the best approach to ensure you avail yourself of the most objective and impactful counsel possible.

Gain Multiple Mentors

It's beneficial to establish three to four intentional mentoring relationships: your immediate superior, someone within the company but not directly in your chain of command, someone external to the organization with expertise in your function or industry, and a leadership coach specializing in assimilation and integration.

Let me say a few words about each category.

1. Your Immediate Manager *(or a Board Member if You're the CEO)*

Cultivating a solid relationship with a reliable and committed superior is crucial for your professional growth and success in a new role. Establishing an effective mentoring relationship requires high trust and high competency, as the mentor should be willing to invest their time and effort in guiding you through the multifaceted aspects of the organization's culture, advising you regarding key stakeholders, and providing in-depth insights into the company's history, achievements, and challenges.

It is essential to assess your manager's experience, expertise, and aptitude in the areas of onboarding, assimilation, and integration in order to ensure their capability to mentor you. A successful mentoring relationship will promote a sense of belonging, empower you to contribute more meaningfully, and result in a very strong professional relationship.

Share this book with your manager to provide a deeper understanding of the intricacies of the onboarding, assimilation, and integration process, and the importance of having a supportive mentor.

By fostering a strong mentoring relationship with your immediate manager, built on high trust and competency, you'll benefit from their experience and support as you navigate the challenges and opportunities presented by your new position. This will ultimately lead to increased job satisfaction, improved performance, and a greater likelihood of long-term success within the organization. However, not every manager is a good mentor, so use your good instincts here.

2. A Colleague or Superior Outside Your Division but Within Your Company

Collaborating with a supportive and knowledgeable coworker who is not directly involved in your line of authority can offer valuable context and perspective. However, it is essential to approach this mentoring relationship with caution, as everyone has their own agenda, whether they are aware of it or not. To establish a high-trust, high-competency mentoring relationship, carefully assess your potential mentor's biases and determine whether you can genuinely rely on them for guidance.

Avoid aligning yourself with individuals whose agendas conflict with the organizational objectives you have been assigned to achieve. To ensure that the mentoring relationship remains focused on your professional growth and aligns with the company's goals, communicate openly about your objectives and expectations.

By cautiously selecting a mentor from outside your chain of command, you can gain valuable insights into the broader organizational context, better understand the company's culture, and navigate any challenges that may arise in your new role. Before you proceed, however, you may want to receive input and buy-in from your manager regarding the establishment of this relationship.

3. An External Mentor with Experience in Your Role or Industry

Engaging with a mentor outside your company who has expertise in your specific role or field can provide valuable insights into your responsibilities and the broader industry context. Although they may not be familiar with your organization's internal dynamics, they can offer guidance based on their experience and knowledge. Ensure that you present an accurate portrayal of your situation and select a mentor who is willing to explore the details and nuances with you. Some mentors can't or won't take the time to do this, so choose wisely.

Ideally, you should have a pre-existing, long-term relationship with this person, which can facilitate open communication and foster trust. Assess their knowledge of leadership onboarding and their ability to support you effectively as a mentor. Sometimes, you may find that you have outgrown your pre-existing mentor. In that case, it is time to find a new one.

By forging a strong relationship with an external mentor, you can benefit from their wealth of experience, their industry knowledge, and an unbiased perspective on your role and responsibilities. It is your responsibility to determine if the mentoring relationship will work. The onus is on you to ask for this mentoring, equip them with the right tools, and ensure that they are qualified to help you. Most importantly, it is up to you to set and maintain a useful meeting cadence.

4. A Professional Onboarding, Assimilation, and Integration Coach

In addition to seeking guidance from internal and external mentors, engaging a professional onboarding, assimilation, and integration leadership coach can be instrumental in helping you achieve success in your new role. A well-qualified coach with expertise in this niche can provide you with customized support, unbiased feedback, and actionable strategies to navigate the complexities of your new position.

Here are some benefits of partnering with a professional executive coach who can help you effectively transition into your new role:

Customized support: A professional leadership coach will work closely with you to understand your unique strengths, weaknesses, and objectives. By tailoring their approach to your specific needs, the coach can provide personalized guidance and support that addresses your challenges and leverages your strengths. This customized support can empower you to tackle your new responsibilities confidently and effectively. They are, in effect, paid mentors, and do this type of work all day long. So, you can expect this person to be very time efficient and effective in targeted work to help you where you need it the most.

Unbiased feedback: Unlike mentors within your organization, a professional leadership coach is an external, neutral party. This enables them to provide unbiased feedback on your performance, interpersonal dynamics, and organizational challenges. Their objective perspective can help you gain valuable insights into areas of improvement and growth opportunities that may be overlooked by those more closely involved in your day-to-day work.

Actionable strategies: Professional leadership coaches are experts in developing actionable strategies to help you assimilate into your new role and integrate into the company culture. They can offer practical advice on things such as building relationships, setting expectations, and managing your time and resources efficiently. By providing you with the tools and techniques to address your specific challenges, a professional coach can help you excel in your new role.

Enhanced self-awareness: Through regular coaching sessions, you will gain a deeper understanding of your own leadership style, communication preferences, and decision-making processes. This increased self-awareness can help you adapt your approach, improve your interactions with colleagues, and ultimately enhance your effectiveness as a leader.

Long-term success: A leadership coach not only focuses on your immediate transition but also your long-term success within the organization. By helping you establish a solid foundation in your new role, the coach can set you up for continued growth, development, and advancement within the company.

Leveraging Your Executive Coach

If you already have a leadership coach, it's crucial to ensure that they possess expertise in assimilation and integration coaching. Most leadership coaches concentrate on developing your leadership skills, which will undoubtedly be useful later in your tenure. However, at this stage, you need a specialist in this niche area.

To assess your existing coach's expertise, conduct an interview and inquire about the number of specific assimilation and integration engagements they've handled throughout their career. If you find someone who has managed one hundred or more, you likely have a competent professional to assist you. Otherwise, consider finding another coach who specializes in this unique area of work.

As an experienced onboarding, assimilation, and integration coach with more than three decades of pattern recognition, I want to share some strategies for effectively utilizing someone like me.

First, regularly engaging with your coach is essential, as having a coach you don't communicate with is equivalent to not having one at all. In this case, you are wasting your time and money. It is easy to think that during your first three to six months in the role, you are too busy for coaching. The opposite is true. You can't afford to be too busy to keep focused on the material covered in this book.

Second, the optimal frequency for coaching sessions is once per week for the first three to six months, then twice per month for a total of twelve months. The amount of time required for each session depends on your preferences, your coach's approach, and your workload. Though some coaches prefer hour-long sessions, I recommend half-hours, as they are generally sufficient and more manageable for busy leaders. The key to successful assimilation and integration coaching lies in the frequency of the sessions rather than the number of minutes.

Third, maintaining a consistent schedule is crucial. If sessions are postponed, the gap between them may extend from two to three or four weeks, causing lost momentum and focus, which is detrimental to the coaching process.

Lastly, what you cover really matters. During your coaching sessions, it's vital to concentrate on the assimilation and integration information covered in this book. Resist the urge early on to work on your leadership skills or use your coach for personal development. Instead, keep both yourself and your coach entirely focused on mastering assimilation and integration best practices.

To be fair, leadership coaching may not be suitable for everyone, and the same holds for assimilation and integration coaching. Consider hiring a coach only if you're committed to the process and prepared to put in the necessary work.

From my experience, about half of all organizations currently invest in leadership assimilation and integration coaching for their newly hired senior leaders, but I believe it is much less common for junior leaders.

If your organization doesn't provide this service, pay for it personally. There's significant value in self-funding your coaching, as individuals who invest in their own development tend to derive greater benefits from the coaching process than those who receive it as a perk from their employer. If your organization covers the cost of your coaching and you treat it like just another perk, you are not making the most of the opportunity. By paying out of pocket, you demonstrate a strong commitment to your growth and are more likely to take full advantage of the coaching experience. Many times, I start with a client who is self-funding, and once the organization sees the tremendous results, they start picking up the tab.

Summary

Many successful leaders rely on the guidance of an experienced mentor, leadership coach, or trusted advisor. While most newly appointed leaders acknowledge the theoretical benefits of such support, they often struggle to allocate time and energy toward it during their transition into a new role. This period is typically characterized by numerous conflicting and unpredictable demands, making it challenging for leaders to fully engage with these resources. However, research has shown that you should resist the urge to go it alone. Here are a few reasons why:

- An objective perspective is impossible to achieve independently.
- A safe space to discuss and refine ideas for management changes is crucial.
- Regular strategic reflection is necessary to ensure you are correctly executing your playbook.
- Onboarding, assimilation, and integration is a proven process; there's no need to learn the hard way when expertise is available.

The Manager's Corner: *Gaining Mentorship*

There may come a time when your new leader specifically requests your mentorship. Make the time, and offer your guidance. If not, consider recommending a trusted colleague within your organization or an experienced assimilation and integration leadership coach who can provide the necessary support.

Additionally, encourage your new hire to seek out multiple mentors. This approach ensures that they receive a diverse range of perspectives and advice, which can be invaluable during their onboarding process.

Assist your new hire in achieving quick wins. Ask them which onboarding book they have chosen to read, obtain a copy for yourself, and review it to familiarize yourself with the advice they are receiving.

Taking a vested interest in your new leader's success benefits not only the individual but also you and your organization as a whole. Offer to mentor your leader. You don't have to wait for them to come to you and ask for this. A mentoring relationship will foster a strong foundation for your new leader and promotes a positive, high-trust and productive relationship.

PHASE 2

RESOURCES FOR LISTEN TO CONCERNS AND DELIVER RESULTS

Your first one to three months in your new role have been consumed by the first three imperatives:

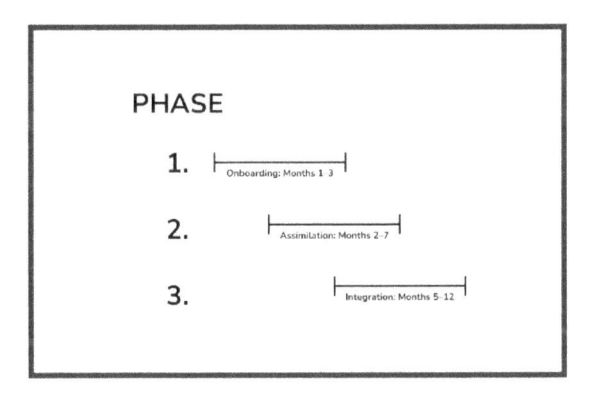

```
PHASE
   1. |—Onboarding: Months 1-3—|
   2.      |—Assimilation: Months 2-7—|
   3.           |—Integration: Months 5-12—|
```

- Build Trust!
- Understand Needs!
- Involve Stakeholders!

Once a solid foundation is in place, it's time to expand your focus inward, refining and honing your personal and leadership capabilities to help you deliver better results. Up until now, my guidance has centered around meticulous onboarding, as thoroughly detailed in Section 2, utilizing the preceding phase 1 resources. However, it's important to note that a one-size-fits-all prescription cannot be applied to determine when you'll be prepared to concentrate on the forthcoming imperatives. The timing will vary for each individual, ranging from the second to the seventh month in the role.

Trust your intuition to recognize the appropriate time for this inward transition. There will come a point where self-reflection becomes instrumental to enhancing your overall performance. In this journey of self-improvement, you'll need a variety of resources, some of which are provided here. This information is by no means an exhaustive treatment on the subject, but I hope it serves as a catalyst for further growth.

As you progress into this pivotal next stage, attention shifts toward listening to concerns. This stage demands a detailed appraisal of your leadership prowess, capitalizing on your strengths while identifying areas requiring refinement. Naturally, throughout the entire process, you are delivering more, better, and bigger results.

As you initiate this introspective journey, it's crucial to address arguably the most formidable challenge in leadership: blind spots. If this issue isn't at the forefront of your concerns presently, it certainly merits prioritizing. After all, these blind spots often become the chief disruptors of successful careers for organizational leaders such as yourself.

These next few chapters will help you remove some blind spots.

CHAPTER 21
ASSESS YOURSELF

Every leader has strengths and weaknesses. Regular self-assessment can help you leverage strengths, address weaknesses, and remove blind spots. To conduct a self-assessment:

1. Review past performance reviews, looking for potential pitfalls in your new role.
2. Solicit unfiltered feedback from previous and current colleagues. A professional coach, manager, or HR department can facilitate this.
3. Seek advice from mentors to refine your leadership style.
4. Schedule time for self-reflection.
5. Consider taking a short break every three months to evaluate your progress.
6. Prioritize self-development. Regularly set time aside for strategic thinking, and keep your developmental objectives visible.
7. Use the opportunity to reinvent yourself. Envision the "new you" and make changes to fit that vision. Write an essay describing your new and improved version of yourself.
8. Identify and address performance-limiting behaviors. Utilize assessments like the ones provided in the next chapter.

9. Minimize surprises. Address any unforeseen issues early in your tenure.
10. Acknowledge the "honeymoon" period. This time can be used to establish yourself as a leader, but beware of becoming complacent, thinking such self-assessment is not needed.

In short, maintain humility, be coachable, and continuously work on self-improvement.

The Manager's Corner: *Assess Yourself*

Support your team members in gaining access to various resources such as tests, assessments, training programs, workshops, and courses that can enhance their leadership skills. Effective leadership development invariably commences with thorough assessments, so make sure these are available to your direct reports. Don't hesitate to utilize these resources for other members of your team and your own personal growth as well.

CHAPTER 22

REMOVE BLIND SPOTS

Following are assessments to help you gain greater insight:

Embarking on the Journey

Blind spots are an inherent part of the human condition. They hinder you from fully realizing your leadership potential. Directly addressing them is essential. Regardless of how deeply you've delved into self-reflection and personal development, it's highly unlikely that you've completely uncovered all your strengths and weaknesses and removed all your blind spots.

We all have areas that are blind to us, waiting to be discovered. Allow me to illuminate this with a personal story.

I built my first house several decades ago. As a novice, I made lots of mistakes. One of the many—or so I thought—was placing the towel rack out of reach, behind the shower door. For years I would step out soaking wet, drench the floor, and reach way behind the shower door for a towel. One day, I accidentally pulled the handle in toward me and discovered the shower door swings both ways, enabling me to grab a towel without leaving the shower. At that moment, a major blind spot was instantly eliminated, and my perspective forever changed. It was a tremendous paradigm shift. You will have similar transformative shifts in your thinking as you uncover your leadership blind spots. One minute you see the world one way, and the next, your view is completely different.

Over the past three-plus decades, I've witnessed several thousand leaders discover new sides of themselves they didn't know existed. These experiences were profoundly transformative, shaping them into much better leaders. Often, these realizations prompted instant actions that radically improved their leadership performance.

However, I have also encountered leaders who never removed their blind spots. Consequently, their growth was severely limited. Many of my clients have been senior leaders who have taken all kinds of leadership tests throughout their careers. My experience is that even the most seasoned and accomplished keep discovering new things about themselves. It's like peeling an onion, one layer at a time.

I hope you will never stop discovering things about yourself. Leadership is a journey with no end. Your task is to persistently strive to identify and eliminate blind spots. Hopefully, I have motivated you to embark on a discovery process to uncover things you don't currently see about yourself and your leadership abilities.

The Johari Window

In the 1950s, two industrial psychologists named Joe and Harry created the "Joe-Harry" model. Now known as the Johari Window, it is highly regarded within leadership development circles primarily because it depicts three sectors where blind spots can exist. Examine each quadrant to see if you can uncover blind spots you may have. The four quadrants are:

	I see	I don't see
You see	WE BOTH SEE	YOU SHOW ME
You don't see		TOTAL BLIND SPOT

1. We both see: This quadrant encompasses the aspects of your leadership that are both self-recognized and readily observable by others. These are the areas of your leadership that are transparent and acknowledged by you and others who know you well.
2. I show you: This sector represents areas that you are aware of ("I see"), but others are not. This highlights the importance of showing others what is true about you or a situation, especially your mentors.
3. You show me: This quadrant depicts areas others see clearly, but you lack insight into ("I don't see"). You need others to show you reality, or at least their perception of it.
4. Total blind spot: This is the most perilous quadrant, depicting areas of which neither you nor others are cognizant. You must remove these to achieve your full potential.

Blind spots are just that—blind. So, if they are blind to you now, how will you uncover them? I believe this process is a journey of continuous discovery, fed by your desire to see reality and empowered by your completion of regular quantitative and qualitative assessments. As you complete these, blind spots will disappear, and you will take your leadership to the next level. You can't eliminate all your shortcomings.

That will never happen. The most effective leader isn't one devoid of weaknesses; rather, it's one who has successfully identified and removed blind spots.

To be your best, you need regular, objective leadership assessments that provide feedback needed to enhance and grow your organizational leadership capabilities. Such feedback allows you to make course corrections where appropriate.

I suggest you engage in some type of assessment process to help gain greater insight. There are several types of assessments included in this book, as well as references to a few others. However, before we delve into them, it is useful to talk about perceptions and how they can impact your ability to lead.

Perception Versus Reality

In the high-stakes arena of professional interactions, we regularly grapple with the intersection of three distinct "realities":

1. The objective reality—the facts, which are indisputably real
2. Others' perceptions of reality, which may align with or diverge from what is real
3. Our own perception of reality, which, like other people's, may be accurate or not

This issue is particularly pertinent to leaders like you because your role requires the following:

1. Recognizing others' perceptions, assessing their alignment with reality, and driving clarity where misconceptions exist. Leaders need to correct inaccurate perceptions of themselves, especially those that negatively affect their ability to influence others and achieve results.

2. Reflecting on your viewpoints, evaluating their accuracy, and continually refining your own understanding. Leaders need to avoid having blind spots.
3. Pursuing an accurate view of reality, untainted by personal biases or subjective distortions.

In short, understanding how you are perceived by others is an important part of your job. To do this, you need to engage in a continuous process of self-discovery and blind spot removal.

Here are two assessments you can take online. They are:

- Gallup CliftonStrengths (not a typo: these two words are melded together)
- The Emotional Intelligence Appraisal, based on *Emotional Intelligence 2.0* by Travis Bradberry and Jean Greaves

My objective is to equip you with the necessary tools for self-assessment, enabling you to attain a deeper understanding of your strengths and areas for improvement. If you've previously completed these assessments, it might be beneficial to formulate a concise summary of each one, emphasizing the blind spots it has helped you identify and overcome.

Gallup CliftonStrengths Assessment

To remove blind spots, you must first understand your strengths. Many leaders, especially overachievers, tend to focus more on their weaknesses and overlook their strengths. The CliftonStrengths assessment is an effective tool for discovering them.

Originally known as StrengthsFinder 2.0, CliftonStrengths is a product of Gallup's belief that optimizing inherent strengths yields better results than trying to overcome weaknesses. It was developed by Dr. Donald Clifton, a pioneer in strengths psychology, and uncovers your top five strengths out of thirty-four potential "strength themes" (if you use the comprehensive version, it will rank all thirty-four).

Taking the assessment is straightforward; after purchasing, you'll answer questions meant to assess your instinctive reactions. Ensure you dedicate fifteen to twenty uninterrupted minutes to the assessment to gain accurate results.

Afterward, you'll receive an in-depth report detailing your dominant strengths with descriptions and suggestions on how to leverage them for success in various aspects. The aim is to improve self-awareness, boost productivity, and foster personal and career development.

As of the time of writing, you can access the CliftonStrengths assessment at https://www.gallup.com/.

Actions to Take to Leverage Your Strengths
1. Embark on a journey of self-discovery by taking the CliftonStrengths assessment, designed to unearth a detailed strengths profile, reflecting the hierarchy and relative power of your unique set of thirty-four strengths. To further deepen your understanding, consider exploring the StrengthsFinder 2.0 eBook. With this comprehensive view of your strengths, you'll enhance your effectiveness, appreciate others' strengths more, pave the way for greater personal and professional success, and help yourself reach your full potential.
2. Post-assessment, spend some time introspecting and reflecting on these key questions:

    - What are the dominant strengths that emerged from your CliftonStrengths assessment?

- Are there any strengths you might be leveraging excessively, to the extent they might become liabilities?
- Did you uncover any strengths that you are currently underutilizing and could harness more effectively for your personal or professional growth?

3. Maximize the benefits of your CliftonStrengths assessment by implementing the following strategies:

- Communicate your top five strengths to your team, colleagues, or managers. Engage in conversations about how these strengths enhance your role and how they could be more optimally applied in your professional context.
- Find a mentor or coach who excels in your areas of desired growth. Discuss your strengths with them and ask for their guidance on nurturing these areas further.
- Craft a personal development plan emphasizing your strengths. Set specific goals tied to each strength and strategize actions to attain those goals.
- Leverage your strengths to tackle work challenges. When confronted with a dilemma, contemplate which of your strengths could guide you toward a resolution.
- Regularly reassess and update your strengths profile. As you evolve professionally and personally, your strengths may also change. Therefore, consider retaking the CliftonStrengths assessment every three to five years to ensure your profile remains relevant.
- Celebrate your strengths! There's no arrogance in acknowledging your capabilities. Embracing your own strengths can elevate your confidence and empower you to embrace new challenges.

- Maintain balance. While highlighting your strengths is critical, don't overlook areas of potential improvement. Treat your lower-ranked strengths as growth opportunities.

This reflective exercise will facilitate a deeper comprehension of your distinctive strengths profile and how to utilize it for success.

Emotional Intelligence Assessment

Emotional intelligence is a critical facet of leadership that goes beyond the confines of intellectual prowess. While traditional intelligence, encapsulated by cognitive abilities and technical skills, can lay the foundation for competent leadership, emotional intelligence sets truly exceptional leaders apart.

Leaders who exhibit high emotional intelligence can better comprehend, manage, and navigate their own emotions and those of their team members. This leads to improved communication, greater empathy, and more effective conflict resolution. Moreover, leaders with strong emotional intelligence can foster a more engaged, motivated, and productive team environment, as they are more adept at understanding and addressing the emotional needs and concerns of their staff. Emotional intelligence allows leaders to connect on a deeper level, building trust and loyalty that can enhance team cohesion and performance. Hence, to truly accelerate growth and effectiveness as a leader, one must invest in developing a robust emotional quotient, complementing and amplifying the value of their intellectual intelligence.

I firmly believe that a significant number of leaders could greatly benefit from enhancing their emotional intelligence. If you think this may describe you, please take an emotional intelligence assessment.

Emotional Intelligence 2.0, a seminal work by Travis Bradberry and Jean Greaves, powerfully advocates for the pivotal role of emotional intelligence in leadership. The authors expound on how individuals and organizations can cultivate emotional intelligence competencies through a blend of self-assessment and the application of empirically grounded strategies. Bradberry and Greaves assert that emotional intelligence accounts for 58 percent of job performance[1] but, intriguingly, only 36 percent of individuals can accurately recognize their emotions in real time[2]—a statistic that I personally can relate to.

Within the pages of this insightful book, you will find online access to the Emotional Intelligence Appraisal, along with sixty-six proposed strategies designed to assist you in uncovering and fostering your emotional intelligence competencies. The evaluation takes roughly fifteen to twenty minutes to complete, and you will receive an immediate report upon conclusion.

This online tool assesses your proficiency in four key skills: self-awareness, self-management, social awareness, and relationship management. In addition, it provides an overall emotional intelligence score and offers recommendations for areas that may need improvement. (Note: They also offer a variety of other assessments, some much deeper and more comprehensive, including a 360: https://talentsmarteq.com/assessments/.)

After completing the assessment, answer the following:

1. What are the top emotional intelligence strengths you identified?
2. Which of your emotional intelligence strengths might you be over-relying on?
3. Are there any emotional intelligence strengths that you aren't fully utilizing?

---
1 Travis Bradberry and Jean Greaves, Emotional Intelligence 2.0 upd. ed. (TalentSmart, Inc., 2009; repr., San Diego: TalentSmart, Inc., 2021), 19. Page references refer to the 2021 edition.
2 Bradberry and Greaves, 11.

By taking these steps, you can gain a greater awareness of your emotional intelligence and how it impacts your leadership effectiveness.

Actions to Take to Grow Your Emotional Intelligence

Following is a top-ten list of suggestions in alphabetical order. If you don't want to take the EQ assessment previously discussed, then review this list, and decide which ones you need to implement.

1. Conflict resolution: Develop the ability to handle and resolve conflicts in a constructive manner. This involves understanding the perspectives of all parties involved and finding a solution that respects everyone's needs and feelings.
2. Constructive feedback: Learn to give and receive feedback in a helpful and positive manner. This can aid in personal growth and foster better relationships with your team.
3. Emotional literacy: Improve your ability to recognize and understand different emotions. Another important skill is labeling your emotions accurately, which can help you understand the nuances of different emotions and how they affect you.
4. Empathy: Develop your ability to understand and share the feelings of others. This involves active listening and recognizing the emotions that others are experiencing. This skill is key to building strong, trusting relationships.
5. Mindfulness: Practice being present and fully engaged in the current moment. Mindfulness can help you remain more balanced and less emotionally reactive, especially in stressful situations.
6. Motivation: Cultivate a positive attitude toward your personal and professional goals. This involves self-motivation, being committed to your objectives, and having a positive outlook, even in the face of adversity.

7. Self-awareness: Start by recognizing your own emotions and their impact. Understand what triggers certain emotions and how your emotional reactions affect your behavior and decision-making. This awareness can help you control your emotions and act more thoughtfully.
8. Self-care: Prioritize your physical and mental health. Regular exercise, a healthy diet, adequate sleep, and stress management techniques can help you stay physically healthy and emotionally balanced, which is critical for maintaining high levels of emotional intelligence.
9. Self-regulation: Learn to manage your emotions effectively. This involves understanding how to control emotional impulses, responding to situations with reason, and staying calm under pressure. Make decisions that are driven by sound judgment, not reactive feelings.
10. Social skills: Enhance your ability to communicate and interact effectively with others. This includes being able to clearly express your own emotions and understanding how to manage social situations and conflicts in a positive manner.

Next, I am pleased to present a series of assessments that I've created specifically for you at this juncture in your career.

The Critical Success Factors Assessment

I've developed this tool after conducting over a thousand interviews with some of the world's most successful CEOs and senior executives. My customary initial question in each CEO or executive coaching engagement is this:

What are the five primary factors that have propelled your success in your senior leadership career, and will remain critical to your success in your future leadership roles?

Do you know the key success factors that will continually elevate your leadership to the next level? Almost all exceptional leaders include one specific factor in their "top five." Is it included in yours? Prepare yourself for a potential paradigm shift.

Take the following evaluative test. You "pass" if that one specific factor is on your list.

Ask yourself, "What are the success factors that have brought me to my current position and will also be scalable to my next level of leadership excellence?" Reflect on these additional prompts: "What soft skills have been instrumental in my success?" "Which of these will I continue to rely on as I further develop my leadership abilities?"

This reflection exercise is designed to provide you with a deeper understanding of the driving factors behind your success, aiding in your continued leadership development and growth.

Make a list of the top five:

1.
2.
3.
4.
5.

Now, take a moment to analyze your list. If you are at an early or middle stage in your career, you might observe that your list comprises mainly personal attributes—specific actions or traits that are representative of you and your personal execution strengths. Indeed, these are areas where you excel. However, take a moment to ponder this: The most accomplished leaders often identify one of their paramount strengths as their ability to nurture, mentor, and coach others. Did this factor feature on your list? If not, I would recommend prioritizing this skill.

After all, your effectiveness as a leader is reflected in the people who work for you, isn't it? The better they are, the more exceptional your organization's performance will be. Thus, at your current leadership level and beyond, it's less about your individual abilities and more about your capacity to elevate others. Recognizing this shift in focus is a pivotal step toward transformative leadership.

Most emerging and mid-career leaders completely fail this test, miss this critical success factor, and, as a result, have a major paradigm shift. They recognize, as I hope you will, that in order to grow to the next level, there are things that they must (1) stop doing, or do less of, (2) start doing, or do more of, or (3) continue doing, or do the same of.

Although your personal skills and abilities are very important, it is even more important that you lead others to do great things and produce awesome results. Agreed?

Top Ten Strengths and Weaknesses

With the DISC (discussed in an earlier chapter) and the assessments from this chapter complete, you are ready to make an informed list of your top ten strengths and weaknesses in rank order.

Understanding your strengths and weaknesses is pivotal in leadership as it builds the bedrock of self-awareness, a crucial attribute of effective leaders. Often, leaders tend to concentrate either on capitalizing their strengths or rectifying their weaknesses. Which tendency defines you?

Leveraging your strengths can fuel your team's inspiration and motivation, steering them toward their objectives. On the other hand, recognizing your weaknesses can avert potential snags and offer avenues for growth. Thus, it is essential to maintain a balance between the two. If you lean too much toward one or the other, this lack of balance can create blind spots, hindering proficient leadership. Drafting a list of your top ten strengths and weaknesses can help you more accurately view your leadership capabilities and pinpoint areas of overemphasis.

Top Ten Strengths and Weaknesses Assessment

Begin by setting aside some quiet, focused time for this exercise. Take a piece of paper or create a document on your computer and divide it into two columns. Label the first column "Strengths" and the second "Weaknesses." Start with the "Strengths" column and jot down the top ten abilities, skills, or traits you believe are your strengths. These could be any of the qualities from our five categories of competency model or others you came up with that were not assessed.

Once you've listed ten, move to the "Weaknesses" column and do the same, but this time focus on areas where you believe you could improve.

Now, you'll rank order these strengths and weaknesses. Starting with the "Strengths" column, look at your list and decide which strength is your top one—the strength you believe is the most dominant or beneficial. Number it as "1." Then, decide your next most significant strength, and number it "2." Continue this way until you've ordered all ten strengths from most to least significant.

Repeat the same process in the "Weaknesses" column, ranking your traits from the area where you need the most improvement to the area where you need the least. This exercise will give you a clear picture of key strengths and weaknesses to work on. It's a valuable tool for personal and professional development, so consider revisiting and updating your lists periodically as you grow and evolve.

As with the other assessments, I suggest you go over these two rank-ordered lists with your manager, mentors, advisors, and/or coach. Pay particular attention to your top strengths and your bottom weaknesses, and answer these two questions:

1. Which of your strengths are you currently overusing, thereby turning into weaknesses? You will recall: a "strength overused becomes a weakness."
2. Which of your weaknesses are actually becoming strengths? You are making progress in certain areas, and it is important to acknowledge this, celebrate your success, and continue that progress.

If you like, you can use the following space to document your work:

Rank	Strengths to Leverage	Rank	Weaknesses to Overcome

Conclusion

With the insights gathered thus far, you now have a clearer understanding of your strengths, weaknesses, and potential blind spots. However, without objective feedback from your manager, peers, and direct reports, this remains a mostly introspective exercise. Blind spots, by nature, elude your perception, and thus, a qualitative, interview-based 360-degree assessment, ideally conducted by an external assessor, is recommended after six months in your new role. This ensures anonymous feedback and greater accuracy.

Invariably, such an assessment will reveal significant blind spots. While it might seem daunting, this process is instrumental to your leadership journey and long-term success. It can highlight what to stop, what to start, and what actions to continue in your role.

The Manager's Corner: *Remove Blind Spots*

This lengthy chapter had a number of assessments that your leader just completed. Ask them to go over the results with you. You may also want to take these yourself. Removing blind spots is essential for any leader, no matter how senior or accomplished.

One of the most effective tools for leadership development and blind spot identification is the qualitative, interview-based 360-degree assessment process. This involves a skilled interviewer conducting in-depth interviews with ten to twenty stakeholders. As you probably know, the "360-degree" name comes from the comprehensive coverage of your professional relationships: north (superiors), south (direct reports), east (external stakeholders), and west (peers or internal stakeholders).

If given the opportunity to participate in one for yourself, seize it. Many of the most accomplished senior leaders I know undertake this process every few years—it's the gold standard for blind spot identification and remediation. And, ensure your leader gets one at or around their six-month mark in the new role.

Do what you can to have your leaders receive one as well. It will be transformational for both of you.

CHAPTER 23
UNLEASHING LEADERSHIP EXCELLENCE ASSESSMENT

Highlights

This chapter features:
- An overview of the five Critical Categories of Competency™
- A list of sixty leadership competencies
- The Unleashing Leadership Excellence ("ULE") Assessment

Completing this assessment will help you immensely in this stage of your assimilation and integration process. Now that you have established yourself in the role, completed some self-assessments, and removed a few blind spots, you are ready to take a more in-depth and serious look at your greatest strengths and weaknesses.

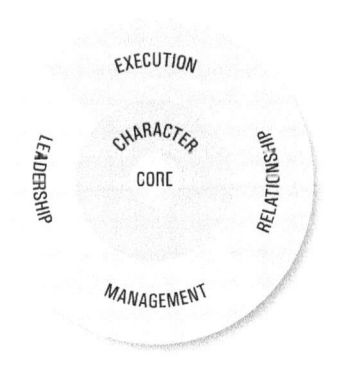

Categories of Competency

Following is a brief description of the categories of competency. I will skip an in-depth explanation, and just provide a quick overview.

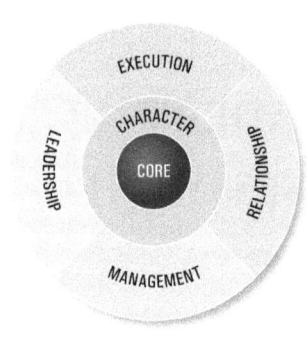

Core

At the center of this model, Core is defined as your true, authentic self.

Your core is the essence of your being. Explore your core and you'll find answers to "Who am I?" and "What's my purpose?"

Beyond competencies, traits, and experiences, your core remains constant. At the center of who you are is your true self and your spiritual nature, however you define that. Within your core live deep-seated values, beliefs, and a sense of purpose. Accessing this core can lead to profound personal insights and a heightened sense of connection with the universe.

While a powerful place for leaders to explore, your core can't be assessed by the Unleashing Leadership Excellence Assessment, or any other, for that matter. Suffice it to say this is a critical component of leadership, and worth spending time on. It just isn't the subject of this book or assessment, so we'll move on. There are other works I have published on this subject. Write me for them.

Critical Categories of Competency™

To be a well-rounded leader, I believe you need to be equally competent in all five of what I call the Critical Categories of Competency™.

They are:
- Character
- Execution
- Relationship
- Management
- Leadership

Character

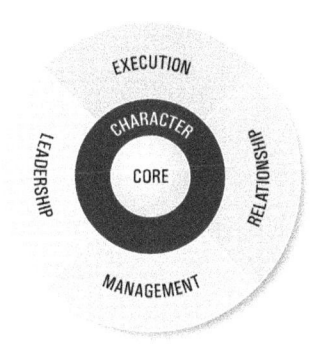

Your character is the most important yet least measured of these five categories of leadership competency.

Notice how it is central to the model, demonstrating that it's foundational to everything you do as a leader, and as a person. I think about it as the metal wheel affixed your axle (core). No matter how perfect your tire is, to use a car analogy, you aren't going anywhere if your wheel is bent. And if your core is broken (think of your axle), no matter how perfect your wheel and tire, you are severely limited in how far you can go in the quest for ultimate success.

Execution

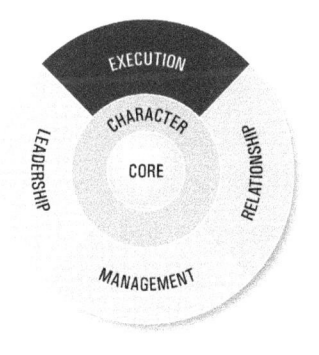

As an organizational leader, your success is rooted firmly in your ability to execute effectively.

You've undoubtedly proven yourself in this category to some extent, which is most likely why you were promoted in the first place. From my experience, it is the most common reason individual contributors and managers find themselves in organizational leadership roles. But "what got you here won't get you there[1]," to quote my friend Marshall Goldsmith, and his best seller, with this as the title. To go to the next level, you need to be strong in Relationship. Note: I recommend you read Marshall's book. And allow me to give a shout out to him for recommending mine!

---
1 Marshall Goldsmith, What Got You Here Won't Get You There: How Successful People Become Even More Successful (New York: Hyperion, 2007), 10.

Relationship

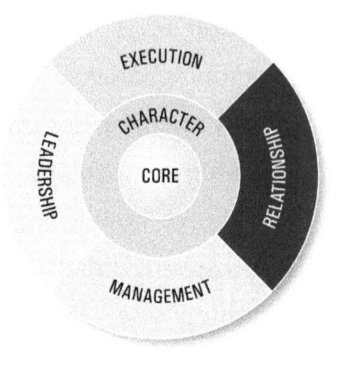

This category of competency is integral to your ability to effectively interact with others—superiors, peers, direct reports, and customers alike. Execution may have elevated you into the leadership ranks, but relationship skills and abilities will help you stay there. But great skills here are not enough. You also need to be progressively stronger in the Management category if you are going to scale yourself to the next level of organizational leadership.

Management

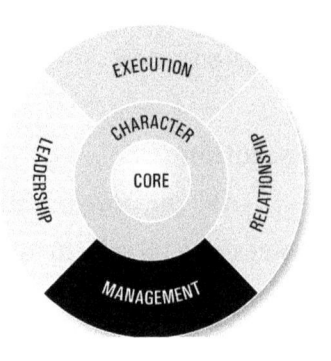

As a leader, you are involved in people management and managing many "things" (the management of everything else). This category of competency is essential to master as you gain progressive levels of responsibility. There are many leaders who are not good managers and many managers who are not good leaders. These are two distinct disciplines.

It is important to be competent in both categories in order to be an effective *organizational* leader.

Leadership

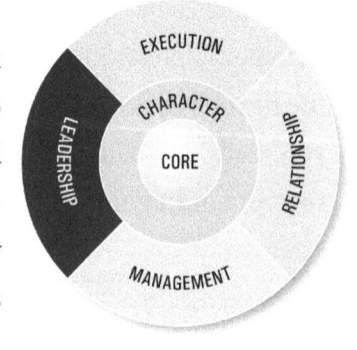

Remarkably, a substantial portion of existing leadership literature fails to comprehensively address the aforementioned four competency categories. This well-established core competency model, widely recognized and adopted by numerous organizations across the globe, seeks to bridge this gap. It is grounded in the collective experiences and practices of thousands of leaders worldwide. Notably, only one segment of this model bears the label "leadership." I encourage you to view this category through the lens of "influence," a term I consider interchangeable with "leadership."

As you grow as a leader, you become progressively more influential, which brings us back full circle to Character. The more influential you are, the more important that your character is aligned with these other four categories of competency. And if your axle is solid, true success that stands the test of time is assured.

The ULE Assessment

Here is an overview of the sixty competencies. It is a statistically valid, benchmarked assessment. The following self-assessment will be very informative and useful. A simple Google search on any of these competencies will yield plenty of information and suggested actions. Write me if you want the version that provides an extensive analysis and action plan for each of the sixty competencies.

Sixty Competencies from the Critical Categories of Competency™ Assessment

	CHARACTER	EXECUTION	RELATIONSHIP	MANAGEMENT	LEADERSHIP
1	Accountable	Analyzing Issues	Actively Listening	Attaining Goals	Aligning Organizations
2	Adaptable	Balancing Priorities	Adapting Behavior	Delegating Responsibility	Building Culture
3	Altruistic	Building Teams	Building Trust	Developing Teams	Casting Vision
4	Compassionate	Driving Results	Communicating Persuasively	Driving Performance	Championing Change
5	Courageous	Implementing Plans	Creating Allies	Embracing Diversity	Leading Innovation
6	Driven	Making Decisions	Cultivating Dialogue	Improving Processes	Driving Strategy
7	Humble	Managing Meetings	Emotional Intelligence	Instilling Accountability	Empowering Performers
8	Positive	Managing Time	Leveraging Networks	Leveraging Financials	Growing Leaders
9	Resilient	Negotiating Outcomes	Managing Conflict	Coaching and Mentoring	Influencing Stakeholders
10	Self-Aware	Solving Problems	Managing Stakeholders	Managing Cross-Functionally	Inspiring Commitment
11	Self-Disciplined	Sustaining Focus	Navigating Politics	Managing Projects	Loving Customers
12	Trustworthy	Taking Risks	Projecting Presence	Thinking Strategically	Serving Others

Core Character Assessment

1: Poor   2: Fair   3: Good   4: Very good   5: Excellent

COMPETENCY	SUB-COMPETENCIES	SCORE
1. Accountable	• **Determined:** Exhibits strong determination to be held accountable for oneself and others. • **Takes Ownership:** Assumes responsibility and completes commitments punctually. • **Reliable:** Possesses reputation as a reliable leader who completes agreed-upon actions.	○ ○ ○ ○ ○ 1 2 3 4 5
2. Adaptable	• **Flexible:** Modifies approach to better align with situational demands. • **Versatile:** Changes behaviors and meets situational needs, adapting to varied scenarios. • **Resourceful:** Responds well to change and ambiguity and pivots with new information.	○ ○ ○ ○ ○ 1 2 3 4 5
3. Altruistic	• **Benevolent:** Prioritizes the needs and welfare of others over personal self-interest. • **Serves Others:** Demonstrates genuine motivation to enhance others' circumstances. • **Unselfish:** Generous with time and attention for others and sets standards to be emulated.	○ ○ ○ ○ ○ 1 2 3 4 5
4. Compassionate	• **Empathetic:** Cares deeply for people and takes actions to alleviate others' suffering. • **Kind-Hearted:** Demonstrates warmth and is considerate, nurturing, and caring. • **Cultivates Compassion:** Champions a culture of compassion within the team and organization.	○ ○ ○ ○ ○ 1 2 3 4 5
5. Courageous	• **Intrepid:** Is unafraid to take calculated risks and faces adversity with courage and resolve. • **Bold:** Exhibits bravery and stands firm in the face of significant challenges. • **Brave:** Is unafraid to step outside the comfort zone and pursue innovative solutions despite fears.	○ ○ ○ ○ ○ 1 2 3 4 5
6. Driven	• **Goal-Focused:** Achievement-oriented with a proactive, internal motivation for excellence. • **Hard-Working:** Strong work ethic with a deep hunger and passion for producing results. • **Ambitious:** Success-motivated, consistently going above and beyond to attain goals.	○ ○ ○ ○ ○ 1 2 3 4 5

1: Poor   **2:** Fair   **3:** Good   **4:** Very good   **5:** Excellent

COMPETENCY	SUB-COMPETENCIES	SCORE
7. Humble	• **Appreciative:** Regularly expresses gratitude and acknowledges the contributions of others. • **Unassuming:** Does not seek unnecessary attention or recognition and is modest. • **Modest:** Downplays personal achievements, instead focusing on others' and teams' successes.	○ ○ ○ ○ ○ 1 2 3 4 5
8. Positive	• **Optimistic:** Embodies hope and confidence and instills these qualities in others. • **Confident:** Energetically believes in self and others and creates a culture of positivity. • **Cultivates Positive Mindset:** Sends positive verbal and non-verbal messages consistently.	○ ○ ○ ○ ○ 1 2 3 4 5
9. Resilient	• **Tenacious:** Persistently and doggedly pursues goals and overcomes obstacles and setbacks. • **Emotionally Stable:** Maintains consistent emotional balance and adeptly manages stressors. • **Mentally Tough:** Maintains determination in adversity and recovers quickly from failures.	○ ○ ○ ○ ○ 1 2 3 4 5
10. Self-Aware	• **Acknowledges Strengths and Weaknesses:** Is regularly introspective, discovering and removing blind spots. • **Solicits Feedback:** Desirous of constructive input; curious, open to self-discovery, and growth-oriented. • **Self-Reflective:** Examines personal beliefs, values, and actions, enhancing self-understanding and development.	○ ○ ○ ○ ○ 1 2 3 4 5
11. Self-Disciplined	• **Self-Controlled:** Has strong willpower and self-mastery, demonstrating a strong ability to control thoughts, emotions, and actions. • **Determined:** Sets clear personal and professional goals and follows through with disciplined focus, persistence, planning, and execution. • **Organized:** Possesses excellent organizational skills, sets and keeps commitments to self and others, and maintains an orderly structure.	○ ○ ○ ○ ○ 1 2 3 4 5
12. Trustworthy	• **Engenders Trust:** Appropriately transparent and has credibility with others for being honest. • **Upholds Integrity:** Demonstrates strong ethical principles and does the right thing. • **Loyal:** Remains faithful to obligations despite challenging or disadvantageous circumstances.	○ ○ ○ ○ ○ 1 2 3 4 5

Total Points (max is 60) _____

Execution Assessment

1: Poor **2:** Fair **3:** Good **4:** Very good **5:** Excellent

COMPETENCY	SUB-COMPETENCIES	SCORE
1. Analyzing Issues	• **Identifies Root Causes:** Systematically investigates issues, determines underlying causes, and analyzes viable options. • **Strategizes Solutions:** Objectively conducts detailed analyses and draws meaningful insights and conclusions. • **Thinks Logically and Rationally:** Uses reason and structured methodology, understands issues, and crafts effective actions.	○ ○ ○ ○ ○ 1 2 3 4 5
2. Balancing Priorities	• **Manages Priorities:** Aligns resources and maintains focus on highest priorities, regularly reassessing organizational needs. • **Thinks Proactively:** Is flexible, responds well to needed change, and proactively adjusts team's workload and focus. • **Leverages Systems:** Utilizes technology to drive high-priority projects to completion on time and under budget.	○ ○ ○ ○ ○ 1 2 3 4 5
3. Building Teams	• **Hires A-Players:** Finds, hires, and develops a diverse team of A-players that becomes a cohesive, high-performing unit. • **Reorganizes Teams:** Moves the right people into the right seats, restructures roles, and proactively exits non-team players. • **Cultivates Teamwork:** Fosters a collaborative and high-performance culture of cooperation and mutual support.	○ ○ ○ ○ ○ 1 2 3 4 5
4. Driving Results	• **Creates Sense of Urgency:** Creates results-oriented culture, drives progress, and achieves targeted results. • **Exceeds Expectations:** Persistently elevates standards, generates momentum, and surpasses expected results. • **Ignites Action:** Inspires others, fosters a results-driven culture, propels progress, and consistently attains targeted outcomes.	○ ○ ○ ○ ○ 1 2 3 4 5
5. Implementing Plans	• **Develops Plans:** Designs comprehensive, actionable plans and contingencies meeting strategic and tactical objectives. • **Measures Progress:** Sets clear, achievable goals and stretch metrics, monitoring and adjusting plans as needed. • **Drives Outcomes:** Aligns plans with desired results, creating milestones and metrics for achieving clear targets.	○ ○ ○ ○ ○ 1 2 3 4 5
6. Coaching and Mentoring	• **Nurtures Potential:** Identifies top talent, intentionally spends time in regular, one-on-one coaching sessions, and employs Socratic method. • **Fosters Mentee/Mentor Relationships:** Acquires, engages with, and leverages mentors, and conversely, invests self in mentoring others. • **Provides Wise Counsel:** Generously offers timely input, valuable insights and good advice based on proven skills, abilities, and expertise.	○ ○ ○ ○ ○ 1 2 3 4 5

1: Poor   2: Fair   3: Good   4: Very good   5: Excellent

COMPETENCY	SUB-COMPETENCIES	SCORE
7. Managing Meetings	• **Drives Agendas:** Prepares and follows well-designed meeting agendas, assigns useful pre- and post-work, and captures actions. • **Promotes Accountability:** Establishes concrete metrics, assigns clear ownership, and sets deadlines, priorities, and follow-up actions. • **Streamlines Meetings:** Drives efficiencies, agendas, pre-work, post-work, punctuality, scheduling, delegation, and decisions.	○ ○ ○ ○ ○ 1 2 3 4 5
8. Managing Time	• **Effective Time Manager:** Prioritizes time and tasks on urgency, impact, and strategic value, without compromising quality or efficiency. • **Manages Calendar:** Implements efficiencies, streamlines tasks, sets effective boundaries, manages distractions, and controls scheduling. • **Leverages Others:** Assigns tasks to assistant and others with priority coding, time-blocks calendar, uses efficient systems, and is punctual.	○ ○ ○ ○ ○ 1 2 3 4 5
9. Negotiating Outcomes	• **Communicates Persuasively:** Convincingly presents viewpoints, assertively sways others, and drives positive, win-win outcomes. • **Finds Common Ground:** Facilitates dialogue, unifies diverse perspectives, builds consensus, and drives compromises. • **Tactful and Diplomatic:** Handles negotiations diplomatically, maintains relationships, and gains needed concessions.	○ ○ ○ ○ ○ 1 2 3 4 5
10. Solving Problems	• **Determines Root Causes:** Thinks creatively, ferrets out root issues, finds solutions, and develops strategic action plans. • **Champions Strategic Problem-Solving:** Uses critical thinking and analysis, optimizes decision-making, and implements solutions. • **Collaborates with Others:** Engages the right stakeholders, gains diverse insight, and develops practical, implementable solutions.	○ ○ ○ ○ ○ 1 2 3 4 5
11. Sustaining Focus	• **Demonstrates Resilience:** Exhibits steadfastness and long-term stamina amidst setbacks or obstacles to goal attainment. • **Tracks Progress:** Persistently monitors and maintains goal-focused accountability and keeps the team focused on objectives. • **Minimizes Distractions:** Mitigates distractions and keeps self and team steadfastly focused on tasks through to completion.	○ ○ ○ ○ ○ 1 2 3 4 5
12. Taking Risks	• **Takes Calculated Risks:** Strategically evaluates opportunities, takes bold steps as needed, and embraces the possibility of failure. • **Seizes Opportunities:** Assesses potential risks and identifies and capitalizes on well-calculated, potentially risky opportunities. • **Analyzes Risks:** Gathers data, makes informed risk assessments, understands risk drives innovation and growth, and takes action.	○ ○ ○ ○ ○ 1 2 3 4 5

Total Points (max is 60) _____

Relationship Assessment

1: Poor   **2:** Fair   **3:** Good   **4:** Very good   **5:** Excellent

COMPETENCY	SUB-COMPETENCIES	SCORE
1. Listening Actively	• **Empathetically Present:** Internally recreates others' feelings and perspectives and gleans underlying meanings and nuances. • **Patiently Listens:** Avoids interrupting, "hears" non-verbal messages, asks clarifying questions, and paraphrases accurately. • **Responds Thoughtfully:** Processes information thoroughly before responding, offering useful insights, suggestions, and feedback.	○ ○ ○ ○ ○ 1 2 3 4 5
2. Adapting Behavior	• **Aware of Behavioral Styles:** Understands own behavioral style, different behavior patterns, and how to identify styles of others. • **Willing to Adapt:** Consciously expends effort to modify own behavioral style to better meet the behavioral needs of others. • **Able to Adapt:** Is behaviorally versatile and able to adjust behavioral style to better meet the demands of situations and relationships.	○ ○ ○ ○ ○ 1 2 3 4 5
3. Building Trust	• **Engenders Trust:** Shows empathy, is consistent, and values others' experiences, viewpoints, concerns, and feedback. • **Honest and Supportive:** Communicates transparently, openly collaborates, explains decisions, and handles mistakes fairly. • **Rewards Team Trust:** Encourages and rewards trust-building behaviors within the team, acts reliably, and follows through.	○ ○ ○ ○ ○ 1 2 3 4 5
4. Communicating Persuasively	• **Articulate Speaker and Writer:** Expresses ideas concisely, clearly, and convincingly, adapting style to the audience's needs. • **Persuasive Communicator:** Makes precise, relatable points, shares a clear vision, and gains shared understanding. • **Evidence-Based Presenter:** Uses data and stories to persuade others with compelling presentations that inspire action.	○ ○ ○ ○ ○ 1 2 3 4 5
5. Creating Allies	• **Builds Relationships:** Garners a loyal following, cultivates influence with key stakeholders, and grows relational equity. • **Collaborates Cross-Functionally:** Creates alliances, garners and nurtures support, and drives organizational synergy. • **Influences Outcomes:** Secures backing, continually builds and expands allegiances, and cultivates organizational influence.	○ ○ ○ ○ ○ 1 2 3 4 5
6. Cultivating Dialogue	• **Facilitates Dialogue:** Creates a safe space for expressing ideas and encourages, respects, and celebrates diversity of thinking. • **Attentively Listens:** Patiently and accurately interprets verbal and non-verbal messages and provides thoughtful responses. • **Asks Insightful Questions:** Stimulates conversations, draws out participants, and guides dialogue toward constructive outcomes.	○ ○ ○ ○ ○ 1 2 3 4 5

1: Poor   2: Fair   3: Good   4: Very good   5: Excellent

COMPETENCY	SUB-COMPETENCIES	SCORE
7. Emotional Intelligence	• **Demonstrates Empathy:** Understands and considers others' feelings and perspectives, mediates conflicts, and resolves issues. • **Emotionally Observant:** Grasps and navigates others' emotions, responds appropriately, and helps the team to do the same. • **Self-Regulated:** Controls own emotions, connects with others on an emotional level, fosters positive relationships, and is resilient.	○ ○ ○ ○ ○ 1 2 3 4 5
8. Leveraging Networks	• **Actively Networks:** Cultivates, nurtures, and connects an ever-expanding network of influential relationships to best help others. • **Leverages Contacts:** Altruistically and strategically connects stakeholders to benefit others and drive organizational outcomes. • **Marshals Resources:** Gains and freely shares information, resources, and support to collaborate and achieve common goals.	○ ○ ○ ○ ○ 1 2 3 4 5
9. Managing Conflict	• **Mediates Disputes:** Facilitates open dialogue and mutual respect and develops timely, shared agreements between conflicting parties. • **Negotiates Solutions:** Employs diplomacy, maintains composure, instills calmness, and orchestrates constructive outcomes. • **Resolves Conflicts:** Identifies and proactively addresses conflict, quickly and fairly settles disputes, and preserves relationships.	○ ○ ○ ○ ○ 1 2 3 4 5
10. Managing Stakeholders	• **Sets Expectations:** Influences, manages, and level-sets stakeholder expectations, driving effective communication, rapport, and trust. • **Builds Bridges:** Forms positive relationships with stakeholders, provides swift responses to concerns, and gains needed buy-in. • **Delivers Timely Communication:** Provides needed updates, project status, and decisions to stakeholders, garnering support.	○ ○ ○ ○ ○ 1 2 3 4 5
11. Navigating Politics	• **Organizationally Aware:** Identifies and respects the formal and informal networks and power structures of an organization. • **Employs Discretion:** Decodes and navigates the intricacies of organizational politics, cultural differences, and sensitive issues. • **Savvy Diplomat:** Maintains confidences, employs diplomacy, provides respect, and recognizes and navigates political issues.	○ ○ ○ ○ ○ 1 2 3 4 5
12. Projecting Presence	• **Commanding Aura:** Displays an authoritative and engaging demeanor, capturing attention and inspiring confidence. • **Magnetic Influence:** Radiates a compelling, powerful presence that draws people in, fostering a sense of respect and admiration. • **Instills Trust:** Exudes humility and credibility, combined with a strong, authentic presence and engaging, confident demeanor.	○ ○ ○ ○ ○ 1 2 3 4 5

Total Points (max is 60) _____

Management Assessment

1: Poor   **2:** Fair   **3:** Good   **4:** Very good   **5:** Excellent

COMPETENCY	SUB-COMPETENCIES	SCORE
1. Attaining Goals	• **Aligns Objectives:** Clarifies goals, creates concrete objectives, sets metrics, engages stakeholders, develops plans, and achieves results. • **Leverages Team:** Works through others, empowers team, and attains strategically aligned goals. • **Overcomes Obstacles:** Solves problems, removes barriers, manages priorities, collaborates with others, and asks for help when needed.	○ ○ ○ ○ ○ 1 2 3 4 5
2. Delegating Responsibility	• **Empowers Ownership:** Delegates freely, demonstrates trust, supports initiative, and gives team latitude to achieve results. • **Promotes Initiative:** Matches abilities to tasks, provides support, encourages proactivity and risk-taking, and provides feedback. • **Creates Accountability:** Sets clear expectations, creates systems, develops accountability culture, and regularly inspects progress.	○ ○ ○ ○ ○ 1 2 3 4 5
3. Developing Teams	• **Champions Teamwork:** Manages team dynamics and drives team clarity, communication, conflict resolution, and mutual respect. • **Develops Team Health:** Drives focus, identity, bonding, unity, camaraderie, morale, cohesion, collaboration, agility, and harmony. • **Bolsters Resilience:** Inspires, motivates, and nurtures a positive, energetic, and inclusive work environment, celebrating successes.	○ ○ ○ ○ ○ 1 2 3 4 5
4. Driving Performance	• **Drives Performance:** Provides regular recognition, rewards, 1:1s and team meetings, support, performance reviews, and feedback. • **Develops Standards:** Creates a performance culture, sets clear goals, metrics, and expectations, and addresses underperformance. • **Improves Execution:** Provides actionable constructive and positive feedback, coaching, and mentoring and creates improvement plans.	○ ○ ○ ○ ○ 1 2 3 4 5
5. Embracing Diversity	• **Culturally Aware:** Understands, appreciates, and supports cultural differences and similarities within and outside the organization. • **Advocates for Diversity:** Inclusive, avoiding biases of race, gender, age, cultural background, sexual orientation, and physical abilities. • **Creates Inclusivity:** Promotes a welcoming culture where all are respected, accepted, and valued for their contributions.	○ ○ ○ ○ ○ 1 2 3 4 5
6. Improving Processes	• **Champions Change:** Engages stakeholders, gathers insights, charts performance, gains alignment, and enhances systems and processes. • **Analyzes Systems and Processes:** Utilizes process-management tools and improves productivity, consistency, and predictability. • **Optimizes Efficiency:** Conducts workflow analysis, streamlines processes, minimizes waste, and cultivates operational efficiency.	○ ○ ○ ○ ○ 1 2 3 4 5

1: Poor   **2:** Fair   **3:** Good   **4:** Very good   **5:** Excellent

COMPETENCY	SUB-COMPETENCIES	SCORE
7. Instilling Accountability	• **Creates Culture of Accountability:** Instills ownership mindset, provides fair rewards and consequences, and celebrates successes. • **Monitors Performance:** Sets and tracks SMART goals, manages measurable outcomes, and provides regular performance feedback. • **Drives Continuous Improvement:** Helps team learn from mistakes and continuously strive for individual and team growth.	○ ○ ○ ○ ○ 1 2 3 4 5
8. Leveraging Financials	• **Possesses Financial Acumen:** Conducts financial planning and analysis, using data to evaluate and make strategic choices. • **Optimizes Costs:** Proactively uncovers opportunities, reduces costs, and uses financial insights to inform strategic decisions. • **Manages Budgets:** Is adept at budgeting, financial reporting, and making positive contributions to the organization's overall financial results.	○ ○ ○ ○ ○ 1 2 3 4 5
9. Making Decisions	• **Decisive:** Analyzes and mitigates risks, proactively makes choices despite incomplete or ambiguous data, and takes reasonable risks. • **Leverages Logic and Instinct:** Makes effective, sound decisions through a combination of logic, past experience, and intuition. • **Balances Speed and Accuracy:** Makes timely decisions without compromising on the accuracy and quality of those decisions.	○ ○ ○ ○ ○ 1 2 3 4 5
10. Managing Cross-Functionally	• **Aligns Cross-Functional Goals:** Facilitates shared engagement and commitment toward achieving organizational objectives. • **Advocates for Resource Sharing:** Navigates hierarchies and interdisciplinary relationships and resolves potential conflicts. • **Manages Shared Resources:** Designs solutions, gains support and alignment, and delivers results in complex, matrixed organizations.	○ ○ ○ ○ ○ 1 2 3 4 5
11. Managing Projects	• **Designs Initiatives:** Creates clear scope, timelines, ownership, budget, checkpoints, communication strategies, and deliverables. • **Manages Project Risks:** Proactively identifies potential risks and implements strategies to mitigate them throughout the project lifecycle. • **Employs Agile:** Embraces agile practices and collaboration and enables adaptability, responsiveness, and iterative delivery to completion.	○ ○ ○ ○ ○ 1 2 3 4 5
12. Thinking Strategically	• **Applies Strategic Mindset:** Is a strategic thinker that sees the bigger picture, anticipates future trends, and considers long-term implications. • **Balances Tactical with Strategic:** Focuses on both short-term tactics and long-term vision, making strategic decisions aligned with both. • **Seeks External Resources:** Gains strategic perspectives, accessing mentors, industry experts, thought leaders, and researchers.	○ ○ ○ ○ ○ 1 2 3 4 5

Total Points (max is 60) _____

Leadership Assessment

1: Poor **2:** Fair **3:** Good **4:** Very good **5:** Excellent

COMPETENCY	SUB-COMPETENCIES	SCORE
1. Aligning Organizations	• **Leads Alignment:** Cultivates cultural support, creates and champions strategic priorities, drives organizational vision, and achieves goals. • **Collaborates Cross-Functionally:** Facilitates dialogue, promotes the agreed strategy, removes barriers, and gains full goal alignment. • **Aligns Structures:** Ensures people, leadership, processes, resources, metrics, systems, and innovation are aligned across organizations.	◯ ◯ ◯ ◯ ◯ 1 2 3 4 5
2. Building Culture	• **Creates Norms:** Lays the foundation and expectations for the organization's values, practices, attitudes, and way of functioning. • **Nurtures Culture:** Sustains and enhances existing culture, drawing out those aspects that are desired and identifying those that are not. • **Shapes Environment:** Determines what parts of the culture do not serve the organization's best interests and leads desired change.	◯ ◯ ◯ ◯ ◯ 1 2 3 4 5
3. Casting Vision	• **Describes Future State:** Clearly lays out a desirable, inspiring, and compelling future state and why heading in that direction matters. • **Engages Stakeholders:** Garners support, champions direction, and ensures strategies, plans, and actions align toward the vision. • **Inspires Followers:** Actively and persistently articulates a vision, which motivates followers to embrace the direction and take action.	◯ ◯ ◯ ◯ ◯ 1 2 3 4 5
4. Championing Change	• **Forms a Coalition:** Enrolls stakeholders, creates a sense of urgency, casts a compelling vision, and gains buy-in for the need for change. • **Designs Initiatives:** Creates change initiatives, builds a strong case for change, and gains buy-in from those impacted by the change. • **Implements Change:** Leads effective change management while maintaining focus on operating effectiveness and key objectives.	◯ ◯ ◯ ◯ ◯ 1 2 3 4 5
5. Leading Innovation	• **Identifies Opportunities:** Recognizes strategic opportunities for innovation, takes risks, tries new ideas, and is not afraid to fail. • **Cultivates Innovation:** Creates a cultural environment and mindset conducive to innovation, fresh perspectives, and breakthrough ideas. • **Invests in New Ideas:** Encourages diverse thinking and creativity, leverages data, promotes experimentation, and balances risk/reward.	◯ ◯ ◯ ◯ ◯ 1 2 3 4 5
6. Driving Strategy	• **Designs Strategy:** Develops a compelling and competitive strategy and translates it into specific goals, objectives, and action plans. • **Conducts Strategy Sessions:** Engages key stakeholders in the strategy design, development, and implementation process. • **Institutes Strategy:** Formulates strategic plans, inspires implementation, aligns organizational actions, and tracks performance.	◯ ◯ ◯ ◯ ◯ 1 2 3 4 5

	1: Poor 2: Fair 3: Good 4: Very good 5: Excellent	
COMPETENCY	**SUB-COMPETENCIES**	**SCORE**
7. Empowering Performers	• **Creates Empowered Culture:** Leads a climate and culture that inspire everyone to stretch beyond what they thought possible. • **Provides Latitude:** Conveys confidence in others' ability and desire to do their best and provides independence for producing results. • **Communicates Trust:** Provides autonomy, delegates authority, builds self-efficacy, and encourages innovation and initiative.	○ ○ ○ ○ ○ 1 2 3 4 5
8. Growing Leaders	• **Grows Staff:** Actively mentors, coaches, and/or develops leaders, providing regular developmental meetings and growth assignments. • **Identifies Future Leaders:** Engages in succession planning and sets clear expectations, goals, and objectives for promotions. • **Delivers Feedback:** Provides ongoing actionable feedback, both positive and constructive, in regular performance reviews.	○ ○ ○ ○ ○ 1 2 3 4 5
9. Influencing Stakeholders	• **Inspirational Leader:** Is passionate, empowering, engaging, motivating, and influential as a visionary and strong communicator. • **Engaging Personality:** Has charisma, projects confidence and a positive attitude, and is encouraging and emotionally expressive. • **Authentic Influencer:** Is genuine, empathetic, and likable, cares about people, is good with relationships, and inspires confidence.	○ ○ ○ ○ ○ 1 2 3 4 5
10. Inspiring Commitment	• **Purpose-Driven Leader:** Exudes passion and connects stakeholders emotionally to a larger sense of passion, purpose, and meaning. • **Challenges Others:** Inspires others to commit to higher levels of performance than were thought possible and champions success. • **Asks for Commitment:** Role models behavior, sets stretch goals, and gains commitment to achieve aspirational objectives.	○ ○ ○ ○ ○ 1 2 3 4 5
11. Loving Customers	• **Serves Customers:** Has an expansive 360-degree view of customers, including external and internal (superiors, peers, and subordinates). • **Customer-Centric:** Demonstrates deep commitment to customers (internal and external) in words and actions and leads others to do the same. • **Listens to Customers:** Takes time to listen to customer needs, is responsive, and leads the organization in passionate customer service.	○ ○ ○ ○ ○ 1 2 3 4 5
12. Serving Others	• **Trusted Steward:** Acts responsibly and ethically for the good of the organization and everyone involved in it, with a long-term perspective. • **Servant Leader:** Leads by example, embodies organizational values, promotes ethical behavior, and serves others before self. • **Other-Centered:** Prioritizes needs of stakeholders over self-interest and humbly and passionately pursues excellence.	○ ○ ○ ○ ○ 1 2 3 4 5

Total Points (max is 60) _____

Summary of the Unleashing Leadership Excellence Assessment

Now you are ready to pull this all together in a summary of your leadership competencies to see how you stack up in each of the five categories.

Instructions: Review your results, transfer your scores from each of the five preceding assessments, and total across.

CHARACTER	EXECUTION	RELATIONSHIP	MANAGEMENT	LEADERSHIP	TOTAL
Score:	Score:	Score:	Score:	Score:	
Strengths to Leverage	Strengths to Leverage	Strengths to Leverage	Strengths to Leverage	Strengths to Leverage	
Weaknesses to Overcome	Weaknesses to Overcome	Weaknesses to Overcome	Weaknesses to Overcome	Weaknesses to Overcome	

As you review your work, what patterns do you see? Go over these with your manager, advisors, mentors, and/or coach.

I believe you need to have a very strong character and a balanced set of competencies in the other four categories.

Overreliance on a particular category can lead to significant blind spots, inadvertently turning your category strengths into category weaknesses and causing issues with your overall effectiveness. Throughout many coaching interactions, I've consistently identified multiple overused strengths that contributed to leadership challenges. Consequently, the straightforward advice of "playing only to your strengths" is misleading.

While this strategy might prove beneficial for roles involving individual contributors and entry-level management, it's insufficient for organizational leadership. The responsibilities and expectations at your level require a comprehensive, balanced skill set that aligns with this five-category competency model.

Avoid over-dependence on one or two strengths and strive for balance. It helps mitigate the risk of overuse, fosters a versatile leadership style, and identifies potential blind spots that could become weaknesses. Proactive self-evaluation and continuous improvement are essential components of effective leadership development. Therefore, for those aiming to succeed in organizational leadership, possessing a well-rounded skill set isn't just beneficial—it's essential.

Revisit the scorecard above and evaluate how balanced your scores are across different areas. Let this analysis guide your Leadership Development Plan, which we will discuss shortly.

CHAPTER 24
LEADERSHIP DEVELOPMENT PLANS

The Leadership Development Plan (LDP) clearly defines your developmental goals.

Your LDP will explicitly outline your growth goals. You'll use it for harnessing underutilized strengths and bolstering existing ones. It will aid you in addressing areas of weakness that demand dedicated efforts. Creating a written plan is crucial to enhancing your leadership skills. Then, regular revisions will keep your soft-skill leadership development goals top of mind.

Upon finalizing your LDP, share it with your manager, advisors, mentors, and/or coach. This transparency will not only solidify your objectives in your own thinking but also create accountability, keeping your goals at the forefront.

Instructions: Build your LDP by following these steps. Use a spreadsheet, Microsoft Word, Google Docs, or any other means that would be easy to share electronically.

At the end of this chapter is a sample plan for your reference.

Step 1: Set a Goal

Formulate a concise goal statement. It should be a succinct declaration of two to seven words, encapsulating your ultimate objective. Strive for brevity, as you will be asked to:

- Commit it to memory.
- Display it in various places to keep it at the forefront of your thoughts. Consider placing a sticky note on your computer monitor, bathroom mirror, or any other frequently viewed spot.
- Create a recurring calendar appointment named "Review LDP." Regularly reminding yourself of your goal will significantly aid your achievement of it.

Example: Delegate more.

Notice that this starts with an action word and is super succinct.

Create a goal now, based on the work you have done thus far. Ask yourself, "What is the most powerful goal I can set right now that would help me grow as a leader?" Write out a very brief statement that will be easy to remember.

Step 2: Create a Goal Summary

Following that, provide a summary of your goal. Construct a one- to three-sentence description of your objective, commencing with "I can and will," followed by an action verb. The rationale for beginning with this phrase is:

- "I can..." expresses belief in your capacity to reach the goal. If stating "I can" isn't feasible, the goal likely isn't right for you. If you lack conviction in achieving the set goal, seek an alternative that you can confidently affirm.
- "I will..." denotes intentionality, resolve, and tenacity. It signifies your commitment to achieving this goal, irrespective of whether it takes six months, twelve months, or even several years. With perseverance, you will attain your goal.

Example: I can and will delegate more responsibilities to Wanda, Susie, and Charles, offloading tasks to them that they are capable of handling, even if one is a stretch goal or requires me to train them. Also, I will establish an accountability system to ensure their execution of delegated tasks and conduct weekly check-ins during our staff meetings to verify progress and ultimate completion.

Step 3: Create Three "Observable Change" Indicators

Next, you need to describe a future state that gives you a vision for making progress toward your goal. If you were making progress, what would be the observable changes that you or others would notice?

Ask yourself, "If I were to enact these changes (in this instance, delegate more), what tangible and observable changes would occur in my behavior and actions or my thinking and thought processes?" Focus on the keywords "tangible" and "observable." Creating these examples tends to be challenging. Persevere until you have three concrete examples. Consider seeking assistance from your manager, advisors, mentors, and/or coach. Crafting these "Observable Change Indicators (OCI)" is crucial to devising a truly effective LDP.

Examples:

1. "Wanda, Susie, and Charles express that their workload has significantly increased since I began delegating more to them." This OCI clearly validates that you have indeed delegated a considerable number of tasks to them.
2. "My manager, without prompting, mentions that she's noticed I've been assigning more work to my direct reports recently." The key phrase here is "without prompting." Whenever possible, include one such type of unsolicited feedback as an OCI. Another example could be if a significant other or family member spontaneously comments, "I've noticed you seem less stressed and aren't working

as late these days." This comment may demonstrate that you are giving more work to others.

3. "I observe that I have considerably more time on my calendar to block out periods for strategic planning, a task I'd been postponing due to a backlog of tactical tasks that my direct reports could (and should) handle." The increase in your available time is tangible evidence of progress. Alternatively, "I find that I'm entrusting my team with more of my responsibilities than ever before." This realization provides concrete, cognitive evidence of progress toward your "delegate more" goal.

Step 4: Categorize and Prioritize Your Goal

Fill out the sections for "Category" and "Level of Priority," ensuring to include the "Why" in each section. While you can use simple High, Medium, and Low priority coding, I recommend using L1 for Highest, followed by L2, L3, L4, and L5. This offers more nuanced levels of prioritization. The "Category" should be drawn from the Unleashing Leadership Excellence Assessment you completed earlier.

Step 5: Chart Results

Document your major results and "wins" as depicted, and make it a habit to log your successes somehow. This habit consolidates your learning and highlights your achievements, providing a satisfying sense of accomplishment. Share these "wins" with your manager.

NOTE: As you rise to higher leadership roles, you will find less and less external recognition for your performance. Excellence is implicitly expected at elevated levels of responsibility. External validation decreases, so you must learn to be a self-validator. Maintaining a record of achievements is a good method of teaching yourself self-validation. Acknowledging progress to yourself is a priceless tool for boosting your self-confidence and self-esteem.

Step 6: Set Two to Six More Goals

With your initial goal established and the first five steps complete, set additional goals. From my experience, some leaders are capable of tackling many goals simultaneously, while others can only handle focusing on just two or three. Understand your capacity and experiment to find what works best for you.

Example of a completed LDP for Goal #1:

Goal #1	
Goal	One-sentence goal statement: Delegate more.
Summary	One to three sentence(s) that amplify your goal; start with "I can and will . . .": I can and will give more delegation to Wanda, Susie, and Charles and offload some non-essential things off my task list that they can do. I will create an accountability system to hold them accountable and will check weekly with them in our staff meetings to ensure that they are getting that work done.
Category	Category of Competency (Core Character, Execution, Relationship, Management, or Leadership): Management
Priority	Level of priority and why: L1. It is critical to my success to move to the next level as a leader. If I am bogged down by tactical execution, I will not have time to do the strategic work that is most important to my manager and her manager.

Observable Changes (OCI)	What you want to happen to prove you are making progress. See examples in the step 3 instructions). Concrete, tangible, and measurable results: #1: #2: #3:
Results	Charting major results. They should be significant and noteworthy. Results: Date: _____. I had a conversation with my manager and was told that she is very happy that I am delegating more to my direct reports. Date: _____. Etc. Track for 6 to 12 months
Journal	Journal (you can write notes to yourself about this): I notice that my fear of letting go is decreasing, and I am pleasantly surprised by how enthusiastic my direct reports are about receiving more work from me. They are doing a better job with my delegation than I expected. I am now able to use my additional free time to be more strategic.

The Manager's Corner: Leadership Development Plans

Ask each of your direct reports to formulate their own Leadership Development Plan (LDP). Create a safe, no-judgment zone where they feel at ease sharing their LDPs with you. I suggest a purely developmental monthly—quarterly at a minimum—half-hour one-on-one with each of your direct reports. During this time, avoid talking about tasks or projects they are working on. Stay focused on their development. Take on the role of "leadership coach" and help them grow their soft skills during this meeting.

For a detailed guide on creating an effective LDP, refer back to this chapter. Note that step 3 often presents a significant challenge when tackled individually; extend your assistance here. Your help will be enthusiastically received by your top performers, gratefully endorsed by most others, and reluctantly accepted by your lowest performers. In most cases, you'll forge a stronger connection and cultivate deeper trust with your future leaders. It will also be very telling as you stack-rank your team.

PHASE 3
RESOURCES FOR SERVE WITH EXCELLENCE

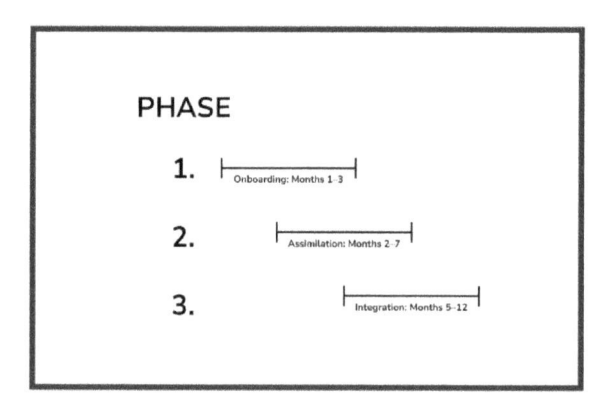

```
PHASE
  1.  |—————|
      Onboarding: Months 1-3
  2.       |—————|
           Assimilation: Months 2-7
  3.            |—————————|
                Integration: Months 5-12
```

Once you've been in your role for five or six months, you'll likely be in a continuous cycle of execution and improvement.

For the final topic, I've chosen from a multitude of options the one I deem most crucial for you to flourish in your new position. Accordingly, information from one of my other books, *Your Customer Compass*, will serve as the ideal concluding chapter for you in *The Art of Your Start*.

In *Your Customer Compass*, I utilize the compass model depicted, showing that you have four distinct customer vectors, with only one being external to your organization. The subsequent chapter is a revised excerpt from *Your Customer Compass*, entitled "North."

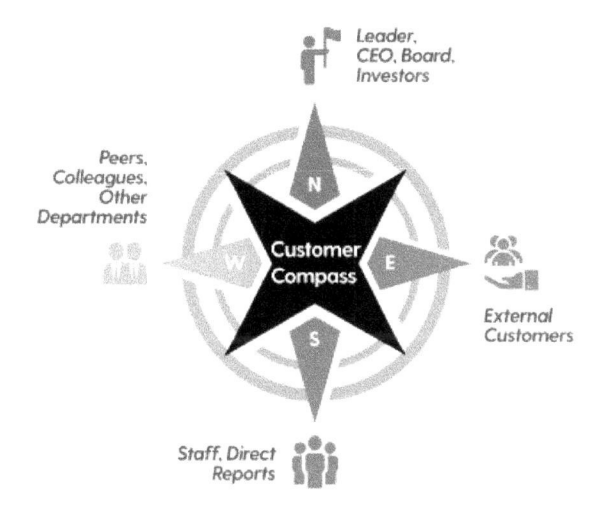

Customer Compass diagram: North — Leader, CEO, Board, Investors; West — Peers, Colleagues, Other Departments; East — External Customers; South — Staff, Direct Reports.

The number one reason for failure in the first year is a failed relationship with those in the "north" vector. I'm sharing this information with you in the hopes that you build and maintain a thriving relationship with your boss. Doing so is the foremost way I know for you to avoid failure. This vector represents anyone in authority over you, not just your immediate manager.

We are about to talk about serving. You will recall the chapter in Section 2, "Serve with Excellence!" This is an extension of that thinking. You may want to read that if you are doing what I often do: reading the last chapter of a book first to see if the book is worth my time.

Adopting the correct "serving up" attitude, perspective, and actions will help you exceed expectations and truly excel.

CHAPTER 25

SERVING UP

Projecting a commanding presence, Art sat quietly in the back of the room. His tall, slender frame, enhanced by his tailored, pinstriped suit and perfectly positioned designer tie, portrayed a proud CEO. He was dressed to impress. His over-starched, fancy cuff-linked shirt, Gucci glasses, and expertly trimmed beard drew the attention he desired. He was an acclaimed entrepreneur, well-known throughout the business community.

The seriousness etched on his face underscored the magnitude of the weight on his shoulders. Underperformance. That's how it is if you're only accustomed to seemingly unending success. Failure was not an option for Art, a local celebrity known for the Midas touch—and if you didn't know that about him, Art would happily bring you up to speed.

Making a rookie mistake, I left the cap of the whiteboard pen off too long, and my writing became unreadable. My marker squeaked to its death on the giant whiteboard in front of me. Clumsily, I rummaged for another in my consultant's bag of tricks. Back then, the standing joke went: "What's the definition of an expert?" "Fifty miles from home with a briefcase." Today, that's replaced by "A plane flight and a backpack." I was indeed far from home, and out of my comfort zone, on that rainy January day in 1987.

Art's stoic stare pierced me like an arrow as our eyes met for a nanosecond. We quickly looked away. His furrowed brow and deep frown clearly indicated his unhappiness. "Is it what I'm saying?" I wondered. Easing up on the OD jargon—Organization Design and Development for those not in the field—I decided to change the focus of the offsite. This was supposed to be my introduction as Art's new OD consultant. From the skeptical looks I was getting, it wasn't going well.

As a novice OD consultant in my late twenties, the marker was my control stick of the meeting. Clutching a fresh marker, I breathed a sigh. To say I was nervous would be grossly misrepresenting reality. I was terrified. This was my largest engagement to date, and I was oversold to Art by another client. Not wanting to screw up the sale, I let Art think the best, despite my deep inner belief that he was a hopeless case. Art was Art. Unless he changed, I saw no hope for his company turning the corner. But how would a kid thirty years his junior help him see that he was his own problem? I had no clue.

All of Art's top executives were in the room, and this over-the-top, dominant CEO had seemingly cloned himself in his lieutenants. They had killer instincts and smelled fresh bait. I could feel it. Hired to reorganize his company, I had to gain buy-in from the tough crowd staring up at me from the front row: COO, CFO, CIO, CMO, and all the GMs. This alphabet soup caused my stomach to do flips. Everyone was so serious, and no one was giving any positive vibes. Understandably. Business was not great, no one was getting bonuses, and Art was impatiently wanting change—now. Making matters worse, a youngster half everyone's age with no industry experience was going to tell these seasoned veterans what they were doing wrong. Gulp.

When in doubt, ask a question. Advice from my mentor buzzed through my head. "Who's the most important person in this organization?" I blurted out. I immediately guessed this was the stupidest question I've ever asked.

"Art," came the dutiful chorus from his loyal staff. The answer was a foregone conclusion, a truth that Art would remind them of, in subtle or not-so-subtle ways, whenever possible. Art was more than their CEO; he was the fulcrum on which every department balanced. Hundreds of employees were interwoven into his grand tapestry, each dependent on Art's direction. He was the glue holding it all together, and he didn't know how to do it any other way. Nor did he want to. He craved control.

In consulting, if you still don't know what to do, ask another question. "Who's next most important after Art?" I queried. The room grew awkwardly silent. That question visibly unsettled Art; he folded his arms across his chest. Long story short, I persevered, drawing out Art's organization chart, which finished with sales and service individual contributors at the bottom of this pyramid.

Before me, Art's kingdom depicted in a top-down org chart. Innocently I asked, "Have we left anyone out?"

From the back of the room, an audacious soul yelled out, "The customer!"

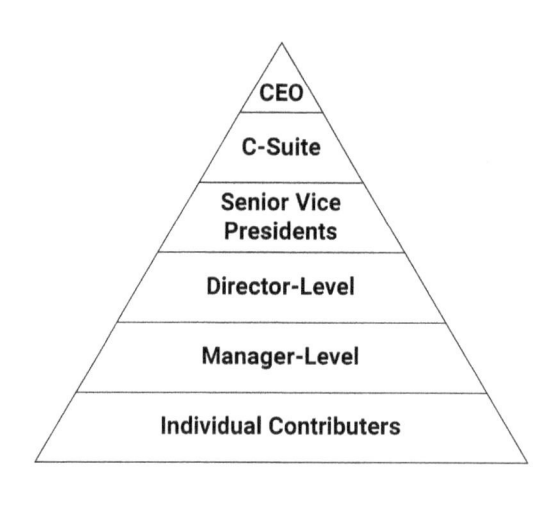

"Good!" I declared and wrote "Customers" in large letters across the bottom.

Immersed in highlighting the need for restructuring, I could have never anticipated what would happen next— the epiphany that would influence the trajectory of my career. I was trying to show that Art needed to relinquish some control. He didn't trust his leaders to protect his interests or believe they could match his passion, intensity, and resolve to "get it right" without his constant oversight. Today, we call that micromanagement. Back then, I called that "Art."

Suddenly, divine inspiration hit like a bolt of lightning. I said, "Considering we mentioned the customer last, I guess they're not that important." With a quick stroke, I erased "Customers."

That was all Art needed. Jumping up, he declared, "If they go away, we go away!" Art shot to the front of the room and proceeded to give a fifteen-minute lecture about the importance of customers.

After several failed attempts to get a word in edgewise, I spoke over him, asking another divinely inspired question: "Art, can we redraw your org chart in order of importance, with the customer on top?"

"Great idea!" he said. Wow, positive feedback. Buoyed, the upside org chart for Art's company was born.

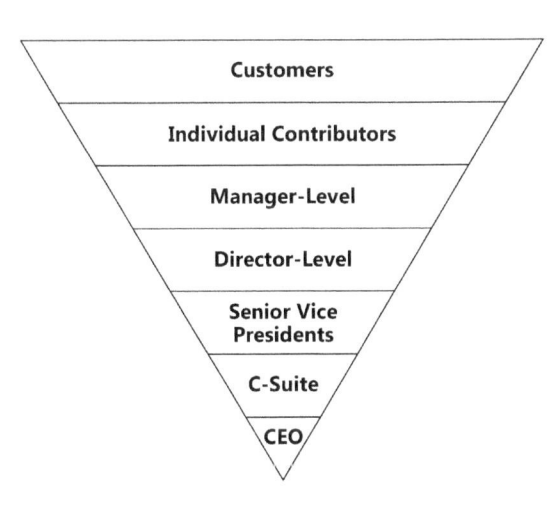

With enthusiasm, we recrafted the diagram, with the "Customers" box spanning the entire top of this inverted triangle. I instantaneously realized where Art was to end up. Indeed, the team determined that the next vital groups were sales and service, as they had the most interaction with the customer. After several layers, we finally reached Art's direct reports, and at the very bottom: Art. I timidly asked, "Art, how does it feel to be at the bottom?"

"Fantastic!" he exclaimed. "This is exactly what we're missing—a total focus on the customer.

"I want this organization to be obsessed with our customers. I want to know beyond a doubt that everyone in this room is as fanatical about serving our customers as I am! Especially when I'm not around."

Surprised, I quickly replayed the meeting I had when Art hired me. "Daniel," he had said, "I want my team to seize control, to be proactive rather than respond to my prodding. I'm sick and tired of having to manage them."

Leaders frequently find themselves entangled in this complex power struggle. It's akin to balancing on a high wire, swaying between the desire to nurture a self-reliant team—much like what Art wished to establish—and the inherent impulse to maintain a firm grip on control until there's absolute certainty it's safe to let go. The mere thought of loosening that grip, surrendering substantial control, and potentially risking your team's performance, accountability, and authority, is a haunting prospect that looms over many exceptional leaders at every level.

Back in the offsite, a realization struck me: If we are all here primarily to serve the customer, doesn't it mean we're also here to serve those who are directly "above" us? This question sparked an enlightening exchange, and for the rest of the day, we designed a model of internal customer service. We came to an agreement: Art existed to serve his C-suite as his primary customer. The purpose of the C-suite was to serve their VPs. The VPs were there to serve the managers, and ultimately, everyone's goal was to serve the individual contributors, who played the crucial role of serving the external customers. As the day elapsed, the transformation occurred right before my eyes. To this day, I have hardly ever seen such a profound shift from top-down autocracy to bottom-up empowerment. For all his issues, Art was a smart businessman. He knew, in his heart of hearts, he had struck gold.

We finished the day with a comprehensive action plan centered around empowerment and servant leadership, laying the groundwork for concepts that would be proven successful and become mainstream decades later. The model is what I call "serving up."

After the offsite, Art and I met in his lavish corner office for a one-on-one coaching session.

"Art," I began, "how do you feel about the outcome of today's meeting?"

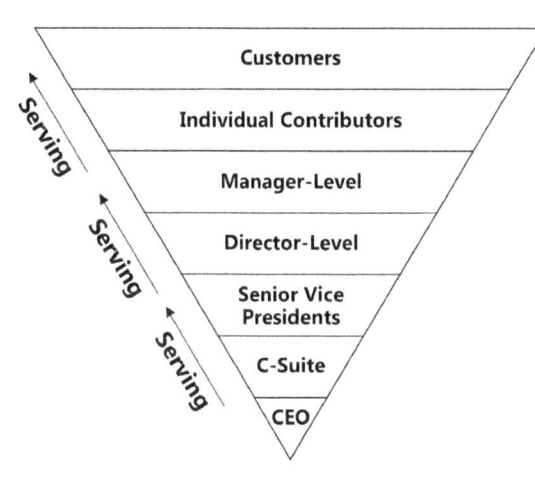

"Intriguing," he replied. "I'm not sure everyone truly grasped the implications of what they just signed up for, but I'm enthusiastic. If it works, it's a game changer for our company and for me. I'm eager to give it a go."

"Art," I delved deeper, "what steps can you take to ensure that this works?"

"That's a good question. Give me a moment to articulate my thoughts."

An hour later, Art had constructed a robust action plan, which he promised to execute diligently. The work he did in the subsequent year of our engagement turned around his company and his life. Thrilled with the transformation, Art and I collaborated for several more years to implement "serving up."

Since that memorable day in 1987, I've performed this illuminating exercise countless times. The concept of the inverted organizational chart has garnered considerable acknowledgment and is now broadly utilized. I don't claim to have invented it—I simply discovered it in the heat of the moment. When you discover a profound truth, it's always timeless and rooted in universal life principles (I call them ULPs for short). Here is the ULP: "It is better to serve than to be served."

To this day, I continue to be amazed by the reactions this concept elicits from organizational leaders like yourself. Instead of expressing discomfort at the thought of being moved from your lofty position, you display an inspiring readiness to position yourself at the base, allowing others to be rightly placed at the top. However, the same enthusiasm isn't quite mirrored when the situation is reversed. In a moment, I'll share a story that demonstrates this—a story that truly underscores the main point of this chapter.

Leaders often find themselves ensnared in a challenging web of responsibilities, pulled in four distinct directions. You probably relate to this predicament. Let's explore two of these contrasting forces, imagining them as points on a compass. In this particular instance, we'll focus on the north-south vectors.

Before delving further, it's worth noting that this "serving up" perspective likely resonates with the prevalent mindset within your organization. Your board of directors and CEO, assuming you aren't holding one of those positions, view serving up as essential for your organization's success. Most senior leaders are keen to adopt this concept of the inverted organizational chart, emphasizing service to their internal customers. However, even if this concept is deeply embedded within the culture of your current environment, it doesn't necessarily guarantee that every leader in your organization subscribes to this leadership approach.

You may find yourself working under a manager like Art. Art's focus was primarily directed toward one vector—the external customer, symbolically located to the east. However, despite the transformation at his company, Art still struggled with wanting to be served. But the improvements he did make made all the difference in the world for his company, his employees, and himself. Soon, he was playing more golf and going into the office less, and the company experienced tremendous growth. For the shareholders, it was also a major win when the company was sold for a premium to a strategic buyer.

Servant Leadership

The most inspirational leaders I've had the pleasure of encountering innately exhibit the principles of servant leadership, irrespective of whether they're consciously aware of this particular model. They shun the seduction of a regal pedestal. In our increasingly enlightened era, they comprehend the crucial importance of providing service to everyone in all four vectors.

So, when you look northward, what is your perspective? Do you see your manager as someone you should serve? Do you perceive your role as enabling your boss's success? When you look to the north, do you identify your manager as your customer? I would argue that they are. If I were to simplify your job description to its purest form, I might say, "Your role is to make their job easier." Therefore, my suggestion for you is to delve into leadership resources that teach concepts like this and enhance your capacity to make your manager's job more manageable. The following story details when I learned this firsthand.

When All You Want Is to Be Served

Back in 2002, I had the opportunity to provide leadership coaching to Eileen Kamerick, CFO of Heidrick and Struggles, which to this day is one of the world's most prominent and successful executive search firms. Eileen had recently recruited a VP of Finance, Kevin, who was extremely talented. With formidable intelligence, an impeccable professional history, and an esteemed educational background, Kevin was, on paper, a superstar.

Despite these glowing credentials, there was one glaring problem: Kevin was stretching Eileen's patience thin. His unyielding quest for change was causing considerable upheavals within the team. While some aspects of Eileen's department required improvements, Kevin's approach was so disruptive that it eclipsed all else, leaving Eileen with the piercing noise of shattering glass.

I suggested Eileen have me conduct an interview-based 360-degree assessment of Kevin. In doing so, the issues swiftly emerged into sharp focus. Kevin was deficient in the art of listening, and he lacked a well-rounded customer compass. His efforts were directed toward serving Wall Street. Those were the only stakeholders that mattered to Kevin. Thus, he did an exceptional job of galvanizing the entire accounting and finance department to expedite the quarterly close, which they ultimately accomplished in record time, in addition to other improvements in reporting.

Westward, his peers were struck with admiration. "Great job, Kevin!" many of them commended. Yet to his north, Eileen, his direct manager, was grappling with distress, as she was incessantly caught in a barrage of complaints from the south about Kevin's overbearing demeanor. The staff hated working for him.

I presented Kevin with the findings of the 360-degree assessment and mediated several meetings wherein Kevin was confronted with the adverse effect he was inflicting on his northern and southern borders. Despite these interventions, Kevin found himself unable to comprehend the idea that Eileen and his direct reports were his customers, too, whom he needed to serve with the same fervor he showed to his eastern and western vectors. Predictably, he was exited a few months later, still perplexed about where he had gone wrong.

A strength overused becomes a weakness. Overemphasizing any single vector inevitably leads to complications in the others. Kevin's east-west focus was very well established. His bridges with Wall Street and his peers were exceptional. He was essentially an east-west kind of individual. I've encountered many such people in my tenure as an external change agent. Their time in an organization tends to be short-lived, and if they do manage to hold on, it's usually due to a miscalculation on someone's part.

If your compass only accounts for east and west, you're neglecting two critical stakeholder groups that make or break your success. As a side note, this is precisely why 360-degree feedback is so valuable. If you are overcommitting to serving one vector and neglecting another, this assessment will illuminate that issue.

To summarize, maintain balance. Over- or under-indexing on any vector will cause magnetic disturbances and distort your compass bearings.

Many leaders grapple with these two opposing vectors: the manager (north) and direct reports (south). Neglecting either one can potentially derail your organization and your career. For the purpose of helping you thrive in the second half of your first year, I'll limit my focus here to your northern vector. As mentioned earlier, this is the number one reason a newly appointed leader leaves the organization.

Your Primary Job

I've had the privilege of mentoring Eileen through multiple prominent CFO roles within public companies over the past two decades. I dare say I gleaned more from her than she ever did from me. The most crucial lesson she imparted was the concept that a subordinate's primary responsibility is to make their manager's job easier. This notion brings forth the question: Do you perceive this as your primary duty? Can it be asserted that you are an individual who simplifies your manager's job? Do you consider your manager as your customer? As you look north, how many customers do you identify? How effectively are you serving them?

A Difficult "Ask"

I understand that for some, the notion of serving your manager might not be readily digestible. It might seem like a tall order. You might ask, "Shouldn't my leader consider me their customer? Aren't they in place to serve me?" Or, "I have a boss like Art. I don't want to serve a person like this."

My response would be, "Yes. They should see you as their customer. But they might not be aware of it yet. They may not have been exposed to this perspective or delved into such concepts." Perhaps your manager hasn't embraced this philosophy. Maybe they haven't explored the idea of servant leadership—that you are to serve equally in all four vectors. Perhaps they're so swamped with trying to stay afloat that they haven't spared a moment to reflect upon the idea of you being their customer. Maybe you haven't considered the possibility of your direct reports being your customers either. Have you?

As we move forward, I request that you momentarily put aside any judgments of anyone in your northern vector. Release any frustration you might be harboring due to a perceived lack of perfect leadership. Let go of any resentments you may have for behaviors that have failed to meet your expectations of being served.

Likewise, extend the same grace to yourself and acknowledge your own imperfections. Accept that you might not have served your team to the best of your ability, either. Once that's acknowledged, release it. The crucial question now becomes, "What actions will you take moving forward that will transform the way you work together with your north-south vectors?"

I understand that merely requesting you to alter any negative perceptions through a few simple words may seem difficult. However, it is possible. You can achieve it. A considerable aspect of leadership is nurturing the right mindset. The battle often is decided in the realm of your thoughts. Triumph in this battle and suspend your preconceived notions about who serves whom. Visualize your manager as a primary customer you are there to serve. How would your behavior alter if you sincerely adopted this viewpoint? How would your interaction be transformed? If you truly believed that your most crucial customer was not from the east, west, or even south, but from the north, what would you do differently?

With this altered mindset, let's explore how you can optimally serve your manager. This leads us to a concept that is likely familiar to many—managing up.

Managing Up

It is commonly understood that managing up is necessary at times to guide your manager and those in your northern vector toward taking the right actions. Isn't that the case?

Allow me to confess something to you. Despite teaching the principles of "managing up" for over three decades, I realized only a few years ago that I had it all wrong. There is no such thing as managing up! It is a complete misnomer. Why do I say that?

The term "management" implies control. As a manager, you oversee people and projects, exerting authority over your direct reports' workflows and project functioning. However, when it comes to your manager and those above, you have no control whatsoever. Thinking in terms of "managing up" is a fallacy.

You may ask, "If you are not managing up, what are you doing?" The paradigm shift I experienced a few years ago is that you are actually "leading up." After all, what is leadership, if not the skill of influencing others to move in a direction you believe is best? Thus, you are leading your manager, through your influencing skills, to make the best possible decisions and take the best possible actions that align with your organization's vision, mission, and core values.

Leading Up

You can and should influence your manager and others in the north vector. If you act in their best interests, as well as those of the organization, then you are fulfilling your role. However, if you neglect to serve this vector, then you are falling short. I recommend assessing your motives before exerting your influence. If your intentions are pure and focused on the well-being of your manager and the organization, then proceed. If you are driven by a selfish agenda, seeking personal convenience, gain, or comfort, be aware. People tend to see through such attempts, and it can harm your relationships with those you depend on most for support.

Returning to an earlier question: "Shouldn't my manager see me as their customer? Aren't they here to serve me?" Though the short answer is yes, you must also do your part in serving them. You cannot control your manager, nor should you try. Serve them to the best of your ability by using your influence.

Be deliberate in your approach to leading up. Aid your manager in becoming the best version of themselves. Regard it as part of your responsibilities. I believe they will take notice of your efforts and reciprocate accordingly. True transformation begins to unfold when both the manager and the direct report view each other as customers and strive equally to serve one another. This is the ideal everyone should aspire to achieve, whether you are the CEO, a mid-level leader, or in leadership for the first time.

In summary, shift your perspective from "managing up" to "leading up." See your immediate manager as a customer you are there to serve. Endeavor to make their life easier. Assist them in being the best they can be through influencing up.

The North-South Vectors

As you contemplate your relationships in the north-south direction, you'll observe that you occupy a similar position with your direct reports as your manager does with you.

As you explore the dynamics of "serving up" applied to your manager, it becomes apparent that the same principles are applicable to your role in serving the needs of your direct reports. This brings us back to a saying that holds true: "People join companies and leave bosses." Don't be the kind of boss that your people leave. The extent to which your manager views you as a customer will greatly influence the level of loyalty you develop toward them. Similarly, the extent to which you serve your direct reports and fulfill their needs will greatly influence their level of loyalty to you.

The quality of your tenure depends heavily on the quality of the relationships you foster in both north and south directions. A lot is within your control and shaped by the value you place on these vital stakeholder relationships. There is no better way to cultivate strong and mutually beneficial relationships than by recognizing and treating these two vectors as highly valued customers you are there to serve.

Questions to Ask Yourself

When considering your manager, several questions to ask yourself are:

1. If you were to ask your manager to evaluate the quality of your service to them, what feedback do you anticipate you would receive?
2. Apart from your immediate manager, which other customers do you serve as you look north? What do you believe they would say about the quality of your service to them?

3. Reflecting on your performance in leading up, do you feel you have done a commendable job? How can you enhance your approach in this area?
4. Regarding the north-south journey, how successful have you been in navigating this path? Where have you failed? What steps can you take to address and mend those failures?

Take a moment to contemplate these questions, as they can provide valuable insights into your relationships, your leadership effectiveness, and areas for improvement in serving your customers in both the north and south directions.

The Manager's Corner: *Serving Up*

As your leader's leader, role modeling "serving up" is more important than the words you use to express your expectations for them as they serve stakeholders.

I suggest you read this chapter from beginning to end. If you don't have time, here are the key points:

1. Finding balance: In the practice of upward leadership, it's essential to strike a balance between empowering your team and retaining control. Successful leaders cultivate an autonomous workforce while wisely navigating the apprehension associated with surrendering control.
2. Customer centricity: Both external and internal customers are fundamental to organizational success. Prioritize and incorporate their needs into key decisions.
3. Servant leadership: Uphold servant leadership values, prioritizing team support and growth and promoting empowerment.
4. North-south relationships: Recognize that your manager is a primary customer in the north, while your direct reports are

your customers in the south. Build quality relationships and strive to meet both vectors' needs, fostering loyalty and effective collaboration.
5. Quality relationships: The quality of relationships influences loyalty and productivity. View your manager and direct reports as customers, striving to serve them with genuine intentions and focusing on their best interests.
6. Navigating the north-south journey: Reflect on your performance navigating the north-south journey. Assess the quality of your service, identify areas for improvement, and address any potholes along the road to enhance collaboration and communication.

By embracing "serving up" principles, you will cultivate more effective relationships, create a greater customer-focused mindset, and drive more positive results within your organization.

CHAPTER 26

SECTION 3 CONCLUSION

Here are parting thoughts.

To the Leader

Thank you for allowing me to help you during your first year in a new leadership role.

I hope you find the playbook and resources most helpful. Remember, this is a one-year journey. It's easy to lose sight of this perspective, but the aid of mentors, advisors, your coach, and/or your manager will keep you on track. Encourage these individuals to read this book, particularly the "The Manager's Corner," for a succinct understanding of its essence.

The journey toward effective onboarding, assimilation, and integration is a marathon, not a sprint. Safe travels on your new road to greater success.

To the Manager

You've dedicated considerable effort to guaranteeing a seamless onboarding, assimilation, and integration process for your new leader. Indeed, navigating this process requires a balance of art and science.

For optimal outcomes, equip all incoming leaders in your organization with a resource like this book before their journey begins. Assigning them a preliminary task of reading about this subject significantly increases their likelihood of success. This proactive approach can ensure a lasting and mutually beneficial relationship between the new leaders and your organization.

EPILOGUE

I would be lying to you if I told you that the wisdom found in these pages came from me. It did not. For my entire career, leaders have shown me the way. Maybe leaders like you.

Friends, we stand on the shoulders of giants to reach new heights of excellence in leading others. We have been enriched by the wisdom of those who have gone before us. Therefore, I refuse to take credit for the leadership insights presented. Recognition is due to the truly great leaders who have shown us all what it means to effectively lead others.

It has been the privilege of a lifetime to help great leaders become even greater. As I reflect, several top ones come to mind, and they all have one thing in common. It can be well said that the best leaders are also great followers. Whom you follow matters. If you are following yourself, it is the surest way to get lost. Follow the very best leaders you can find, and you are sure to make a significant contribution to the art, and science, of great leadership.

You might be curious about whom I follow.

For me, the greatest leader who ever lived was a humble carpenter, who quietly built things out of wood, until the day he was told to build things that would stand the test of time. He followed. His Father led him. It cost him his life. My life is devoted to serving, to the best of my ability, like He served me. I will leave you with this quote to ponder, from one of my favorite books on leadership, and the "S" of SOLID:

For even the Son of Man came not to be served, but to serve, and to give his life as a ransom for many. — Mark 10:45 NIV

Your aspiring servant,
Daniel "Coach D" Mueller

BIBLIOGRAPHY

Masters, Brooke. "Rise of a headhunter." Financial Times, March 30, 2009. https://www.ft.com/content/19975256-1af2-11de-8aa3-0000779fd2ac.

Goleman, Daniel, Richard Boyatzis, and Annie McKee. *Primal Leadership: Realizing the Power of Emotional Intelligence*. Boston: Harvard Business School Press, 2002.

Cappelli, Peter. "Talent Management for the Twenty-first Century." *Harvard Business Review* 86, no. 3 (March 2008). https://hbr.org/2008/03/talent-management-for-the-twenty-first-century.

Bradberry, Travis, and Jean Greaves. *Emotional Intelligence 2.0*. TalentSmart, Inc., 2009. Updated edition, San Diego: TalentSmart, Inc., 2021. Page references are to the 2021 edition.

Goldsmith, Marshall. *What Got You Here Won't Get You There: How Successful People Become Even More Successful*. New York: Hyperion, 2007.

INDEX

accelerated performance review, 55
actionable steps, 42, 79, 123
active listening, 110, 111, 122, 126, 158–9, 180, 211, 242
alignment, 32, 40–4, 57, 61, 72, 75, 93, 96–8, 118–9, 123, 126, 138, 140, 157, 197, 236
allies, 117–20, 123–4, 129,
behavioral adaptability, 202, 207
behavioral style, 99, 101, 127, 135, 188, 199, 200, 202–10
blind spots, 66, 81, 127–8, 146–7, 160, 163, 206, 213, 230–1, 233–7, 245, 247–9, 265–6
board member, 20, 30, 62, 64, 136, 168, 221
board of directors, 100, 282
build trust, 44, 88, 90, 94, 98, 105–6, 122, 134, 150, 166, 170–1, 177, 186–7, 199, 229
BUILDS™ Playbook, 6, 16, 88–9, 153, 163, 166
build trust playbook, 105
business background, 176, 179, 182
change approach, 74, 79
common failure points, 44, 46–7, 80
common pitfalls, 6, 8, 119
competency, 89, 126–8, 162, 206, 221–2, 246, 249, 251–3, 266, 271
concerns, 31, 61, 64, 88, 91, 96, 121–2, 125–6, 128–36, 151, 166, 170, 177, 187, 215, 229–30, 240
conflict, 51, 76–9, 212, 222, 240, 242
Connecting the Pieces, 175
constructive conflict, 76–7, 79
constructive criticism, 28, 159, 161, 168,

core character, 271
core values, 51, 102, 109, 120–1, 127, 287
corporate leadership coach, 38
Critical Categories of Competency™, 162, 249–50
Critical Success Factors Assessment, 243
culture, 5–6, 22–8, 28, 30–2, 35, 38, 47, 51, 53, 57, 71–2, 76, 78–9, 90–1, 97, 102–3, 118–9, 122, 126–7, 138, 140, 158, 164, 168, 181, 215, 221–2, 224, 282, 296
Deliver Results Playbook, 152
DISC behavioral assessment, 188, 199, 213
four quadrants of the DISC, 200, 201
Observation-Only-Based DISC Assessment, 210
early wins, 68, 79, 173
ego, 32, 38–9, 41, 60, 65, 67, 70, 77, 104, 110, 112, 129, 139, 143, 217–8
emotional intelligence, 99, 111, 127, 160–1, 207, 240, 242–3, 296
Emotional Intelligence Appraisal (EQ), 237, 241
executive career coaching, 29
executive team, 38
expectations, 5, 22–4, 28, 32, 35, 37, 40–3, 47, 53, 56, 60–2, 64–7, 74, 83, 90, 93, 95, 97–8, 102, 118, 138, 141, 146, 164–5, 181, 184–7, 195, 197, 218, 222, 224, 266, 275, 286, 290
expected deliverables, 42
external placements, 54 failure to execute, 69
fast failures, 52
feedback, 65, 75, 77, 80–1, 93, 97–103, 109, 117, 119, 126–30, 132–4, 146–7, 153, 157, 160–1, 164–5, 167–8, 182, 192, 196–7, 206, 215, 223–4, 231, 236, 242, 247, 269, 279, 285, 289
first thirty days playbook, 96
Gallup CliftonStrengths Assessment, 237
goals, 36, 41, 44, 72, 76, 93, 95, 98, 111, 131, 142–3, 145, 148–51, 157, 159, 161, 164, 168, 181–2, 184, 187, 192–3, 195–6, 198, 216, 218, 222, 239, 242, 267, 271
Hangman for Leaders™, 144
high-trust relationship, 43–4, 94–6, 106, 110, 115, 122–3, 199
honeymoon syndrome (savior syndrome), 62, 64
hundred-day onboarding plan, 42, 55, 69, 192, 196–7
integration and assimilation, 15, 51, 20,

internal promotions, 35, 54
interview, 66, 72, 119, 127, 146, 178, 225, 248, 284
involve stakeholders playbook, 123
job description, 42
Johari Window, 234
key priorities, 42, 191
key stakeholder, 69, 106, 179, 194
Leadership Excellence Assessment, 103, 147, 163, 249, 250, 265, 270
leadership coaching, 2, 5, 31, 147, 200, 226, 283
Leadership Development Plan (LDP), 141, 147–8, 150, 154, 266–7, 272
leadership role, 5–7, 16, 18–21, 23, 27, 37, 52, 54, 77, 82–3, 89, 93, 95, 121, 166, 174, 186, 215, 292
leading leader, 157
leading up, 132, 287–8, 290
Listen to Concerns Playbook, 135
listening and learning approach, 108
lone ranger approach, 40
managing up, 133, 287–8
mentorship, 159, 167–8, 171, 182, 215–8, 220, 227
milestones and metrics, 42, 142, 195
misalignment with values or strategy, 68, 79
new job, 2, 6, 33–4, 45, 49, 61
north-south vectors, 282, 286
objective reality, 97, 236
onboarding coaching, 20
onboarding plan, 42, 55, 69, 97, 192–3, 196–7
onboarding, assimilation, and integration coaching, 55 onboarding, assimilation, and integration failure, 44
onboarding, assimilation, and integration process, 5, 21, 34, 49, 62, 88, 221, 292
onboarding, transition, and assimilation process, 16
overconfidence, 38, 74
overexertion and burnout, 44,
perceptions, 62, 98–99, 101, 123, 236, 286
performance feedback, 27, 77, 127
periodic assessments, 102

personal background, 176–8
personal development plan, 161, 239
planning, 21–2, 45, 56, 57, 74–5, 79, 93, 151, 154, 173, 194, 270,
politics, 38, 57, 63, 133
poor performers, 73, 79
positive impression, 122, 104
promotion, 2, 37, 54, 141

public shareholders, 37
quadrants of competency, 162
quick wins, 27
reasonable transparency, 66
red flags, 33, 78, 80, 82
relational dynamics, 57
relationship assessment,
relationship-building tactics, 104, 105, 106, 175, 185
retention, 20, 25, 35, 44, 48, 59, 189,
say no, 70,
Seemingly Unimportant Decisions (SUDs), 56, 58, 59,
self-assessments, 157, 249,
self-care, 44, 243,
self-esteem, 70, 79, 270
servant leadership, 39, 157, 158, 161, 164, 280, 283, 289, 290
servant-leader, 158, 161, 163, 164,
Serve with Excellence Playbook, 163
shareholders, 37, 107, 114, 282
significant achievements, 142, 179,
sixty competencies, 253
skill set, 17, 44, 133, 146, 149, 161, 162, 266
stakeholder meetings, 104, 106, 109, 177, 185, 188, 191
strategic direction, 23, 51, 80,
strategic objectives, 137
strategy development, 69
strengths and weaknesses, 6, 43, 66, 146, 148, 160, 163, 231, 233, 245, 246, 249
style diversification, 209
successful transition, 25, 45, 166, 168, 198

SWOT analysis, 161, 195,
take charge, 52, 71, 79, 159, 201,
team meetings, 112, 186, 187, 188, 189,
terminations, 19, 46, 77, 135, 172,
thirty-day playbook, 55
three envelopes, 139
three-phase process,
time off, 49, 50, 92,
Top Ten Strengths and Weaknesses Assessment, 246
Total Quality Management (TQM), 141
trust test, 45
Understand Needs Playbook, 113
unforced errors, 101
Unleashing Leadership Excellence Assessment, 103, 147, 249, 250, 265, 270
valuable resources, 16, 136, 170, 171
venture capitalists (VCs),
video communication, 46

ABOUT THE AUTHOR

Daniel J. Mueller is one of the earliest and most active pioneers of the executive leadership coaching industry. Starting in 1987, he has provided executive coaching for more than two thousand CEOs and executives, delivered over fifty thousand hours of one-on-one executive coaching, and been privileged to support and witness major transformations in the lives of most clients.

Passionate about serving leaders at every level, Daniel is dedicated to helping executives and leaders at all levels become more effective. Before specializing in executive coaching, he was CEO of a management training company, then CEO of a business advisory firm, and finally CEO of an organizational development consultancy—all three of which heavily influenced his unique approach to leadership coaching. An avid student of leadership, he regularly speaks and publishes on subjects critical to leadership peak performance.

Since his first executive coaching engagement in 1987, Daniel knew he had found his passion and calling and had a meteoric rise to the top of the emerging executive coaching profession. However, the more outwardly successful Daniel became, the greater the internal pain grew of feeling like an imposter. Naively, he chose to numb his pain with alcohol, which led him into recovery from alcoholism—his sobriety date is March 4, 1996. Humbled and broken, Daniel began diligently working to attain personal transformation from the inside out. This story of amazing success, total failure, and complete redemption has led to one of his favorite sayings: "I coach from a place of weakness, not strength." From the wreckage emerged a tried and proven methodology for helping any leader grow to the next level—if they are willing to do what it takes. Daniel is a good example of, "If he can do it, anyone can."

He can be reached at Daniel.Mueller@SOLIDleaders.com.